TECHNOLOGY IN THE L2 CURRICULUM

Stayc DuBravac
University of Kentucky

Series Editors
Judith Liskin-Gasparro
Manel Lacorte

Boston Columbus Indianapolis New York San Francisco Upper Saddle River
Amsterdam Cape Town Dubai London Madrid Milan Munich Paris Montréal Toronto
Delhi Mexico City São Paulo Sydney Hong Kong Seoul Singapore Taipei Tokyo

Editor in Chief: Bob Hemmer
Editorial Assistant: Jonathan Ortiz
Executive Marketing Manager: Denise Miller
Associate Managing Editor: Janice Stangel
Senior Vice President: Steve Debow
Production Manager: Fran Russello
Full Service Production: Chitra Ganesan/PreMediaGlobal
Art Director: Jayne Conte
Cover Designer: Bruce Kenselaar
Printer/Binder: RR Donnelley and Sons Company

Credits and acknowledgments borrowed from other sources and reproduced, with permission, in this textbook appear on the appropriate page within text.

Catalogue in Publication data available from the Library of Congress

10 9 8 7 6 5 4 3 2 1

ISBN 10: 0-13-238512-0
ISBN 13: 978-0-13-238512-1

*To my wife, Christina, who has made
my work better,
my days more joyful,
and my life more complete.*

CONTENTS

PREFACE

The goal of this book is to provide an up-to-date overview of computer-assisted language learning (CALL). With the growing presence of computers and internet connections in foreign language classrooms, the need to use CALL effectively in language instruction has increased significantly. This book targets pre-service and in-service instructors of second languages (L2), sometimes referred to as world languages (WL), including English as a second language (ESL), with the aim of facilitating the use of computers in and out of the classroom. The audience for this book also includes advanced undergraduate or graduate students earning degrees in CALL, TELL, applied linguistics, or L2 or WL education, as well as longtime professional educators looking to improve their instructional skills in using the available technological tools. A number of graduate programs in foreign language and linguistics now include courses in CALL/TELL methodology. These courses focus on various aspects of technology in a second language classroom, from evaluation of technology to production of applications for use in the classroom. This book aims to satisfy the needs of these courses in the areas of software and webware, second language acquisition (SLA) theory, language teaching methodology, and assessment strategies that relate to technology and language teaching.

If this book is used in a college course (whether graduate or undergraduate), it is important to organize the course so that students have the opportunity for both discussion and practice of the topics presented. Group work can encourage students of similar experience and varying talents to pool their knowledge and enhance learning (Mason & Rennie, 2008). Instructors are encouraged to model the technologies presented in this text. For example, comments and discussion about the chapters can be posted on a class listserv, threaded discussion, newsgroup, blog, wiki, and/or student web pages. As instructors model the use of the tools, students can familiarize themselves with each technology, and more time during class can be devoted to learning current applications and how to design, create, and evaluate activities. The sections within each chapter include tasks designed to deepen understanding of the concepts, foster linking theory to practice, and investigate the technologies and practices.

The first three chapters focus on the history of CALL and Web 1.0 technologies. Chapter 1 discusses the history of technology and language teaching and includes the basic technologies available to language teachers. Chapter 2 concentrates on evaluating and using the wide array of technologies available to instructors. Chapter 2 also looks at copyright law and fair use in relation to digital media. In Chapter 3, we investigate the history and use of the web for teaching languages and examine a variety of types of sites and activities such as dictionaries and online translations, WebQuests, and other presentations for both instructional and management purposes.

Chapters 4, 5, and 6 set technology in the methodological and instructional context that guides how languages are taught today. Chapter 4 offers an overview of key concepts in SLA as they relate to CALL and suggests teaching guidelines for using electronic media. Chapter 5 presents activity theory to support a task-based pedagogy for CALL. The taxonomy of CALL tasks presented in this chapter aims to clarify options that are available to instructors. Chapter 5 also discusses participation structures and how technology supports a range of interaction and task types. Chapter 6 addresses national standards for language learning, language teaching, technology for students, and technology for teachers. Chapter 6 has two main goals: (1) to identify approaches to using computers to meet the student standards in language learning and computer usage and (2) to explain how computers can be used to create personal learning networks for professional development for instructors.

Chapters 7 and 8 focus on the advantages and disadvantages of synchronous and asynchronous tools and how to design and implement learning tasks using these tools. Chapter 7 analyzes synchronous tools such as MOOs, chat, text messaging, instant messaging, and VoIP. Chapter 8 considers asynchronous technologies including email, discussion boards, blogs and microblogs, RSS feeds, podcasts, vodcasts, wikis, and social networking sites.

Chapters 9 and 10 address online methods of traditional and alternative assessment. Chapter 9 illustrates the advantages and disadvantages and the future of computer-assisted language testing (CALT). Chapter 10 presents three modes of alternative assessment: performance, projects, and electronic portfolios (ePortfolios) and how technology can support them. As alternative assessments generally require rubrics to facilitate grading, Chapter 10 also discusses rubrics and checklists in detail. The concluding chapter, Chapter 11, describes the state of CALL today and the future potential for CALL in the classroom.

Instructors at all levels and in a variety of context should find the contents of this text useful for teaching students in face-to-face settings, in hybrid courses, or in courses that are delivered online. Readers need not gain mastery over all of the tools presented in this book, but rather should familiarize themselves with them to develop a toolbox of techniques and technologies to use for instruction both inside and outside of the classroom.

ABBREVIATIONS USED IN THE BOOK

ACTFL—American Council on the Teaching of Foreign Languages
CAI—Computer-assisted instruction/Computer-aided instruction
CALICO—Computer-assisted language instruction consortium
CALL—Computer-assisted language learning
CALT—Computer-assisted language testing
CAT—Computer-adaptive testing
CBI—Content-based instruction/Computer-based instruction
CBT—Computer-based testing
CEFR—Common European framework of reference
CLT—Communicative language teaching
CMC—Computer-mediated communication

CMS—Course management system
DMCA—Digital Millennial Copyright Act
F2F—Face-to-face (as opposed to CMC)
FAQ—Frequently asked questions
GUI—Graphical user interface
IALLT—International Organization of Language Learning Technologies
IL—Interlanguage
IM—Instant messaging
IRC—Internet relay chat
IRT—Item-response theory
ISP—Internet service provider
ISTE—International Society for Technology in Education
IT—Instructional technology
L1—First language
L2—Second language
LPD—Language program director
MSIE—Microsoft Internet Explorer
MUDs—Multi-user domains
MOOs—MUD object-oriented
MUSH—MUD shared hack, habitat or hallucination
MUVE—Multi-user virtual environment
MUSE—Multi-user shared environment
NETS-S—National educational technology standards for students
NETS-T—National educational technology standards for teachers
PLN—Personal/professional learning network
PM—Private message or one-to-one text message in a chat room
Podcast—iPod + broadcast; it is an episodic online audio publication
RSS—Really simple syndication, a method for subscribing to online content.
SCT—Sociocultural theory
SLA—Second language acquisition
SMS—Short messaging service, also known as text messaging, or texting
TEACH—Technology, Education, and Copyright Harmonization Act
TELL—Technology-enhanced language learning
URL—Uniform resource locator, or web address
Vodcast—video podcast
VoIP—Voice over IP uses the internet for voice communications
WBT—Web-based testing
WL—World languages
ZPD—Zone of proximal development

ACKNOWLEDGMENTS

Technology in the L2 Curriculum has undergone numerous changes since its inception. I am grateful to those who contributed significantly to my changes in thinking. I owe a debt of gratitude to my graduate students at Florida Atlantic University and the University of Kentucky who were willing to implement many of my suggestions in their classes and return with reports of their successes and shortcomings.

I would also like to thank Manel Lacorte and Judith Liskin-Gasparro for their prompt and thought-provoking feedback and unceasing encouragement. I also thank Bob Hemmer at Pearson Education for his patience and support.

CHAPTER **1**

Introduction

OVERVIEW

Instructional technology (IT) has grown rapidly since the 1990s as a result of technological advancements and the ubiquity of personal computers. Second language acquisition (SLA) has also experienced significant development as a field of inquiry since the 1980s, when several prominent publications began to separate SLA from general linguistics (e.g., Canale & Swain, 1980; Ellis, 1986; Krashen 1982, 1985; Long, 1985b, 1996; McLaughlin, 1987; Swain, 1985). These two relatively young fields have made extensive contributions to computer-assisted language learning (CALL). Because they draw on a number of fields (e.g., psychology, computer science, teaching methods), they have facilitated an eclectic approach to teaching second languages using computers. This chapter is designed to introduce readers to some broad concepts in the area of IT, discuss aspects of the historical development of CALL, and familiarize readers with some key terms.

The development of teaching methodologies has often coincided with the available technology; the relationship between teaching methodologies and technology encouraged numerous mechanical exercises when CALL debuted. The continual development of technology that enabled multimedia, interactivity, and real-time communication corresponded to developments in teaching methodologies that emphasized authenticity, interaction, and learner control. Both technology and the push for a learner-centered approach have led to changes in the role of the instructor as learners have taken a more central position in the language learning process.

This chapter also briefly discusses online security and identifies practices and two important tools to protect users' identity and files. Loss of data is common even for the most proficient users; the sources of loss are innumerable: theft, flood, lightning, accidental deletion, hard drive failure, and so on. Worse than loss of files may be loss of identity because of poor online security practices. One of the easiest yet most violated methods of security is a good password. We discuss how to create and maintain good passwords as well as introduce tools to increase users' efficiency.

DEFINING TERMS

CALL involves several fields that inform best practices. SLA is the study of how and why humans acquire language. SLA also includes the study of what language is and how the acquisition of a language is represented in the human mind. IT often refers to the theory and practice of using technology to overcome educational challenges both in the classroom and in distance learning environments. Computer science, often abbreviated as CS, is the study of information and computing and how to implement applications in computer systems. The fields of SLA, IT, and CS abound in acronyms; putting these fields together only intensifies the profusion of truncated forms and abbreviations. This section identifies frequently used acronyms and discusses terms that appear throughout this book.

The term *CALL* appeared during the 1960s, and it has developed along with technological advancements and pedagogical improvements (Bonk & Cunningham, 1998; Delcloque, 2000). CALL denotes the use of any type of computer hardware or software that helps learners develop their language skills. CALL can refer to applications designed to teach both first language (L1) and second language (L2), but this text uses the term only as it applies to L2 instruction. CALL may refer to the use of computers in the classroom or in a language lab in conjunction with a course, and it also refers to language learning that may not be associated with a course, an instructor, or other individuals. CALL stems from a cross-disciplinary foundation of CS, IT, linguistics, SLA, and L2 pedagogy. In other words, users evaluate the quality of any given CALL software beyond its initial functionality (computer science) from several perspectives, such as its ease of use or navigability (instructional technology), its accuracy (linguistics), its scope and sequence (SLA), and its intersection with other course materials (L2 pedagogy). Computer-aided instruction (CAI) differs from CALL in that it not only includes language learning, but also extends to all fields, such as math, science, and anthropology.

The introduction of technology-enhanced language learning, or TELL, can be traced to Bush and Terry (1997), who argue that technological innovations are a means of complementing instructors' teaching methodology, not supplanting it (as may be inferred from the term CALL). TELL is similar to CALL, but it includes other types of technology in addition to computers, and it specifies the role of these technologies as enhancing agents. The term *enhanced* is preferred to the term *assisted*. The latter can imply that some help was required to accomplish the task or that instructors are somehow inefficient without the computer; the term *enhanced* implies that the instructor uses technology to improve the overall language learning experience. In the case of TELL, the technology component is ill-defined but usually refers to electronic media or computers. Technology in this case can include any electronic objects such as an overhead projector, a computer or mobile device, an interactive video, an audio conference, a videoconference, or any combination of these.

Computer-mediated communication, or CMC, refers to any type of communication that uses a computer. During the 1960s and 1970s, the Defense Advanced Research Program Agency linked computers owned by the Department of Defense and several research universities to share information (this infrastructure gave rise to today's internet). Sharing information initially took the form of electronic mail, but the realization that some information should be shared among multiple individuals gave rise to mailing lists and electronic bulletin boards. Although CMC had existed for years, its use for learning a L2 became widespread only in the 1990s (Warschauer, 1996b). The popularization of CMC in language learning can be largely attributed to Warschauer (1996a), who provided both theoretical impetus and research to support the benefits and possibilities of CMC in language learning. Textual, audio, and video chats are all tools used for CMC that have gained a significant research base over the past decade on which to draw when designing CMC activities. The technology for CMC has also improved significantly in the past five years to provide user-friendly CMC applications (e.g., Skype, gchat, Instant Messaging), which are discussed in Chapters 7 and 8.

In contrast to CMC applications, stand-alone applications require only a computer or handheld device (not a network connection). Stand-alone applications normally run from portable storage (i.e., CD, DVD, or flashdrive) and are generally self-starting applications once the storage device has been inserted in the computer. Stand-alone applications generally target individual learning such as tutoring, rote practice of grammatical forms, introduction to cultural aspects of the target language, and reading activities. The difficulty with stand-alone applications is that even though they are convenient for some learners, they are insufficient to learn a foreign language according to most theories of SLA, which emphasize the importance of interaction and negotiation of meaning. In addition, many publishers are moving away from stand-alone applications to online or mobile applications (or apps).

Many applications are now delivered through the internet. The internet is a loosely connected global network of computers that allows individuals to communicate and collaborate in ways never before possible. The internet has been compared to familiar concepts such as a library, university campus, or bazaar-type marketplace. Many people use the terms *internet* and *World Wide Web (WWW)* interchangeably as if they refer to the same concept. However, the WWW is only a subset of the internet; the internet includes email, chat, instant messaging, the World Wide Web, Gopher, and TELNET, for example. The latest metaphor for the internet is a cloud, and *cloud computing* has become in important concept for many businesses (Lai, 2009). The thought behind cloud computing is that many computers can be plugged into the cloud to retrieve information, applications, and services available only on the internet (see Figure 1.1).

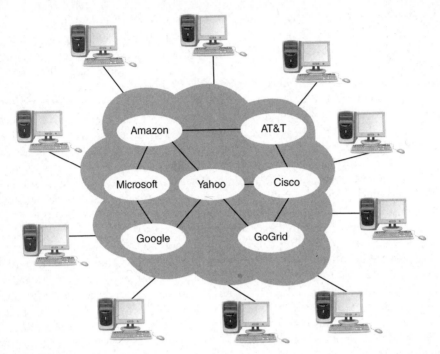

FIGURE 1.1 A Model of Cloud Computing

Many people may already think of the internet as a cloud without calling it that. The general idea is that when you turn on your machine (or computer) and connect it to the internet (cloud), you theoretically have access to everything that is connected to the internet. With a cloud model, many users do not need to understand much of the technical infrastructure and types of connections used in the cloud. Nonetheless, users can still profit from knowing more about how computers are connected and how the internet actually provides these services. Just as humans use a language to communicate, computers use a protocol. Some popular protocols include Hypertext Transfer Protocol (HTTP) used for accessing the WWW, Post Office Protocol (POP3) and internet message access protocol (IMAP) used by most email services, or File Transfer Protocol (FTP) used for transferring files from servers to clients. Once documents are in the cloud, they are accessible to all, barring any specific precautions such as password protection or a firewall. Cloud computing refers to the ability to use infrastructure from outside one's firewall (i.e., after the user connects to the internet) to support computing activities. Cloud services can include virtual computers and storage, email, web and file servers, remote database and management servers, and any number of distributed transaction servers. In reality, the computational requirements for the personal computer are diminishing because more functions can be performed in the cloud rather than on the desktop. Thus, personal communication devices such as the iPad and smartphones can be weaker (computationally) because the computation happens in the cloud, and users simply access the data from a communication device rather than run the entire program.

HISTORY OF LANGUAGE LEARNING AND TECHNOLOGY

The following discussion is designed to introduce some key concepts and broad perspectives on the history of language teaching and technology. A fuller description of SLA theories appears in Chapter 4, and the history of various specific technologies is presented throughout the book.

Early Language Laboratories (1960s–2000s)

The early language laboratories that inundated colleges and universities in the 1960s made use of the available technology of the time, that is, recorded tapes and, eventually, computers that were capable of creating text. The development of multimedia, HyperCard, email, videodiscs, speech recognition, the WWW, and artificial intelligence and the overwhelming ubiquity of personal computers produced significant changes in both the language lab and the conception of how languages are learned (e.g., more attention to collaborative work and CMC; Belz & Thorne, 2005; Liu, Moore, Graham, & Lee, 2002; Palloff & Pratt, 2007; Shrum & Glisan, 2010). Not surprisingly, the technology used for CALL has consistently been compatible with the most popular language learning theories at any given time. Grammar translation and eventually the audiolingual method (ALM) dominated language teaching methodologies during the heyday of language laboratories. The following section discusses past and current trends in CALL beginning with the grammar–translation method and ALM. This discussion is followed by some reflections on the changing roles of the learner, the instructor, and the computer, specifically how these three dimensions interact with the coming of age of CALL and the ever-evolving computer classrooms.

Early Methodologies

The grammar–translation method is the oldest recorded methodology for teaching and learning a foreign language. This method was used regularly during Roman times, throughout the Middle Ages, and up through the middle of the twentieth century (Omaggio Hadley, 2001). In fact, some would argue that it remains a popular method of teaching second languages (Ellis, 2008; Thanasoulas, 2002). The grammar–translation method compelled foreign language learners to examine a text in the L1 and translate it to the L2 with the help of an expert speaker. During the Middle Ages, this methodology was the norm for the clergy learning Latin, the noble English learning French, and the noble French learning English, for example (Musumeci, 1997). Even in the early 1900s, students learned bilingual vocabulary lists and the rules of grammar as a means to learning the language. Comprehension and production skills were generally tested through translation, and there were relatively few opportunities for speaking, negotiation of meaning, or meaningful discussion. This methodology was pervasive through the first half of the twentieth century, until the publication of Skinner's (1957) behaviorist studies.

The rise of behaviorism brought with it the notion that all learning was a result of repetition and habit. This notion of the importance of repetition promoted the concept of drill-and-practice techniques, also known as drill-and-kill exercises by contemporary practitioners (Warschauer & Healey, 1998), which were characteristic of the ALM, which was founded on the assumptions that language was primarily oral in nature, that linguistics involved recurring patterns, and that language acquisition was achieved mainly through the overlearning of those patterns (Chastain, 1976). The focus shifted from speaking about the language to speaking in the language. ALM encouraged repetition with considerable attention to correct linguistic forms but provided little opportunity to create with the language. Students were merely required to parrot the expert speaker and, according to Omaggio Hadley (1993), "even when drills were meaningful the monotonous repetition eliminated the effects of meaningfulness and contextualization" (p. 98).

Traditional Roles of Learners and Instructors

Advances in SLA research and progress in language teaching methodologies led to the evolution of the roles of learners and instructors between the early 1960s and the beginning of the twenty-first century; the importance previously accorded to the instructor has gradually shifted to the learner (Hall, 2001; Horwitz, 2008; Nunan, 1999). The change has occurred slowly over the past 50 years, and technology continues to aid the shift toward more responsibility to the learner (Collins & Halverson, 2009).

The grammar–translation method posited that the text was the basis for learning the language. The creation of tasks and usefulness of the language relied largely on the instructor (or expert speaker); the instructor decided which tasks the learner should complete, determined the value of the language, and evaluated the ability of the speaker.

ALM provided for a minimal shift in the roles of learner and instructor. The expert speaker still provided the input and tasks and to a large extent determined what the learner needed to know about the language and culture. In many cases, ALM resulted in the instructor initiating all speaking tasks and correcting inaccurate grammatical forms produced by the learner. The learner, on the other hand, did not need to initiate any type of speech (i.e., create with the language), but rather responded to the stimulus provided by the instructor.

As a response to the roles assigned to the teacher and the learner during the audiolingual period, the 1980s and 1990s saw increasing emphasis on the learner (see Nunan, 1988) and learner processes (Cook, 1991) so that learners' needs could guide the curriculum via needs assessment and curricular evaluation. Popular L2 learning methodologies encouraged creative use of the language, meaningful practice, and authentic tasks. The role of the learner was emphasized in methodologies that posited reducing learner anxiety, allowing autonomy and independence, and increasing motivation. Instruction in the 1990s continued to give more autonomy to the learner and focused on more constructivist models of teaching and learning while starting to emphasize more attention to the tasks that students complete to learn language (Nunan, 1999).

In addition to focusing more on the learner, much literature from a variety of theoretical perspectives has stressed the importance of meaningful interaction

(Doughty & Long, 2003; Ellis, 1994; Mitchell & Myles, 2004; Saville-Troike, 2006; VanPatten, 2007). Regardless of the theoretical focus (e.g., comprehensible input, negotiation of meaning, activity theory, or strategy use), the classroom practice that applies many of the theoretical principles is meaningful interaction among students (see Chapter 4 for a discussion of SLA theories).

Indeed, the overriding L2 methodology of the early twenty-first century is eclecticism, in which instructors experiment with a collection of activities that work for them and their students (Horwitz, 2008). Part of the reason for the eclectic approach to teaching languages may come from the variety of fields that inform language teaching methodology, such as sociology, psychology, general education, and linguistics. Along with SLA, the development of these fields has contributed significantly to language teaching methodologies since the 1960s. Nevertheless, many questions persist, and there is by no means consensus on most of the methodological solutions offered to date. Language instructors and researchers largely agree that *no one true method* exists to teach a second language but that emphasis on the learner and interaction is paramount to the task (Curtain & Dahlberg, 2010; Omaggio Hadley, 2001; Shrum & Glisan, 2010).

Role of Computers and Limitations of Technology

The availability of technology has often, but not always, coincided with the dominant metaphor that drives the methodology for language learning. Table 1.1 shows a brief overview of the development of technology and language learning methodology and a rough timeline of their occurrence. Davies, Walker, Rendall, and Hewer (2012) offer several typologies and phases of CALL's development that classify it according to task (e.g., gap filling, multiple choice, tutorial programs, simulations, text mazes, cloze), skill (e.g., reading, writing, vocabulary, listening), area of use (home, office, school, library), conceptual metaphor (behavioristic, communicative, integrative), and technology (text, multimedia, Web 1.0, Web 2.0). This historic presentation reveals the parallels in available technology and tasks for learning an L2. We begin with simple models of learning machines and grammar translation, move quickly through the development of personal computers, and finish with web-based or cloud-based resources to manage and teach language courses.

CALL got its start with the early learning machines of the 1920s (Desmarais, 1998), but significant technological developments in the 1960s allowed more frequent use of computers in language learning contexts (Delcloque, 2000). Early learning machines presented questions to the learners and would not let them proceed to the next part of the lesson until they had answered the questions correctly. The language machine model gave way to twenty-first-century ideas of programmed instruction, whereby learners must pass a test or quiz after each learning module before continuing to the next module, a sequential model of learning that is still popular in online and distance instruction today. According to Paramskas (1999), even during the 1960s and 1970s, computers offered limited feedback and a "resolutely grammar-based approach" (p. 13). Fitting the computer into the role of instructor under a grammar–translation

TABLE 1.1 Timeline of Technology and Teaching Methodology

Technology	Typical Activity/Methodology	Timeline
Learning machines	Grammar translation	1920s
Mainframe computer	Grammar-based tasks	1960s–1970s
PLATO (Programmed Logic for Automatic Teaching Operations)	Stimulus–response tasks, audiolingual method	1960s
TICCIT (Time-shared Interactive Computer-Controlled Information Television)	Multimedia, learner control, communicative activities	1970–1980
Personal computer and stand-alone authoring tools (e.g., HyperCard, ToolBook, Wida) and videodiscs	Learner-directed drills, communicative activities, information gap activities	1970s–1990s
Personal computers and the WWW	Learner-directed activities, communicative activities, shared resources	1990–2010
Personal computers and Web 2.0	Project-based learning, community construction	2000–present

paradigm was not difficult; the computer merely had to provide tasks and corrections, and it could easily do so in a text-only environment from a mainframe or nonnetworked computer.

The computer was easily able to assume the role of the instructor under the ALM vision of instructor and learner roles because computers could be programmed to provide any number of drills on grammar, vocabulary, or pronunciation. The PLATO (Programmed Logic for Automatic Teaching Operations) program provided stimulus–response–modeled teaching for much of the 1960s. These types of activities allowed the computer to play only a minimal role in the classroom, because learners typically went to language labs to complete the drills, and valuable class time could be devoted to oral practice.

> Both CALICO and TICCIT are closely associated with Frank Otto, professor of linguistics at Brigham Young University (BYU) in Provo, Utah. The TICCIT program was used at BYU initially (1975) for math and English, but it was used through 1994 for languages including Dutch, German, French, and Chinese.

Although IBM was established in 1924, the use of computer technology did not become widespread until the late 1970s when Apple and Microsoft made the personal computer more affordable and accessible to instructors and students. Coincidentally, L2 methodologies also began to emphasize the individual role of the L2 learner during this same period. The late 1970s and early 1980s saw the creation of CALICO (Computer-Assisted Language Instruction Consortium), the first association dedicated to L2 instruction and computers in the United States, and TICCIT (Time-shared Interactive Computer-Controlled Informational Television), which is arguably the first multimedia L2 computer application. One of the most important tenets of TICCIT was learner control. Students used control buttons to select examples or rules, and to opt for hard or easy questions. The ability of the learner to control the program, novel at the time, influenced many CALL applications that followed, including most HyperCard and ToolBook applications, as well as interactive videodisc adventures such as *Oscar Lake* and *À la Rencontre de Philippe*.

In the early part of the twentieth century, programmers, mathematicians, and physicists were the main users of computers. A graphical user interface (GUI) allowed nonprogrammers to dabble with computers without knowing all of the needed commands. However, it was not until the 1980s that the computer, and specifically CALL, began to take its current form. Personal computers spread across most universities and schools; in 1982, the personal computer was voted Machine of the Year by *Time* magazine. Since then, individuals, rather than only large research institutions and businesses, have bought and used computers at increasing rates. HyperCard was introduced in 1987, and other less well-known authoring systems followed shortly thereafter. The WWW was created in the 1980s, and enormous progress occurred in speech recognition, machine translation, artificial intelligence, natural language processing, and CALL throughout the 1990s (Delcloque, 2000).

Thus, the 1990s witnessed an explosion of personal computers and internet usage, specifically email and the WWW. The *Computer Industry Almanac* estimated 147 million internet users in 1988, and Internet World Stats (http://www.internetworldstats.com, 2011a) claims 361 million internet users in 2000 and more than 2.26 billion in 2011. The World Wide Web's ease of use allows novice users to search for information, intermediate users to publish information, and expert users to manipulate information in a way that was not previously permitted. The 1990s also saw a number of advances in videodiscs and other stand-alone material (Bush & Terry, 1997). GUI and multimedia allowed for easily understandable user interface and considerable change from the drill-and-practice, text-based exercises of the earlier decades.

Despite these numerous advances in both technology and language teaching, many developers failed to harmonize their language learning products with the methodological trends of the day, and a number of CALL applications merely masked drill-and-practice activities with bells and whistles. It is important to note that although the addition of multimedia was unable to improve poorly designed activities, it was indeed able to improve good activities. The addition of multimedia also made it more difficult for instructors to anticipate which applications would be the most effective for their students. Before the advent of multimedia, instructors normally evaluated CALL software simply on the basis of text, feedback, scope, and usability. Following the introduction of multimedia, instructors began to evaluate CALL applications according to text; feedback; scope; usability, sound and video quality; cultural appropriateness; hardware and software limitations (i.e., memory, storage space, speakers, video drivers); and, finally, the distraction factor, or how the bells and whistles might detract from the actual task of learning the language.

Interface versus Interaction

Interaction occurs between two live beings, whereas *interface* occurs between a human and a computer. These terms seem to refer to the same general phenomenon, but they have historically been exclusive. During the 1990s, SLA researchers and language teaching methodologists focused increasingly on interaction and the reasons why interaction facilitates SLA while CALL advocates emphasized interface and task types (Davies et al., 2012). Bush and Terry (1997) demonstrate that CALL researchers sought to answer questions such as How easy is X to use? How can we get the learner to do X? What should the learner be able to do at this point? Yet rarely did CALL designers ask the question Why? It was not until the late 1990s and the early 2000s when the design of CALL began to coincide with the demands of language learning specialists (Arnold & Ducate, 2006). Besides the natural progression of technology (first, "Look what we can do!" and then "Look what works better!"), the web created a relatively standard and intuitive interface for users (i.e., the same type of functionality on various machines using a variety of software packages). Language specialists learned this standard interface easily and because they could publish their own materials, many technophile language specialists created their own activities and published them online during the 1990s (Gonglewski & DuBravac, 2006). Many design applications also became available to aid in the creation of webware such as Blackboard.com, HotPotatoes.com, and Quia.com. These design applications allowed instructors with little knowledge in coding or network communications to develop online activities for their courses (e.g., matching pictures, online quizzes, word/sentence jumbles, multiple-choice questions). Even today, many instructors use online design tools to augment their course activities. In addition to the helpful online design tools, services such as Geocities.com (now Yahoo.com) and most universities offered free online web space to publish web pages for both students and instructors. The accessibility of the WWW for students and instructors enables any student or professor to have an online presence or to use the web to create activities or presentations that are accessible from any computer at any time. Davies et al. (2012) note that CALL took a step backward during this period, and numerous sites emerged with drill-and-practice activities and point-and-click exercises simply because they were easy activities to create online.

It was not until the turn of the century that the technical aspects of the WWW allowed for video, audio, and Web 2.0 interactions such as chat, instant messaging, and social networking sites. Several early web sites began offering keypal connections (email exchanges between native speakers). These keypal connections permitted students learning a language in one school to communicate asynchronously (i.e., via email) with students from a target language school. Eventually chat programs became popular because they allowed students to communicate synchronously with others in the target language and also provided impetus for numerous academic studies (see Chapter 8).

The development of technology helped move the teacher out of the center of the classroom activity because the instructor no longer controlled the interactions. Indeed, email, social media, and the variety of information on the web make it impossible for instructors to control the amount or type of input that students receive. The instructor moved from controlling and maintaining the classroom environment to facilitating and directing students' choice of topics, mode of discussion, and method of presentation. Admittedly, instructors could still dictate the quantity of the interchange between students (e.g., two emails per week, one tweet per day, 10 minutes of Skype), but their ability to structure the interaction (e.g., only present tense, or focus on food) was seriously reduced with the arrival of Web 2.0 applications. Even with WebQuests (an activity whereby students search for information on the web, generally attributed to Dodge, 1995), instructors have little control over the content of the web pages that their students stumble upon.

This change in locus of control for the instructor as a result of technological advancements coincided with a push for "learner-centered approaches" (Horwitz, 2008). Such approaches encourage instructors to concentrate on teaching students to govern and direct their own learning rather than follow the instructor. In fact, the model of learners as agents coincides with what digital natives have come to expect in education (Collins & Halverson, 2009). *Digital natives*, a term coined by Marc Prensky (2001), describes those who were born during or after the general introduction of digital technology. They have interacted with technology from a young age and have a greater understanding of its uses and concepts. Digital natives expect to be agents of their own learning and to use technology frequently and for a variety of purposes.

The modern instructor in technologically enhanced environments seeks to implement technology when it provides significant advantages over traditional instructional methods, particularly in light of the distinct orientation of those who grew up with the internet, also known as the *net generation* (Oblinger & Oblinger, 2005). Technology should not be used simply for technology's sake, but rather because it facilitates tasks better than other teaching tools. For example, a teacher may decide to conduct a brainstorming session with students using a PowerPoint slide or a wiki page as a method of recording and displaying the answers offered by the students. On the other hand, if the goal is to demonstrate accurate orthography, chalk on a chalkboard may be easier and cheaper than an overhead projection system. For the modern instructor, the task drives the use of technology.

Modern Smart Classrooms or E-Classrooms

Smerdon and Cronen (2000) reported that in 2000, only half of teachers who had computers in the classroom used them for instruction. Rother (2005) echoed this report five years later from a survey that reported that although 80% of high school teachers used computers for administrative functions, only a little more than half regularly used them for instructional purposes. The *Chronicle of*

Higher Education (Young, 2010) reports similar statistics for colleges and universities: 76% of respondents use technology that supports classroom management (e.g., Blackboard/Moodle, plagiarism detection tools), but fewer than 17% use technology that supports teaching (e.g., blogs, videoconferencing, games/ simulations, wikis [web sites that can be edited and changed by anyone], chat).

These findings are not surprising because there is significantly more support for the use of management applications than for teaching applications. Many high school teachers identified the need for more computers in their classroom (Rother, 2005) because students would each need their own computer (called *one-to-one computing environments*) if the goal were instruction, but one computer for the entire class suffices for management purposes. Teachers may often find it difficult to rely on a media center or language lab that might require more planning for scheduling, using software updates, logistics, and so on. This argument may no longer be valid because the student-to-computer ratio is changing as schools move toward using mobile devices available to all students.

At the postsecondary level, planning and support also influences the types of technology that faculty adopt. Management systems such as Blackboard or Moodle often provide significant support, whereas other forms of technology may be less stable or less supported (e.g., Twitter, video conferencing). Moreover, these systems offer explicit and simple instructions on using the management aspects of the systems (e.g., how to post an announcement, enter grades, or send a mass email), but the teaching content tends to be more general and require more extensive experimentation (i.e., using a wiki for brainstorming, using group sites for project completion, using journals or blogs).

Modern computer classrooms are often called *smart classrooms* or *e-classrooms*. The nomenclature is unimportnt, but it is necessary to define the technology used in a classroom. Some classrooms offer one computer per individual, whereas students share computers in others; some have a computer station of three to six computers; still others have only one terminal in the back of the room. In 2005, three out of four high school teachers reported that they work in an environment with limited computers in the classroom (Rother, 2005). Some institutions offer rotating schedules for a single computer classroom; for example, instructors are able to take their classes to the computer lab no more than once a week. Yet increasingly K–12 classrooms are using mobile devices (e.g.,

---

TASK 1.1

Select a nearby institution (e.g., a high school, community college, or your own university) and report on the available technology for that institution. Report on these three categories: hardware, software, and human support. Here are some possible questions: What type of technology is available (e.g., computer classrooms, projectors, speakers, microphones, video cameras) and how accessible is it? What types of software are available? How much support is there for a teacher (e.g., workshops, a help desk, a lecture series in educational technology, Blackboard course creation)? What kind of support is there for students? Compare your findings with those of others in the class.

iPads, iPods) to satisfy their computing needs (Roscorla, 2011). Whatever the case, evaluation of the technological capabilities and availability of computing resources will determine to a large extent how learning is improved through CALL.

Just as the 1960s saw the creation and development of language labs, the twenty-first century is seeing the creation and development of computer classrooms. Today's computer classrooms are increasingly equipped with software and hardware that allow students to direct their own learning and use a variety of personalized tools, both in class and at home. The development of language labs and the exercises done in the language labs of the 1960s and 1970s gave more control to the instructor because they encouraged a teacher-fronted classroom. In contrast, today's computer classrooms have diminished the preeminence of the instructor, giving precedence to the language task (often done outside of class). Instructors still have significant control over the language learning activities but not direct control they had earlier; today, instructor control stems from structured tasks assigned to the students.

Recent trends in teaching encourage small-group cooperative work, attention to learning styles, the use of authentic tasks and language, empowerment of students, and creative use of the language (Horwitz, 2008). Technology facilitates these goals in many ways when implemented properly (Collins & Halverson, 2009). One of the most important ways to ensure that technology facilitates the communicative goals rather than distracting students' attention is to verify that the task drives the technology and not vice versa. Although this mantra seems obvious, it is not always easy to apply. The most successful technophile instructors often push the technology to the limit and create bleeding-edge applications (i.e., those that are even newer than cutting-edge technology) that do not provide the communicative support for which they were designed. However, once these technologies are fully examined through experimentation, they can be paired with tasks that are more suited to the technology. Thus, it is wise to experiment with the technology, but the communicative task should dictate the technology used in class.

TECHNICAL CONSIDERATIONS

During the 1990s (i.e., the so-called information age), enormous amounts of hype surrounded CALL and the capabilities of computers. Much of that hype has now become reality, even ordinary. Among the more commonplace and usable technologies in the classroom today are the WWW (i.e., online courses, student publications, and web activities), synchronous communication (e.g., Internet Relay Chat, text messaging, Skype, and instant messaging), asynchronous communication (e.g., email, blogs, wikis, and bulletin boards), and online communities (e.g., Facebook, Second Life, Yahoo!/Google groups, Twitter, Flickr). The number of online services available today is astounding; Apple.com (2012) reports over 500,000 apps in their app store. Instructors who explore these options while striving to become proficient in the use of electronic resources discover quickly that they accumulate a large number of login IDs and passwords for these sites. In fact, readers who explore the resources mentioned in this book and the accompanying web site will find that they need more than 100 login IDs and passwords.

To maintain the dizzying array of passwords and still uphold a threshold level of security, instructors can make use of two important tools. First, a backup tool is indispensable. There are local (or offline) and online backup options depending on the need to back up to a spare partition, a flashdrive, an external drive, or an online drive. Second, a password manager can help instructors manage online information safely without the need to constantly create and maintain hundreds of passwords.

Backup software has been around for many years, yet stories persist of students or instructors who find themselves with unrecoverable files. Loss of files can result from accidental deletions, viruses, or hard drive failure (and all hard drives crash, it is only a matter of time). Many instructors believe that storing files on a flashdrive and copies on the computer hard drive is sufficient. However, making regular backups of the files can be spotty at best without a backup program. There are a number of free software tools for local storage. Windows and Mac systems come with free backup utilities. Additionally, FBackup (fbackup.com) and Comodo backup (comodo.com) are both free and easy to use. Backup programs compare file systems and make sure that the file system on the hard drive is identical to the backup file system. They also have settings that allow users to set the backup frequency (e.g., daily, twice a week, monthly).

Using online services such as Mozy (mozy.com) or Dropbox (dropbox.com) is also an excellent option for storing files because they are available for both Mac and PC, they are free, they are easy to configure, and users will be able to access their files on any computer. If users run out of the free space, they can subscribe to the service for additional storage. Users can often set which files to back up and how frequently to check for new versions. Admittedly, setting up backup software takes effort, but it takes much less time and effort to set it up than to seek professional help when trying to retrieve lost or damaged files.

The second important tool to use on a regular basis is a password manager. The two main advantages of a password manager are security and ease of use. Security is important because an increasing amount of our information is online that, if left unprotected, can be used for any number of malicious purposes. Many individuals prioritize ease of use over security, however. In a given day, one must remember passwords to access the desktop computer, email, Facebook, Blackboard, online banking, Skype, or any number of other online services. It is much easier to have weak passwords (e.g., 12345), the same password for all accounts, or passwords that incorporate personal information (e.g., your phone number, name, or address).

Although many readers may already be aware of how to make strong passwords, it bears repeating because some users still do not protect their accounts appropriately. Passwords are the easiest method of protecting sensitive information, and a few key points may help facilitate good security practices:

1. Strong passwords tend to be longer, contain more variety (called *entropy* or *bit strength*), and are difficult to guess.
    a. Do not create short passwords. Longer, more complex passwords are more difficult to crack than a short, simple password. Length refers to

the number of characters in a password, and the length should be at least 8 characters; however, passwords between 10 and 14 characters are more secure. Complexity refers to the sets of characters that are included in the password. These sets include lowercase letters (a, b, c), uppercase letters (A, B, C), numbers (1, 2, 3), punctuation (!, @, #, %), and alt-characters (¢, £, ç, ¿).

b. Do not use dictionary words. Password-cracking software often works by comparing lists of words against passwords until they find a match. If a password can be found in a list (of words, proper names, foreign words, numbers, etc.), then it can be cracked very easily.

c. Do not include personal information. Personal information is alarmingly easy to find on the internet. Hackers can, and often do, use this information to crack passwords and gain access to accounts. This includes name, nickname, the names of family members or pets, address, phone number, or important dates (e.g., marriage, birth).

2. Do not store passwords in an unencrypted format. UserIDs or passwords stored in manual or digital format are easily stolen. In most cases, allowing an IM client or internet browser to remember passwords enables anyone to access the account if they have physical access to the machine.

3. Do not use the same password across accounts. Although a number of sites store users' passwords in an encrypted format on their servers, they are not required to do so and many sites simply store passwords in a plain text file. For example, when users log in to a blog to post comments and if the blogging site stores passwords in a plain text file, then a hacker can gain access to usernames and passwords by simply stealing that file from the server. If users have the same password for banking sites, PayPal, or email accounts, then the hacker now has access to those accounts.

Conventional wisdom also suggests another practice that really does not improve security enough to justify the trouble it creates for users: Change your password regularly. The need for frequent password changes is a result of *password aging*, a method used to eliminate discontinued accounts in organizations with frequent turnover; although it used to be important to change passwords frequently (every 30, 60, or 90 days), it is no longer considered valuable protection against password theft, cracking, or sharing. The best defense is a strong password, and the only reason that instructors would want to change their passwords each semester is if they must share their password with someone (e.g., a student at the help desk or a teaching assistant) who ends up in their class and could potentially change his or her grade online using the professor's password. However, it would be better to change the password after the student no longer needs access, rather than wait 90 days.

Some individuals do not adhere to these security standards because they struggle to come up with a sufficient number of strong passwords, and have even more difficulty remembering them. Most security experts recommend choosing a passphrase instead of a password (Granger, 2002). This means choosing a phrase (e.g., "I like green eggs & ham. Sam-I-am does not.") and using the letters from the phrase as the password—Ilge&h.SIadn. Adding some characters and numbers (e.g., replacing "l" with "1," "e" with "3," and "s" with "$")—*I1g3&h.$IadØ*—results in a strong password (bit strength = 81) compared to *iloveyou* or *princess* (bit strength = 5 for each). *Bit strength* refers to the amount of entropy (or unpredictability) of a given string. The lower the entropy or bit strength, the more susceptible the password is to being guessed through trial and error. Burr, Dodson, and Polk (2006) of the National Institute of Standards and Technology recommend at least 80 bits for secure passwords; however, even 64 bits would take around four years to decrypt using contemporary machines working 24 hours per day. Users can check the strength of their passwords at PasswordMeter.com or by searching "password checker" in any search engine.

The most important tool you can have at your disposal to help you maintain good passwords is a password manager that enables users not only to create, maintain, and organize passwords, but also to set a date to change the password. The dominant password managers such as KeePass (keepass.info [crossplatform]), 1Password (agilewebsolutions.com/products/1Password [for MAC]), and Roboform (roboform.com [for PC]) have numerous advantages, as summarized in Table 1.2.

Password managers allow a user to store sensitive information in a secure location and remember only one master password, the password for the database. The userID/password combinations are stored in an encrypted format to protect the file if it is ever lost or stolen. It would still take an incredible amount of time to hack (depending on the master password/passphrase). If users have difficulty creating a secure password, many password managers will generate a random password according to criteria selected by the user (e.g., lowercase, uppercase, symbols, numbers, alt-chars, spaces, brackets, repeated characters). Moreover, this password can be complex and forgettable because a password manager can also take users directly to the site and auto-fill the login form so that the user never types the password again. If users feel more secure changing their passwords on a regular basis or if IT management policy requires employees to change their passwords periodically, users can set the password manager to remind them when it expires.

In short, there are few drawbacks compared to the number of advantages offered by a password manager. The biggest drawback is that if the master password for the database is lost or forgotten, it cannot be recovered. Now it may become clear why we began this discussion with the importance of a good backup utility. This tool in conjunction with a password manager can improve security, ease of use, and overall efficiency with the amount of online resources that a technologically savvy instructor uses on a regular basis.

Instructors who wish to access their information both at home and at school can use portable versions designed to be stored on flashdrives or mobile devices as well as online options (e.g., clipperz.com, passpack.com). They all perform the same basic functions and guarantee the same level of security.

TABLE 1.2 Advice and Password Managers

Advice	Problem	Password Manager Solution
Use strong passwords. (passphrases)	Passwords are too long or too random to remember.	Passwords are easily accessible in one file (either on the hard disk or on a portable flashdrive). Users need to remember only one master password for the file.
Do not store passwords in an unencrypted format.	Most users cannot encrypt their own files.	Passwords are stored in an encrypted, password-protected file that can be opened only with the master password.
Do not use the same password for different accounts.	a. Too difficult to create strong passwords	Password managers can generate random passwords to be used. Passwords can use the characters you designate (lowercase, uppercase, symbols, numbers, alt-chars, spaces, brackets) with the length you want.
	b. Too difficult to remember which password goes with which site	Many password managers allow you to go directly to the site from the password manager so that you do not need to retype your userID/password combination.
Do not let the program/website remember your password.	Too painful to input your userID and password every time you go to a site	Password managers often let you go directly to the website, auto-fill the password, and enter multiple sites without ever typing your password.
Change passwords regularly (if you feel the need to do so).	Too lazy to change	Password managers can remind you to change your password or let you know when the password expires.

TASK 1.2

Begin using a backup program and password manager

1. Download or sign up online for a backup utility that you can use for at least the next month. Decide which folders you will back up and how frequently.
2. Download or sign up online for a password manager. For the rest of this book, each time you are asked to evaluate or try out a new online resource, store your userID and (strong) password in the password manager.

TASK 1.3

Search your institution or school district and identify who or where one can go for technological help (e.g., IT help desk, technology specialist). Identify at least three resources that you can use to learn about the technologies available to you.

Conclusion

The emphasis on communication in language learning has mirrored the developments in technology. Early models emphasized reception skills evident in translation and reading web pages. The focus on reception shifted to production, as seen in Swain's (1985) output hypothesis and the increase in individual web pages (e.g., personal sites, blogs, Twitter). Negotiation has become a buzzword in language teaching methodology and a focus for many social networking sites (e.g., Facebook.com) and conferencing software (e.g., Skype, AdobeConnect.com).

Most institutions offer web space for instructors, and many offer online course products such as Blackboard or Moodle (called learning management systems [LMSs]). Many of these services are moving to the cloud rather than being housed by proprietary servers. For example, a wiki used to depend on the server on which the application was loaded. Today with free sites such as WikiSpaces.com and PBWorks.com, instructors do not need to rely on server space to run a wiki; they simply sign up for the service provided on the web. Blogs are no different in that very few people house their own blog; rather, they rely on online services such as Blogger.com, or wordpress.com.

The remainder of this book examines a variety of services and technological resources (such as web pages, email, wikis, blogs, chat, and portfolio management sites) in an attempt to clarify the options available to instructors. It may be more prudent for instructors to develop a technology toolbox to use rather than trying to master all of the technologies or implement all of the services in a single course. The purpose of the following chapters is not to convince readers that the all-inclusive use of technology is advantageous to learning a foreign language, but instead that certain technologies provide significant advantages for selected activities in particular situations. The goal of this book is to help instructors acquire a knowledge of how, when, and why to use certain technologies to enhance language learning and facilitate their own teaching.

Practical Work

This section contains questions for review and suggestions for developing computer skills.

1. What do the following acronyms mean?

a. CALL	**e.** L2	**i.** ISP	**m.** DVD
b. TELL	**f.** CAI	**j.** FTP	**n.** LMS
c. SLA	**g.** ALM	**k.** IRC	
d. CMC	**h.** CALICO	**l.** GUI	

2. According to the chapter, how do language teaching methods and technology relate to each other?

3. What are some of the recent major developments in L2 instruction that have affected CALL?

4. Name three of the most frequent activities that you do using technology (in or out of school). If you teach, how is this different from or similar to your students' use of technology?

5. Define, as you see it, the roles of the learner, the instructor, and the computer in a foreign language course.

6. How many local drives does your personal computer have?

7. What is the difference between the internet and the WWW?

8. Name five ways you could use the internet in a class you are teaching.

9. Having a presence on the web is an important first step to feeling comfortable and making it easy to use the internet more frequently in a class you are teaching. Choose one of the following to complete this week:

a. Create your own web space if you have not already established a presence on the web.

Most ISPs (internet service providers) offer free space that accompanies your monthly connection payment, but a number of online services also provide free web space such as http://www.wix.com, http://www.pbworks.com, or Google sites (http://sites.google.com). If your institution does not provide web space to students, these sites are excellent resources. The most common problem encountered when students open a web account is that they forget their userID and password, so novices should write this information on a card and keep it where it is easy to access.

A web site is simple to create and maintain if the initial organization of the site is clear. The first step toward good web design is to flowchart the site, showing where each page will lead. It is wise to create separate directories for separate concepts. For example, an instructor may decide to have a separate directory for each class. It is also wise to create a separate directory for all images. The reason is to reduce the need to search through hundreds of pages on the server to find the one that needs updating. Begin with the end in mind.

b. Set up an online Blackboard or Moodle for your class.

Many schools, colleges, and universities now offer learning management systems (LMSs) such as Moodle, Blackboard, or Sakai. These LMSs allow instructors to post and delete items online. The main advantage to LMSs is that instructors do not need to learn how to transfer files, write web pages, or maintain security for the information they have posted. Most learning management systems also allow online testing (including timed tests), online grade books, chat, and other beneficial automated processes that make the instructor's life much simpler.

c. Begin a blog.

Teachers and students are increasingly using blogs (or Weblogs, see Chapter 8) to maintain their presence on the web since maintaining a blog is as simple as filling out a form on the web.

10. Subscribe to a listserv.

A good listserv can be a regular source of reliable, useful, and timely information for professional development. Some good listservs are FLTEACH and L-TESOL. You can find these and others by searching "foreign language listserv" or "language learning listserv." Instructions for joining the listserv will be included on the sites that you find.

Suggestions for Further Reading

Arnold, N., & Ducate, L. (2006). CALL: Where are we and where do we go from here? In L. Ducate & N. Arnold (Eds.), *Calling on CALL: From theory and research to new directions in foreign language teaching* (pp. 1–20). San Marcos, TX: CALICO.

Chapelle, C. A. (2001). *Computer applications in second language acquisition: Foundations for teaching, testing, and research.* New York: Cambridge University Press.

Davies, G., Walker, R., Rendall, H., & Hewer, S. (2012). Introduction to computer assisted language learning (CALL). Module 1.4 in G. Davies (Ed.), *Information and communications technology for language teachers (ICT4LT),* Slough, Thames Valley University [Online]. Available from http://www.ict4lt.org/en/en_mod1-4.htm

Delcloque, P. (2000). *The history of computer assisted language learning, Web edition.* Available from http://www.ict4lt.org/en/History_of_CALL.pdf

Levy, M. (1997). *Computer-assisted language learning: Context and conceptualization.* New York: Oxford University Press.

Musumeci, D. (1997). *Breaking tradition: An exploration of the historical relationship between theory and practice in second language teaching.* Boston: McGraw-Hill.

Warschauer, M., & Healey, D. (1998). Computers and language learning: An overview. *Language Teaching, 31,* 57–71.

ANSWER KEYS

a. Computer-Assisted Language Learning, b. Technology-Enhanced Language Learning, c. Second Language Acquisition, d. Computer-mediated Communication, e. Second Language, f. Computer-assisted Instruction, g. Audio-lingual Method, h. Computer-Assisted Language Instruction Consortium, i. Internet Service Provider, j. File Transfer Protocol, k. Internet Relay Chat, l. Graphical User Interface, m. Digital Videodisc (originally) or Digital Versatile Disc (current), n. Learning Management System.

CHAPTER 2

Evaluating and Using Software, Online Applications, and Hardware

OVERVIEW

One direct influence on computer-assisted language learning (CALL) is the wide array of available software products ranging from the latest language-specific application to programs as ubiquitous as the word processor. This chapter addresses two important dimensions of software evaluation: the selection of appropriate technologies and some legal considerations behind their use. Specifically, the first part of the chapter helps facilitate decisions concerning the adoption of various technologies based on their anticipated use. After reviewing the history and development of early CALL activities, we discuss some widely accepted guidelines on how to evaluate language learning software and offer a set of characteristics for evaluation that includes underlying assumptions, goals, content, and technical requirements. Along with their use of commercially published packages, many instructors may want to create their own CALL activities using online resources, which brings copyright issues into play. Most teachers benefit from a number of laws that address educational purposes specifically. The second half of the chapter deals with rules and regulations that govern and protect educators and online artists including copyright law, the notion of public domain, fair use, and the TEACH Act. The chapter ends with some technical considerations that touch on selecting and creating software from both hardware and user perspectives.

EVALUATION

The guidelines for evaluation presented in this chapter focus on but are not limited to stand-alone software and online applications. Stand-alone applications run on a computer that does not have to be connected to the internet. A good example of a stand-alone application is *À la rencontre de Philippe* (Furstenberg,

1994), a computer application with videodisc support. The user's goal was to track down and help Philippe (he was trying to get other tasks completed). The user navigated a series of interactions that led to a different ending of the storyline depending on the decisions he or she made. Users needed to listen and respond appropriately to achieve the most positive story ending for Philippe.

Online apps are applications in which all or some parts of the software are downloaded from the internet each time the application is run (e.g., web pages, eBooks, rich applications). The majority of software applications, particularly those written for mobile devices, are now available as online apps. Moreover, many of the older stand-alone applications have become online apps in order to facilitate content and software updates and feedback to the developer.

Most publishing houses in the foreign language market prefer to have their software programs available on the web (i.e., as online apps). All of the major publishers want to maintain electronic versions of their world language textbook products and ancillaries (e.g., workbooks, audio and video files). Many have adopted online support such as Quia (www.quia.com) or created their own support such as MyLab (www.pearsonhighered.com/elearning/mylabs/index.html), and they all offer video, audio, and online exercises at the ancillary site for any given textbook. The purpose of this section is to discuss software characteristics so that those adopting multimedia language learning software have the background needed to make decisions concerning their educational effectiveness.

Early CALL Applications

Early CALL applications (mostly stand-alone software) either demonstrated little knowledge of language learning principles or contained incorrect assumptions concerning language learning and teaching. As discussed in Chapter 1, early models of CALL followed grammar–translation, audiolingualism, or behaviorism methodologies (Reeder et al., 2004). These models tended to promote concepts such as *mastery learning* or *programmed instruction* (stemming from the learning machines described in Chapter 1) while ignoring both communicative interaction and exposure to the target culture. The lack of communication between instructors and software designers during the 1980s and 1990s led to what Hubbard (1992) identified as gaps among design, development, and classroom implementation. The gaps occurred mainly because software designers focused on what the software could do rather than on what the learner should do. Admittedly, instructors also contributed considerably to the gap between design and use because they did not always use the software in the ways it was designed to be used. In the early years of CALL, technical limitations also determined how much authentic language and interaction could be included in the program using multimedia (video, audio, speech recognition, etc.), whereas today multimedia and ubiquitous networks have enabled a new orientation to CALL's use (Warschauer, 2004).

The 1990s generated a flood of authoring software that enabled instructors to produce their own stand-alone software (e.g., HyperCard, SuperCard, Authorware, ToolBook, Flash). The internet and the number of web pages also experienced enormous growth during the 1990s, and many instructors turned to the World Wide Web (WWW) for authentic materials and activities. Davies,

Walker, Rendall, and Hewer (2010) state that CALL took a step back during the early 1990s, and a behaviorist model reappeared. Nonetheless, improvements in technology and the advent of Web 2.0, or the social web, enabled two-way exchanges (see Chapter 3). Also during this period, some notable books and web sites took advantage of the easily accessible authentic material on the web as a springboard for language learning activities. The best known of these is Dodge's (1997) web site for WebQuest's activities in English as a Second Language (ESL) and a series of books called *Surf's Up* for French (Moehle-Vieregge, Lyman-Hager, DuBravac, & Bradley, 1997), German (Moehle-Vieregge, Bird, & Manthegi, 1997), and Spanish (Moehle-Vieregge, James, & Chuffle, 1997). The Center for Advanced Research on Language Acquisition (CARLA) also maintains a sample of WebQuest activities for less commonly taught languages (www.carla.umn.edu/technology/resources/languages.html). These activities for the web benefited many instructors because their creators invested significant time and research to determine appropriate web sites and accompanying tasks (see Chapter 3 for further discussion on this topic).

Decisions concerning which CALL resources to use should be based on best practices in language teaching methodology. The problem for some beginning instructors is that they may decide to use technology in the classroom because of administrative pressures or because they are excited about new products or services and end up using technology for technology's sake rather than as a tool for mediating language-based tasks. Thus, evaluating any language learning software or online apps according to an established set of criteria may be necessary.

TASK 2.1

1. Chapter 1 mentioned the importance of deciding on a technology palette rather than trying to master all of the tools available. The first step in developing a set of tools is to decide what you want to do with them. Which technologies are most enticing to you right now and which language learning tasks do you envision doing with them? Name two major advantages of the technologies you have selected. Name two major disadvantages of these technologies.
2. Another important step in determining benefits of certain practices is to articulate your own assumptions and beliefs about language learning. Decide if you agree or disagree with the following statements and justify your response.
   a. Learners acquire a second language faster if the instructor gives explicit grammar instruction.
   b. Learners acquire a second language better with more repetition.
   c. Learners acquire a second language better when they can negotiate meaning with others.
   d. Adult learners learn a second language faster than preadolescent learners.
   e. Younger learners learn a second language faster than older learners.
   f. Learners need to be corrected often in order to acquire the language.
   g. Learners acquire more language than they are taught.
3. What other assumptions can you identify about how you believe language is learned?

Methodical Evaluation

Although the number and type of characteristics that instructors use to evaluate an application may vary significantly, the following discussion signals some important points to consider in adopting and using software or online apps in the classroom. In their framework of modules for evaluation, Susser and Robb (2004) include language acquisition, materials design, learning styles, multimedia instructional design, and online instructional design. Although this framework is extremely thorough and provides significant guidance for evaluating software and online apps, the sheer number of items to consider may be overwhelming. In addition, many instructors may not have a strong enough background in each of the modules to feel comfortable identifying strengths and weaknesses in a given category. Hubbard (2006) argues for a methodological evaluation of software (i.e., one that strives to match technology with the teaching methodology of the institution) that includes technical considerations, operational considerations, teacher fit (how well the teacher can use it), learner fit (how well the students can use it), implementation schemes, and appropriateness judgments (or costs and benefits of a particular software program). Chapelle (2001; see also Jamieson, Chapelle, & Preiss, 2005) proposes an evaluation based on six categories: language learning potential, learner fit, meaning focus, authenticity, impact, and practicality. Chapelle's taxonomy provides an excellent basis for evaluating software in general but ignores, to some extent, the design of the program. (See Appendix A for an overview of Chapelle, 2001; Hubbard, 2006; and Susser & Robb, 2004.) Given the taxonomies listed previously, the following discussion offers questions to ask and provides possible responses. These points are presented in a taxonomic fashion and should be useful to instructors. Those with specialized and technical concerns, such as language center directors, will want to take additional factors into consideration when evaluating software.

A few principles concerning CALL evaluation are generally accepted. First, CALL adoption is situational and depends largely on the institutional context; that is, each institution must take into account its local characteristics (Angell, DuBravac, & Gonglewski, 2008; Burston, 2006; Chapelle, 2001; Davies, Walker, Rendall, & Hewer, 2012; Hubbard, 2006; Reeder et al., 2004). All of the frameworks mentioned previously include learner fit or the method of program implementation in the institutional setting. Surprisingly, Angell and colleagues (2008) found that few decision makers referred to the goals and purposes of the language departments when adopting new materials. Evaluation should include some reference to the particularities of the institutions and their student populations. Second, most of these frameworks refer to both subjective and objective criteria (Chapelle, 2001; Davies et al., 2012; Hubbard, 2006). Terms such as *ease of use* and *cultural appropriateness* tend to be highly subjective and dynamic concepts, whereas price, user satisfaction, and technical requirements tend to be easily measurable characteristics. The prominent evaluation frameworks attempt to include both types of measurements. Third, the evaluation process should be structured (Angell et al., 2008; Burston, 2006; Davies et al., 2012; Hubbard, 2006; Jamieson et al., 2005; Reeder et al., 2004, Susser &

Robb, 2004). Much of the content in a CALL package may be invisible to users unless certain procedures are used. Therefore, checklists, forms, and rubrics are particularly helpful for the evaluation of CALL software. Software packages can also contain a dizzying array of presentations, exercises, activities, and quizzes; a methodological approach enables evaluators to examine each type of task and assess each according to a predetermined standard (e.g., yes/no, good/ bad, or a rating scale). If adoption is a committee decision, checklists may be particularly helpful in enabling multiple evaluators to address the same aspects of the software. Finally, most faculty agree that the main objective of any CALL software should be its ability to enhance language learning (Angell et al., 2008; Blake, 2008; Burston, 2006; Chapelle, 2001; Davies et al., 2010; Hubbard, 2006; Jamieson et al., 2005; Reeder et al., 2004; Susser & Robb, 2004). Historically, a number of checklists have dealt with fonts, navigability, and grammatical scope and sequence, but these concerns have given way to a greater focus on how software develops intercultural competence and bilingual skills (Blake, 2008). Table 2.1 summarizes the key guidelines discussed earlier.

The following evaluation schema in Table 2.2 is divided into four major sections: underlying assumptions, goals, content, and technical considerations. Evaluation forms are useful because they may enable instructors to see beyond initial presentations and adopt the appropriate software for their classes based on fit and effectiveness rather than appearance.

TABLE 2.1 Guidelines for CALL Evaluation

Guideline	Implication
1. Adoption depends on institutional context.	Evaluators should determine the needs, learner characteristics, and goals of their particular situation to determine how technology (or a particular CALL application) fits into their language program.
2. Evaluation should use both subjective and objective criteria.	Evaluation should include a variety of methodologies (both pre and post) to determine the efficacy of using technology rather than other traditional tools (e.g., worksheets, dry-erase board). That is, how do you know if it is better than what you are currently doing?
3. The evaluation process should be structured.	Checklists, forms, or rubrics should inform the criteria and procedures for evaluating CALL.
4. The main focus of the evaluation should be on the efficacy of the application for language learning.	Criteria should concentrate on both theoretical and practical models of language acquisition and teaching.

TABLE 2.2 Categories for Evaluation

Major characteristics	Concerns	Questions to ask
Underlying assumptions	Learners/instructors	What is the role of the learner/ instructor in my institution, and what is his or her role for this application?
	Language/culture	How is language/culture represented, and what does the learner do with it?
	Learning process	How is language learned? Does the orientation to language learning coincide with the other materials used in the course?
Goals	Purpose	How will the software be used? How does the software support the overall curriculum?
Content	Accuracy	Is the language/culture appropriate and accurate?
	Relevance	Is the language/culture current?
	Interest	Is the language/culture interesting and insightful?
Technical considerations	Navigation	Is it easy to know what to do?
	Presentation	Is it easy to understand what is supposed to be learned?
	Interface	Are feedback and explanations relevant and accessible?
	Multimedia	Are there a variety of text, images, sound, and video?
	Sequence	Are there options for both a sequenced and a random path?
	Weight	How much hardware support is necessary?

Underlying Assumptions

The underlying assumptions of a software package are far reaching and wide ranging because they involve the learners, the instructor, the language/culture, and the learning process. By examining each category separately, instructors should be able to gain a greater understanding of how and why a particular software package would work for their particular context. More important, instructors may be able to predict how the applications and the use of technology can be integrated into the overall curriculum.

The Learners

Institutions generally attract a relatively homogenous student body; for example, some schools attract mostly local students, some mostly commuter students, and still others students from urban or rural areas. Instructors are usually the best judges of how those students perform in the classroom. Instructors should be able to determine whether the program is compatible with their students' technical abilities, learning styles, or language aptitude.

The technical ability of the students refers to their comfort level with computers, and it may include the capacity to troubleshoot malfunctioning software or the ability to insert diacritics and special characters or to switch to the appropriate foreign language font or keyboard. Some students may take the initiative to repair malfunctions on their own, whereas others may prefer to call on an assistant in the language resource center or the help desk. The technical ability of the students may influence the selection of CALL software by limiting choices to the most stable applications available. As a general rule, students should be able to focus on the language learning activities without having to troubleshoot the software. Institutions that have large resource centers with teaching assistant (TA) support lines may facilitate the use of certain applications that would be problematic in smaller institutions that attract students with less technical ability and may lack a central language resource center to support them.

Learning style is a psychological concept that refers to the general way that a learner approaches learning. Sensory mode preference is probably the most comprehensible example: Some learners are visual learners and need to see the words, whereas others do better with auditory, tactile, or kinesthetic methods. After a considerable review of learning style studies, Ellis (2008) reports that the research is inconclusive as far as language acquisition is concerned; learner preference for a particular sensory mode does not imply that language learning is more efficient through that mode. Empirical support is likewise lacking for many of the other prominent treatises of learning styles; Howard Gardner's (1983, 1993, 1999) widely adopted concept of *multiple intelligences* has no empirical support to indicate that teaching to one intelligence (or learning style) actually improves language learning by increasing either the rate of acquisition or the final state of acquisition. The general consensus is that lessons should include a variety of activities, modes of presentations, and support devices. In short, instructors should look for the following:

- Holistic presentations that allow analysis of specific details (through glossed items or detail-oriented support tools).
- A wide array of multimedia (images, sounds, movies, and a multitude of response mechanisms beyond text entry).
- A system that allows sequenced lessons as well as the ability to explore the language/culture in a random order (i.e., learner control).
- A structure for self-evaluation and direct confirmation of hypotheses about grammatical rules.
- A method of alternating between a competitive mode whereby students compete with others or with themselves in a network and a cooperative mode whereby they work together to complete a task or arrive at the end of the lesson.

TASK 2.2

Describe typical students at your institution (either where you teach/taught or where you are studying/have studied). Are they technologically savvy? Do they have access to a broadband internet connection at home? What is the average age? Would you call them diverse? Why? What would you tell a visitor from another country if he or she were to teach/take your class for a week? Head librarians tend to have a pretty good sense of the technological literacy of library users. Make an appointment to interview your librarian (if there are several, seek out the one responsible for electronic acquisitions or training) and try to verify or clarify the vision you have of the "average" person in your local environment.

Language aptitude refers not only to the ability of the individual to speak the language but also his or her ability to learn the language (Skehan, 1989). Gass and Selinker (2008) argue that aptitude is almost inseparable from seemingly unrelated concerns such as motivation, parental education, social class, and background knowledge. Moreover, with the exception of a few specialized institutions, assessment of language aptitudes is largely avoided because of the consensus that everyone can learn a language (Horwitz, 2008).

The Instructor

Every software package or online app has assumptions concerning the instructor and how the program fits into the curriculum. The main issues that instructors need to examine are the connection to the curriculum and the management tools that enable that connection. Instructors and language program directors (LPDs) should have a clear idea of where a course fits in the curriculum and how that course meets the purposes of the overall curriculum.

To assess the link between a software application and the curriculum, instructors should start with a well-articulated description of the curriculum and what students are expected to be able to do at given points throughout it. Instructors can then ask themselves if the software will be used in a language center or in regular class activity (i.e., Will the students and instructors need to access it during class hours? How will they do this?) and how many instructors will be using the software.

Instructors should strive to integrate the software into the curriculum rather than adopt it as an add-on. There should be a strong connection between what occurs outside of class (i.e., as homework or in the language center or computer classroom) and what occurs in class. Students tend to value their experience online less if they do not see it as central to their language learning experience.

Next, instructors should examine the management tools available for the software. Asking a few key questions can shed light on how instructors will use the tools:

- How will students be graded (quantity vs. quality)?
- Who will assign the grades (the software or the instructor)?

- How many instructors will be using the software, and what access do they have?
- How should they collect data to grade students?
- How are the records kept?
- Will the grade book include other grades in the class, or will it contain only the work from the activities students have completed online?

As a general rule, adopted applications should be able to reduce the amount of work for instructors in comparison to what they would do without the technology. For example, some software applications provide numerous open-response questions that are not self-correcting. If instructors need to supply detailed feedback, it would be easier and less time consuming for most instructors to grade a printed page than it would be to click through all of their students' work and provide feedback online. In an institution that requires detailed feedback on all assignments, an online workbook may not be the best solution.

Publishers make numerous assumptions about how instructors will or should use the software. They seek to develop software that is as flexible as possible, although there is always a bias for one learning context over another (e.g., four-year institution, community college, online courses, hybrid courses). It is the instructor's role to adapt the software to the local environment. If instructors are aiming for full integration of a software package into the curriculum, they must clearly understand their roles and those of their students.

The Language and Culture

Underlying assumptions about the language are evident in how the program views language and the cultural knowledge for which students are responsible. Some of these concepts are revisited in the "Content" section that appears later in this chapter. To address the underlying assumptions of language and culture, ask yourself the following questions:

- Does the program present only the four skills of reading, writing, listening, and speaking?
- How prominent/correct/current is the linguistic and cultural information?
- Is the language an object of study or a tool for studying something else?

The underlying assumptions about culture will also be important in coordinating the cultural knowledge that is linked to classroom activities. Instructors should determine how the program views culture in relation to other aspects of language learning:

- Does the software focus on explaining cultural phenomena (e.g., French people do not generally say "hello" to each other more than once per day), or does it focus on examining the perspectives of the people (e.g., Americans often say "hello" to recognize the presence of someone they know. The French usually say "bonjour" to validate membership in a group [of friends or colleagues for example]. For Americans, not saying "hello" every time you see a friend represents a social snub, because you're ignoring their presence. For the French, saying "bonjour" repeatedly to friends represents a snub, because you're ignoring the initial validation of the friendship)?

- Is there a bias for one country/culture over others (see the "Content" section later in this chapter).
- What are the cultural elements in the program?
- Is culture subordinate to language? Do culture and language complement each other? Does the language take a back seat to the cultural presentations?

The underlying assumptions about language and culture reveal how these two aspects of language learning are related and how much importance is given to each one. In a course with a strong focus on grammar and speaking, it might be advantageous to include CALL support that concentrates on culture. Likewise, in courses that emphasize literature and culture, CALL might support students' linguistic or cognitive ability to express what they learn.

The Learning Process

Assumptions about the learning process are readily manifested in the types of activities that learners accomplish. Some packages that are marketed on the basis of educational games are merely drills in disguise, and programs that tout their technology may lack a solid foundation in learning theory. One concern that inevitably enters into most conversations concerning language learning materials is whether the materials have a communicative approach, or an approach that emphasizes communication as both the means and the goal of language learning. The term *communicative approach* was used so extensively in the 1990s and 2000s that it has lost any significant meaning; it is nearly impossible to find an introductory language book in French, German, or Spanish that does not claim to take a communicative approach. Likewise, most software programs cannot truthfully posit a solid communicative approach simply because the software would depend on other users to make communication possible. A more useful dichotomy is that between focus-on-form activities and focus-on-meaning activities, and it should be clear to instructors if the program has an inherent focus on meaning or only on form. Ideally, some support should be provided for inductive learning and recycling (i.e., using the same language in different contexts) and a clear progression from form-based to meaning-based activities.

Instructors should also examine the theory that governs the learning process. Does the software seem behaviorist? Audiolingual? Constructivist? Sociocultural? (See Chapter 4 for more information on theoretical orientations to learning.) What role does feedback play? What type of feedback is there? How frequent is the feedback? What can students do when they have difficulty with a task? When the philosophy underlying the software aligns with the instructor's philosophy, students are more likely to get a cohesive presentation of how to learn a second language. Unity among the instructor, the materials, and the students is more likely to enable the students to reach their acquisition goals.

Goals

As argued in Chapter 1, a clear vision of the goals of the curriculum can help determine the appropriate use of a given application to meet those goals. Instructors should determine the use of software or hardware for language learning and not vice versa (Angell et al., 2008). Therefore, before beginning the adoption process of any software, instructors should identify goals for the program and point out weaknesses within the curricular structure that can be strengthened through specific CALL applications. Instructors can also determine what the software is intended to accomplish. Is it for pronunciation practice? Problem-solving skills? Exposure to the target culture? Easy correction of homework? Diagnostic purposes? For what level? How does the work done with the software count toward a final grade? Does the activity coincide with the theoretical orientation of the instructors (i.e., authentic language/culture, focus on meaning). Finally, in large institutions, the LPD should evaluate his or her ability to ensure that the TAs use the software appropriately so that students derive the intended benefits of the program.

Content

Content is a major selling point for the majority of contemporary software packages. Most packages offer multimedia presentations and a plethora of authentic texts, images, sounds, and video that are culturally and linguistically accurate and stimulating. The main question to ask for this category is, How does the sequence and scope of the software coincide with the goals of the class?

All software applications have a bias related to the language being learned. For those in francophone studies, there is either not enough information on countries outside of France and Canada or not enough focus on Paris, France; for instructors in Hispanic studies, the bias often relates to insufficient representation of their country of origin; for those in German studies, it is too much or not enough about the Holocaust. In short, it is nearly impossible for developers to create the perfect mix for all institutions. Many vendors offer a modular approach whereby instructors can choose which aspects of a product they wish to include or exclude from a given curriculum. Instructors should determine if modularity is possible, how long does it take to set up the appropriate activities before a course begins, and if the process for setting up activities needs to be repeated every year. LPDs should be sure to ask how customized software can be ported to various instructors.

In addition to determining the quality of cultural and linguistic representation, instructors should also examine the quantity of the content, that is, the amount of material for students. In general, language learning applications should provide many activities that might be invisible to users (because students should be able to accelerate through or skip any activities that are quickly understood and spend more time on or review items that need more practice).

The program should also enable students to explore the culture and not just offer explanations of cultural phenomena. For example, the software might allow intercultural exchanges via email or other computer-mediated communication. One efficient method of evaluating cultural content is seeing how it addresses the American Council on the Teaching of Foreign Languages (ACTFL) categories of products, practices, and perspectives (see Chapter 5). Simply put, which practices and products of the culture does the program present, and does it attempt to explore the perspectives or does it stop with presentations?

Technical Requirements

The design of the application tends to be its most noticeable aspect and thereby receives the initial attention, but it should not receive the most attention. Design considerations are most helpful when comparing apples to apples; that is, design is an important consideration when comparing programs that perform the same function, but not as a deciding factor for which software would be most effective overall. The core of CALL has been and always will be based on sound theories of language learning. The following items may help decision makers gain a clear understanding of usability of a given CALL application or a web site:

1. **Navigation:** Students should have easily accessible and readily understandable instructions and icons. It should be clear where to click to get from one activity to the next and how to find help, see hints, and exit. Accompanying web sites should also be easy for students to locate and use. Does the site have a linear design or a branching sequence of segments? How easy is it for the instructor to guide the students through a page?

2. **Content and visual presentation:** Most applications and web sites strive to be objective and accurate. The content should be culturally inoffensive, show an appropriate register of the language, and be grammatically correct with interesting, current information. Text should be large, have distinct colors, and be visually appealing. Images should include illustrations and be relevant to the overall program and not be so large that they hinder access.

3. **User interface:** Users should intuitively be able to know where to click and what items mean. They should be able to change or delete their answers and profit from the feedback provided. Instructors should look for interactivity with helpful feedback and sufficient time to complete the tasks or exercises. Some web sites are adaptable to group work in class, and others may lend themselves to homework activities.

4. **Multimedia (i.e., sound and video):** Speech should be integral to the program and clear and available in male and female voices. Both music and speech should be culturally relevant. All sounds and video should be available in a standardized format that is accessible to students. Instructors should ensure that headsets, drivers, microphones, and other necessary peripherals are available to students.

5. **Sequence:** Students or instructors should be able to choose between sequenced paths and random paths so that students can decide to be led to discover the language or explore the language/culture with minimal guidance.

6. **Weight:** Design can be laden with extra peripherals, sounds, videos, and other media, and each included item takes up some space on the

machine or as it downloads. Although download speeds are increasing, some web sites may be inappropriate for classroom use simply because of the limited bandwidth in a classroom setting (i.e., the site takes too long to download or requires additional software to function).

Language center directors and LPDs should evaluate software to decide whether instructors who are less comfortable with technology can integrate that software into their courses in a way that is not overwhelming. Choosing to adopt software for a curriculum is similar to adopting a textbook, and the considerations should also be similar. The focus should be on the language learning theories underlying the software (Chapelle, 2001; Hubbard, 1992; Reeder et al., 2004; Susser & Robb, 2004) rather than on characteristics of the design.

A rubric for evaluation is essential, especially if adoption is a committee decision. A rubric can easily be designed to evaluate the elements just noted. One of the best ways of collecting this information is through software reviews in CALL-related journals such as *IALL Journal, CALICO Journal*, and *Language Learning and Technology*. Good reviews are also available in language-specific journals such as *Hispania, French Review, Unterrichtspraxis,* and *Italica.*

In addition to using applications created by others, many instructors may choose to develop their own CALL resources for their institutions. The following section discusses some important legal and ethical uses of online, published, and unpublished resources for those who strive to integrate available electronic resources into their courses. This is a brief but detailed overview of the legal use of technology and technological resources.

COPYRIGHT LAWS AND THE INTERNET

Instructors, coordinators, and administrators should assume that any recorded work (print, analog, digital, or other) is copyrighted. A recorded work is anything that is "fixed in any tangible medium of expression" (Title 17, Section 102[a], U.S. Code) and includes magazine and newspaper articles (online and offline), computer programs, or any other type of file that can be downloaded and then viewed or listened to from a computer or mobile device. The use of these works must comply with copyright law. Two concepts that are useful to instructors are (1) the doctrine of *fair use* set out in Section 107 of the Copyright Act of 1976 (Title 17, U.S. Code) and (2) the Technology, Education and Copyright Harmonization Act of 2002 (TEACH), which delineates specific permissions for educators. This section discusses four means by which instructors can comply with copyright law: public domain, fair use, the TEACH Act of 2002, and obtaining copyright permission.

Public Domain

One of the first steps in determining whether a work can be used is to see if it is still governed by copyright law. There are several ways that a work can enter the public domain, where it can be freely copied or distributed. Authors may place their work in the public domain by making a formal declaration to that effect in the preface. This is common for open-source technology, with which programmers use code from other programmers without requiring permission from the author. Other documents enter the public domain because they are not copyrightable, for example, government documents. The internet is not in the public domain because it contains both copyrighted and noncopyrighted materials.

Most works maintain their copyright for a certain period of time and then enter the public domain. Various countries have different laws and therefore different durations for a copyright. This section focuses mainly on U.S. law with some information about other countries. Unpublished works (letters, journal entries, recordings, etc.) generally have a valid copyright for 70 years beyond the life of the author or 120 years from the date of creation if the author's death date is unknown. Therefore, letters written during World War II (1939–1945) from an author who died during the war did not enter the public domain until 2009 at the earliest, and they will not until 2059 if the author's date of death is unknown.

For published works, the date of publication helps determine if the work is in the public domain. Works published before 1923 are already in the public domain; those published between 1923 and 1989[1] may be, depending on registration and renewal laws; and those published after 1989 maintain copyright protection for 70 years beyond the life of the author, after which they enter the public domain.

The use of the date of publication is the result of international agreements. The Berne Convention (1988) extended copyright protection throughout the world to the life of the author plus 50 years, and many countries in the world adhere to at least that duration. The World Trade Organization (WTO; 1994) extended copyright protection to life of the author plus 70 years, and member countries of the WTO must adhere to this statute.

Instructors who deal with older texts (e.g., medieval or Renaissance studies) or extensive government documents (e.g., French for business) may find that many of the texts they use are already in the public domain, so copyright infringement is not a chronic problem. For most instructors, however, the main attraction of the internet is the plethora of contemporary written, visual, and oral texts. These instructors need to determine if the use they make of these copyrighted works is fair.

Fair Use

The doctrine of *fair use* is codified in Section 107 of the Copyright Act of 1976. Even though the concept was developed well before the flood of technological advances, fair use doctrine is technologically neutral and applies to digital as well as print media. The following four factors need to be considered when determining whether a particular case is fair use:

1. The purpose and character of the use, including whether such use is of a commercial nature or is for nonprofit educational purposes
2. The nature of the copyrighted work

---

[1]The Berne Convention Implementation Act of 1988 eliminated the need for authors to give notice or register copyright on published works.

3. The amount and substantiality of the portion used in relation to the copyrighted work as a whole

4. The effect of the use upon the potential market for or value of the copyrighted work (Copyright Office, 2003, p. 19)

Instructors must consider all four of these demands. Ideally, the purpose, nature, amount, and effect of any fair use will have minimal impact on the copyright holder (i.e., the copyright holder will not lose money, status, or influence).

The purpose of the use is one of the most straightforward for educators to determine. It is not normally fair use when users obtain monetary gain from the use of the work. As such, fair use doctrine favors parodies, academic research papers, interviews, documentaries, and software used for nonprofit educational purposes. Fair use also favors restricted access; that is, the copies of the work will be available only to those enrolled in a course.

The nature of the work focuses on the original work and the motivation behind its creation. The nature of a work is normally easy for educators to determine by asking if the work was originally created to earn money or to educate the public. If the product is a commercial one designed for educational purposes, then copying it for educational purposes does not fall under the doctrine of fair use. In other words, if an instructor discovers some commercial recordings designed to help students' pronunciation, the instructor should not make copies of the recordings for his or her own purposes without permission. Fair use guidelines favor published works over unpublished ones, out-of-print texts over currently published texts, works of a factual nature over artistic creations, nonconsumable over consumable texts (workbooks are considered consumable since they are designed for a one-time use), and printed works over audiovisual and multimedia works.

The amount of the copied work should be considered in terms of quantity and quality. Many have tried to set forth quantitative guidelines such as *the lesser of 1% or 300 words from a scholarly book or journal article,* but the U.S. Copyright Office FL–102 (2009) clarifies that "there is no specific number of words, lines, or notes that may safely be taken without permission" (p. 1). Nevertheless, fair use favors partial copies over copies of complete works depending on the length of the copy relative to the length of the original work. A good rule of thumb is that the more instructors copy, the less likely it will be considered fair use. Copying text is favored over copying photos because parts of photos are not normally available for use. Multimedia and audiovisual materials pose similar problems because even short excerpts may capture the essence of the original work and will therefore be considered a major portion of the qualitative substance of the original work.

Effect is usually the most difficult to determine, and courts have often given it the most weight in deciding copyright cases. The most important questions to ask here are the following: Does the copy prevent the copyright holder from collecting fees? Will someone not buy the original because he or she can get a copy at no cost? In general, if the copy contains something new that causes it to differ significantly from the original, then market effect will be minimal because (theoretically) the new work will appeal to a different audience. Fair use favors copies for individual use (but permits multiple copies for classroom use), texts over multimedia, and both text and multimedia over software because any copying of software may easily have significant impact on the market. Fair use also favors spontaneity over long-term use so that items used during one semester only may fall under fair use, whereas the use of material repeatedly over several years is less likely to be considered fair use.

Fair use is not considered an indisputable factor in whether an instructor can copy materials. Rather, fair use guidelines help instructors recognize preferable practices over questionable ones. Table 2.3 summarizes the fair use guidelines discussed.

The TEACH Act

The TEACH Act of 2002 was intended to clarify copyright law for digital distance education. The Copyright Act of 1976, Section 110, has been modified throughout the years to allow performances and displays in the face-to-face classroom (for example, instructors can use copyrighted recordings in class without seeking permission) but was changed significantly for the purposes of digital distribution of such materials (particularly for distance and online education). The strict guidelines associated with the TEACH Act are intended mainly for educational institutions but also have repercussions for individuals who teach using the internet.

The benefits of the TEACH Act apply only to institutions that are governmental entities or accredited nonprofit educational institutions, thereby including most of the elementary and secondary schools and universities as they currently exist. However, the Act excludes many for-profit language schools and trade schools that may not be accredited. In order to qualify under the TEACH Act, institutions must implement copyright policies that promote compliance with U.S. copyright law and that are made available to those individuals working in the institution.

TABLE 2.3 Fair Use Guidelines

Favored under fair use	Questionable under fair use
Restricted access	Unrestricted access
For nonprofit educational purposes	For industry/business purposes
Published	Unpublished
Out-of-print texts	Currently published texts
Works of a factual nature	Works of an artistic nature
Nonconsumable texts (e.g., textbooks)	Consumable texts (e.g., workbooks)
Printed works	Audiovisual works
Partial copies	Copies of entire works
Text	Multimedia
Text and multimedia	Software
For individual use	For wide distribution
Short-term use	Long-term use
One-time use	Multiple uses

Several restrictions are placed on the work to be used in a course. First, it must contain a copyright notice to the students to alert them that the materials are subject to copyright laws. Second, only those enrolled in the course can have access to the work. Third, retention of the work must be limited to the class session. Limits on access and retention are normally achieved through learning management systems such as Blackboard, Moodle, or a proprietary code from the university or school district. Course management systems enable technology officials to set restriction on availability. As such, the TEACH Act also makes explicit the restrictions on how technology officials may administer those course management systems.

The digitization of analog recordings is restricted in two ways. First, instructors cannot digitize more than they would present in a regular class (e.g., 50-250 minutes per week depending on the meeting times and credit load of the course). This ensures that instructors do not digitize unreasonable amounts of a copyrighted work, thus making it easily accessible and transferable among users. This stipulation is an attempt to maintain the fair use standards of amount and effect. Second, instructors must ensure that a digital copy is not already available. If it is, it will normally have licensing terms, including information on use and transfer that prevail over copyright law.

Instructors have additional leeway about what they can include on their access-restricted sites made available through the institution. Whereas the old law permitted transmission of only nondramatic literary and musical works, the TEACH Act explicitly allows any work in an amount comparable to a typical presentation in a classroom. Two significant restrictions apply to this rule. First, the work cannot be a commercially marketed display designed for transmission over digital networks. Many educational companies design software to function with distance education courses and offer licensing agreements to accompany the purchase and use of these materials. Unlicensed use, in these cases, falls well outside of fair use and is not covered by the TEACH Act. Second, the original copy must be a legally acquired copy; instructors are not permitted to use bootlegged copies or illegally made copies, such as self-made recordings at live concerts, movie showings, or other performances.

The TEACH Act also places responsibility on the instructors to ensure that certain criteria are met concerning the work. Instructors who place material online are accountable for adhering to copyright law, and they must ensure that copyrighted works placed online are for educational purposes and not for commercial or entertainment purposes.

In conclusion, the TEACH Act specifies numerous allowances and restrictions concerning the use of copyrighted material online. The two most important of these are that the institution should be an accredited educational institution and that it has a copyright policy that is available to all faculty. If either of these criteria is not met, faculty do not qualify for TEACH benefits.

Obtaining Copyright Permission

When a work is not in the public domain and its use does not qualify under fair use or the TEACH Act, instructors can normally seek permission to use copyrighted material for educational purposes through the copyright holder.

Acquiring copyright permissions for educational purposes is rarely problematic; directors of language centers who need to make multiple copies of videos, interactive CD-ROMs, or sound files to accompany a textbook most often use this route. Members of the International Association of Language Learning Technologies (IALLT; www.iallt.org) have access to a server that houses many files offered by major publishing companies and permits language center directors to download them at no cost if the institution meets any restrictions (e.g., to download audio files for a textbook, the institution must have adopted the textbook in its curriculum).

It is relatively easy to acquire permission from publishing companies for items that accompany textbooks. Acquiring permission from foreign publishers may be more difficult, but the process is the same. First, instructors need to identify the copyright holder and make informal contact by phone or email. This informal contact should be followed by a formal request that specifies the duration and type of use requested for a work. Instructors may need to pay a licensing fee and responses may take time, so the entire process can easily take 6 to 10 weeks. Sometimes licensing fees can be prohibitive, so instructors must be able to identify alternative materials or limit the requested amount to what can be considered fair use. Finally, once the permission is granted, it is a good idea to obtain a legal review from the institution.

It is important to also note that the acknowledgment of the source of the copyrighted material does not substitute for obtaining permission. Distinct differences exist between plagiarism and copyright infringement. Plagiarism is an ethical issue; copyright infringement is a legal one. The two are not necessarily related. For example, one can avoid plagiarism by citing verbatim an entire chapter of a book and giving appropriate credit to the authors. This use infringes on copyright but is not a case of plagiarism. Likewise, one can copy verbatim major sections of a government publication (such as a web site) and give no credit. This is a blatant example of plagiarism but does not infringe on copyright since government publications are in the public domain.

When in doubt, instructors should seek guidance from their home institution concerning the use of copyrighted material. If no such information is available, instructors should be able to find helpful information from the website of a state university, since these institutions are strongly encouraged to qualify for the TEACH Act by providing copyright policies online.

The Digital Millennium Copyright Act of 1998 (DMCA) is worth mentioning here for language center directors and instructors. The DMCA prohibits circumvention of any antipiracy measures built into software, limits liability of internet service providers (ISPs) that simply transmit information, requires licensing payment by webcasters, and permits the blocking of content for minors. Educational entities maintain some exemptions from antipiracy circumvention for research purposes, if faculty are studying encryption, for example. Universities are also considered ISPs when they provide web space to students and faculty and therefore maintain limited liability for copyright infringements on student and faculty web pages. However, educational web sites or radio stations are not exempt from the licensing fees required by record companies for webcasting music. Most important for elementary and secondary schools, Congress granted the right to incorporate software that blocks certain material on the internet so that it will not be available to minors in the classroom.

TECHNICAL CONSIDERATIONS

The technical considerations for software are generally noted on the package or mentioned by the vendor in a clear manner. These include a specific operating system (e.g., Mac OSX, Windows 7, Vista, XP), minimum random access memory (RAM) or processor speed, and peripherals and screen resolution. In contrast, internet sites rarely indicate requirements unless they are lacking; in that case, a warning or error message normally instructs the user to load the latest version of the necessary plug-ins. CALL resources may require a number of plug-in applications or peripherals such as headphones and a microphone as well as the drivers to run them. Most instructors might be unable to gauge whether these items are accessible on the students' home computers. It is strongly recommended that instructors using a computer classroom or language center ensure that the sites to be used in class are accessible from the students' computers and under student login permissions.

The Learning Curve

Using the web to distribute language learning activities has several advantages: (1) Nearly all of the activities are cross-platform (i.e., they work on Macs and Windows-based and Unix-based computers with no additional versions); (2) they are easily distributed to the class; (3) learning to use tools available on the web tends to be more rewarding than learning a full authoring system such as Macromedia's Flash, Sun Microsystem's Java platform, or Microsoft's Silverlight, because web authors can see results and make changes quickly; (4) it is easy to collaborate with other instructors who enjoy creating online activities for their classes; and (5) instructors can easily correct or personalize the activities for their particular classes. A number of repositories are mentioned in this book and online.

Conclusions

Electronic resources are plentiful in the modern language classroom. As CALL plays a more central role in L2 teaching, its evaluation may eventually merit as much consideration as the adoption of a textbook. The evaluation of CALL software should be systematic and focused on methodological concerns. The guidelines offered in this chapter can provide instructors with a clear method of identifying the assumptions, goals, content, and technical requirements of a CALL application. Furthermore, as instructors develop their own online materials, an awareness of copyright issues can facilitate the use of authentic materials because educational entities can take advantage of works in the public domain, the doctrine of fair use, and the TEACH Act.

Practical Work

1. If you have not done so yet, it is wise to determine your own philosophy of teaching with technology. Take a few minutes to identify some key points about how you believe learners learn, how you believe that languages are learned, and the role of the instructor. Be sure to indicate some important uses for technology in a classroom and for extracurricular work.

2. Several popular internet sites allow instructors to create their own activities using online resources. The most prominent are Quia (www.quia.com) and HotPotatoes (hotpot.uvic.ca/). As a follow-up to the discussion of evaluation and online webactivities, visit one of the sites mentioned and create an activity that you could use with your class(es).

3. Most publishers offer web sites along with their foreign language textbooks. Using the criteria discussed in this chapter, evaluate the web site that accompanies the textbook you currently use.

4. Some of the most beneficial web-based products for management of a second language classroom are learning management systems (LMS). The most widely available products include Moodle.org, Blackboard, and NiceNet.org, but many universities use proprietary applications they have created for their own purposes. Visit these sites and evaluate what they offer.

Suggestions for Further Reading

Copyright Office. (1999). *Fair use* (FL-102). Washington, DC: U.S. Government Printing Office.

Hubbard, P. (2006). Evaluating CALL software. In L. Ducate & N. Arnold (Eds.), *Calling on CALL: From theory and research to new directions in foreign language teaching* (pp. 313–338). San Marcos, TX: CALICO.

Jamieson, J., Chapelle, C., & Preiss, S. (2005). CALL evaluation by developers, a teacher and students. *CALICO Journal, 23*(1), 93–138.

Susser, B., & Robb, T. N. (2004). Evaluation of ESL/EFL instructional web sites. In S. Fotos & C. Browne (Eds.), *New perspectives on CALL for second language classrooms* (pp. 279–295). Mahwah, NJ: Lawrence Erlbaum.

Technology, Education and Copyright Harmonization Act of 2002, Pub. L. No. 107-273, 116 Stat. 1758, 1910 (2002).

Sources for reliable software reviews are available online and in print from *IALLT Journal* (www.iallt.org), *CALICO Journal* (www.calico.org), *Language Learning and Technology* (llt.msu.edu), *Hispania, French Review, Unterrichspraxis,* and *Italica.*

CHAPTER 3

The World Wide Web

OVERVIEW

This chapter documents historical and technical aspects of the World Wide Web (WWW), to explain how to find useful documents on the web and to examine types of activities that can be done with those web pages. The WWW brought significant improvements over previous online communication methods. The importance of search engines continues to grow as the number of servers and web documents increases, with many search engines facilitating a variety of services beyond a simple keyword search.

This chapter focuses on using web-based activities and information from the web to facilitate activity-based language learning. Included are activities provided by publishers, concordance activities, dictionary and translation activities, free surfing, WebQuests, class presentations, and online portfolios. The use of web resources is most effective when accompanied by clear instructions and unambiguous follow-up activities. Many have argued that using the web is highly motivational for students (Dudeney, 2000; Gonzales, 1999; Santore & Schane, 2000; Van Selm & Jankowski, 2006), and others have emphasized the benefits of its simplicity (Ahern, 2005; Johnson, 1998). Yet the web, like any other teaching tool, is rendered inefficient without the proper preparation and execution of the activity. By considering instructional and technical needs, the target content, and the follow-up activities, instructors can integrate web activities seamlessly into their courses. This chapter also addresses other uses of the web, such as classroom management and professional development.

HISTORY OF THE WEB

The internet existed long before the advent of the WWW. In the early 1960s, the U.S. military designed a system of computers that would ensure communication in case of a nuclear attack. The decentralization of this network allowed it to continue to function even if parts of it were destroyed. Eventually, other agencies and organizations began to use this internet as well. Although educational and nonprofit users embraced the internet initially, commercial users encouraged the greatest expansion and overall use of the system for sharing files, sending messages, and storing information. The most-used internet resource is electronic mail. According to Nie and Erbring (2000), in 1999, nearly 90% of all internet users had used email, but only 50% had explored the WWW extensively. These statistics have changed considerably since 2000; according to the Campaign Monitor Email Report (2011), nearly half of email users access their messages using the WWW (e.g., via Yahoo.com, Gmail.com, Hotmail.com, Webmail.MostUniversities.edu) or, not surprisingly, using their mobile devices (e.g., iPhone, iTouch) which have gained market share by nearly 85% since 2009.

The creation of the WWW is generally credited to Sir Timothy Berners-Lee, a British engineer at the Massachusetts Institute of Technology (MIT), in collaboration with Robert Cailliau at Concile Européen pour la Recherche Nucléaire (CERN). The popularization of the web came as a result of some key developments: hypertext, which streamlined the document-sharing process; a graphical user interface, to improve aesthetic appeal and navigability; and a substantial number of documents to share.

Berners-Lee's major contribution was linking hypertext technology to the internet. Hypertext, which enabled the linking of a word in one document to another document, had gained some popularity during the 1980s, but all linked documents needed to be located on a stand-alone computer. Before 1990, the internet allowed sharing of documents, but only after users requested access to documents they wanted (and they needed to know which documents were available); then the owner of that resource could grant permission. The creation of the WWW permitted sharing documents without the express permission of their authors, which meant that links could be made between documents on the internet without the owner of the document having to enable the link each time for each separate individual.

The improved appearance of the WWW is attributable to graphical interface browsers such as Internet Explorer or Firefox. Even the earliest graphical browsers (i.e., Mosaic which became Netscape) simplified users' ability to search the web, making using the web more enticing. Before the advent of graphical browsers such as Microsoft Internet Explorer (MSIE), Firefox, Chrome, Flock, Safari, and Opera, most access to the web occurred through Lynx, a text-only browser. Although the text-only interface was useful for scientists and government officials to exchange information, it was not particularly appealing to nonspecialists, such as most language instructors.

Finally, the early web was also unattractive to nonscientists, not only because of its lack of aesthetic appeal but also because of its limited general information.

During the 1990s, increasingly more individuals began to publish their own material which augmented the amount of information available on the web. By the late 1990s, many companies had established a presence on the web and were taking customers' orders via the web (i.e., Amazon.com, WalMart.com, Dell.com). An enormous amount of hype accompanied the dot.com industry, so much so that all businesses felt pressured to have a presence on the web. According to the U.S. Census Bureau, by August 2000, more than half of the homes in the United States had computers and used the internet on a regular basis (Newburger, 2001). This number has steadily increased: More than 78% of the homes in North America in 2012 use the internet on a daily basis (www.internetworldstats.com, 2012).

The web was initially somewhat static; solitary users could surf the web without contributing to its development, interacting with other users, or personalizing their experience. This interface is often referred to as *Web 1.0*—the read-only web. Web 1.0 applications allow the user to interact with the web site, but the users leave no lasting imprint or contribution on the site. These applications include online journals, institutional and personal web pages, shopping sites, or other information sources (e.g., dictionaries, maps). Web 2.0 applications are generally social in nature—they encourage users to interact and create and share information. The majority of the internet applications discussed in the following chapters are Web 2.0 technologies: blogs, wikis, RSS feeds, social networking sites, social bookmarking (folksonomies), podcasting, and vodcasting. Web 1.0 and Web 2.0 applications are not exclusive (i.e., one could use Web 2.0 applications with only Web 1.0 functionality such as a blog page that does not allow comments, or a wiki page that cannot be edited) and do not refer to the technology as much as they do to the use of the web. Users often employ these two types of applications together, for example, using a restaurant web site to locate the restaurant and see the menu but eliciting recommendations using Twitter.com or FourSquare.com. The remainder of this chapter concentrates on using Web 1.0 applications for language teaching and Chapters 7 and 8 focus on using Web 2.0 applications.

UNDERSTANDING THE WEB

Understanding how information retrieval and storage occur on the internet can help users find the information they need more efficiently. This section addresses how information is indexed, retrieved, and presented on the web. As the web develops, searching for information will be semantically driven from the server side; that is, the browser or site will suggest related terms and popular searches to help users find what they need. A basic understanding of how information is stored on the web can also help instructors evaluate the reliability of the source.

Understanding URL Addresses

A URL or *uniform resource locator* is also referred to as the *web address*. This alternate nomenclature is appropriate because the main purpose of a URL is to direct the browser to the correct location for the desired information. Browsers offer the ability to bookmark certain pages. For those instructors who surf the web at home but need to use the sites in the classroom, online bookmarking sites such as Delicious.com, StumbleUpon.com, or Diigo.com allow them to store the URLs on the web rather than on their personal computers. Users need only log in to their account to retrieve the sites they have bookmarked. Moreover, these social bookmarking sites allow users to see bookmarks from like-minded people, Users can create social networks by joining groups to collaborate on research, share thoughts, ideas, and helpful links. Social bookmarking sites also offer other valuable services such as tagging sites (i.e., associating searchable keywords with each site), autoposting URLs via email, twitter, or blogs, highlighting portions of a web page, creating lists of similar sites, send sites to mobile devices to read later, or add online sticky notes to web pages. Diigo.com even has educator and student accounts available. These sites facilitate the collection of good sites, but at the heart of finding and sharing information on the web is the URL.

A URL reveals much about the quality of a site. The URL has become, for many, an indicator of reliability, bias, and authority in content. Although it does not need to be typed when using most browsers, all web pages begin with *http://*.[1] This prefix indicates the method that the client uses to request and receive information from the server. The next part of the URL is the name of the computer that houses the web document. Most institutions choose a computer and name it *www*. Thus, most web sites begin with www, but not all (e.g., many sites designed for mobile devices have deleted the www from their URL, including twitter.com or getpocket.com). The next part of the address indicates the institution, and the suffix of the URL indicates the type of institution. For example, the site www.uky.edu identifies a computer named www at the University of Kentucky (UKY), which is an educational institution (.edu). The next word in the URL may be an indication of reliability. Web site reliability includes authorial validity (the author is recognizable and the purpose is clear), currency (the web site is up to date), accuracy (the information is correct and biases are clear), and honesty (the user's identity and security are not at risk). Certain sites have a reputation for reliability, such as Yahoo! (www.yahoo.com), Amazon (www .amazon.com/), the *Washington Post* (www.washingtonpost.com), and Ebay (www.ebay.com). It should be clear, however, from the URL how reliable or trustworthy a given site is. For example, a list of cheeses in France from a site such as www.office-elevage.fr/doctech-6/fromage-fr/from-fr.htm is probably a more reliable source than www.persopages.fr/~stephane/trucs/blagues/inventées /fromages.htm. The first example has a clear institutional link (the French Ministry of Agriculture: office-elevage.fr), whereas the second is a site dedicated to personal web pages (persopages.fr) maintained by a fellow named Stéphane (~stephane). The first site appears to contain technical documents (doctech-6), whereas the second appears to have jokes (trucs [things]/blagues [jokes]/inventées [invented]). Finally, the first site may still be available in 2014, whereas the second site will most likely disappear before the publication of this book.

---

[1]The prefix "http" stands for **h**yper**t**ext **t**ransfer **p**rotocol. The prefix "http**s**://" is also available, which indicates that it is a "secure" or encrypted connection to a site.

Major domain suffixes include the following:

Commercial organizations	.com, .biz, .co
Educational institutions	.ac, .edu
Governmental institutions	.gov
Military organizations	.mil
Nonprofit organizations	.org
Networking organizations	.net
Telephone networks	.tel

Suffixes indicate the top-level domain of a site and signify the type of organization. In addition to the standard top-level domain suffixes listed here, two-letter indicators may identify the country of origin rather than the type of institution, such as Canada (.ca) or the United States (.us). Table 3.1 shows country internet codes that may be useful to language instructors in Arabic, Chinese, English as a Second Language (ESL), French, German, Italian, Japanese, and Spanish. Unfortunately, top-level domain indicators do not consistently reference the country. For example, certain countries have licensed their country designators to large companies, for example, Tuvalu (.tv) is used by a few broadcasting companies because television has the same abbreviation (TV) and Niue (.nu), because of associated meanings (*nu* means "now" in Danish, Dutch, Norwegian, and Swedish). In short, what began as identity nomenclature became a market for name recognition, and ICANN (2011: the Internet Corporation for Assigned Names and Numbers)—the group that controls internet naming conventions—decided recently that any company could buy a top-level domain name that was not already dedicated to a country. For

TABLE 3.1 Internet codes for selected countries

.ar	Argentina	.eg	Egypt	.ma	Morocco
.au	Australia	.fr	France	.pa	Panama
.at	Austria	.de	Germany	.py	Paraguay
.br	Brazil	.gp	Guadeloupe	.pe	Peru
.ca	Canada	.ht	Haiti	.ru	Russian Federation
.cn	China	.ho	Honduras	.sa	Saudi Arabia
.cl	Chile	.it	Italy	.sn	Senegal
.co	Colombia	.jp	Japan	.es	Spain
.cr	Costa Rica	.lu	Luxembourg	.ch	Switzerland
.do	Dominican Republic	.mg	Madagascar	.uk	United Kingdom
.ec	Ecuador	.mx	Mexico	.ve	Venezuela

example, the Coca-Cola company could apply for the designator .coke and the company web site could be http://www.drink.coke/ (although at nearly $200,000 per application, the applicants for custom top-level designators should be few). In 2011, ICANN also announced the change that domains could now existe in any script, including Russian, Arabic, Chinese, Korean, or Thai. Since the turn of the century, most internet names have been standardized (as generic top-level domains) and signal the quality and reliability of the site.

A browser can read various types of files. The .html (or .htm) suffix is called an *extension* and indicates how the browser should interpret or render the page. In addition, other popular extensions are Active Server Pages (.asp), PHP: Hypertext Processor files (.php), Cold Fusion (.cfm), and Common Gateway Interface (CGI) files (.pl, .cgi). All web pages must display an extension so that the browser knows how to interpret the information in the document. Generally, if the browser requests a file with an alternate extension (e.g., .docx, .pdf, .mp3), the operating system relies on another program to display the file (respectively, MS Word, Adobe Acrobat, or a media player).

Finding and Using What You Need

The abundance of search engines on the internet allows individuals to find specific information in the target language. For example Yahoo! and Google have sites available in numerous languages including English (www.yahoo.com or www.google.com), French (www.yahoo.fr or www.google.fr) and German (www.yahoo.de or www.google.de). In addition, some engines focus on a target language and culture, such as www.voila.fr (France), www.vigilio.it (Italy), trovator.combios.es and www.ozu.es (Spain), www.mexicoglobal.com/ (Mexico), and www.brujula.net/ (multiple Spanish-speaking areas). Google is the most popular and widely used search engine on the web. In early 2011, Google had the majority market share in the world—about 65% of all internet searches—with Yahoo! (16%) and Microsoft (14%) following at a distance (comScore, 2011). All major search engines allow the user to change preferences so that the search returns pages in only one language or many languages, for example, pages written only in English or pages written in Italian, French, and Spanish.

Instructors should become familiar with the conventions of their preferred search engine, which generally has some type of help section to narrow or broaden a search based on variables such as "+, –" or "and, or, not." For example, when seeking sites that discuss bass fishing, it would be helpful to search for "bass -music," since this search would eliminate any sites containing the word *bass* that are related to music. Likewise, search engines generally offer the ability to add synonyms, limit the search to a specific domain (such as only .de sites or only .edu sites), or language and date of the most recently updated pages. The easiest way to discover the particulars of a given search engine is to click the *Help*, *Advanced Search*, *Preferences*, or *Refine Search* links/buttons. Instructors can save hundreds of hours by learning how a search engine works and how to search effectively using its particular features. Numerous sites can help instructors teach these skills to their students (e.g., Boolify.org or GoogleGuide.com)

Searching the web can be frustrating, and it is important not to reinvent a project that someone else has already begun. Good web sites in various languages for language teaching already exist, and a simple web search will reveal the dominant ones for a particular language. Language-specific associations (American Association of Teachers of French, American Association of Teachers of Italian, etc.) and other organizations (Foreign Language Teaching Forum, Center for Advanced Research on Language Acquisition, etc.) maintain lists of web sites for use in the language classroom. Rather than searching out each individual page for an activity, instructors may find it more convenient to search for established, regularly maintained link lists or even sites with activities that include activities. When these are not available, social bookmarking sites such as those mentioned earlier may be the most efficient method of maintaining reliable links for classroom activities.

USING WEB PAGES FOR TEACHING

The web is also attractive as a delivery mechanism for free authentic texts such as current newspapers, recent magazines, literary texts, dictionaries, encyclopedias, computer-assisted language learning (CALL) software, audio, video,

---

TASK 3.1

Google.com is much more than a search engine, and most search engines are following suit. To investigate what Google.com offers, use basic search delimiters to search the following (more information is available under *Advanced Search Tips* at Google.com).
Basic delimiters include:

- The plus sign (+) requests both items together as in peas +ice cream.
- The minus sign (-) requests exclusion of pages that contain both items as in phoenix -Arizona
- Quotes (" ") request pages that contain an exact phrase as in "to be or not to be"
- The asterisk (*) replaces any word or group of words. A search of "language learners feel * using computers" will yield pages containing the entire phrase but with any word in the position of the asterisk (e.g., happy, content, frustrated, confused, eager)

Note: Most search engines automatically search for synonyms so there is no need to use particular delimiters.

1. Search for tortillas but not potatoes.
2. Search for pages with the exact phrase "Advantages of Second Language Learning."
3. Search for pages with foreign language learning (including French, German, Japanese, Russian and other foreign languages). Hint: ~
4. Search for pages with alot or a-lot or a lot.
5. Search for the most common word (*her* or *a*) that fits in this phrase: "Little Miss Muffet sat on _____ tuffet."

and almost anything an instructor can imagine using in class. The educational literature is replete with advice on how to use the web in and out of the classroom (Blyth, 1999; Clark, 2000; Dudeney, 2000, Gonglewski & DuBravac, 2006; Gonzales, 1999; Kassen, Lavine, Murphy-Judy, & Peters, 2007; Moehle-Vieregge et al., 1997; Lomicka, Lord, & Manzer, 2003; Richardson, 2009; Santore & Schane, 2000; Schaumann & Green, 2003; Son, 2008; Taylor & Gitsaki, 2004; Warschauer, Shetzer, & Meloni, 2000). Numerous web sites as well encourage web-enhanced language learning (www.well.ac.uk, www.webquest.org, or www.halfbakedsoftware.com). Most of the literature emphasizes basic rules for use of the web as well as technical advice for surfing or doing research using the web. This section discusses various types of activities that use the web, explains the basic guidelines for using the web for language learning purposes, and suggests in-class follow-up activities for web assignments.

Technologically savvy novice teachers often have the need to produce their own sites and activities. Those instructors should have no problem finding ways of developing and publishing their materials on the web. This section targets uninitiated instructors and describes the most convenient online applications designed for second language (L2) learners that do not require production of web pages. The activity types mentioned here include publisher-supported activities, online translation, corpus activities, free surfing, WebQuests, Web presentations, and online portfolios. These activities are not meant to be exhaustive, but rather to give an idea of how web resources may be used.

Publishers' Pages

Publishers of L2 textbooks offer companion web sites that provide web-related materials and activities, with supporting services. The materials may include worksheets, games, slides, or WebQuests (described below), and the services increasingly include online language labs or learning management systems (LMS) such as Blackboard.com, Moodle.org, or NiceNet.org. The advantage of these pages is that they coincide with the theme and the grammatical goals of each chapter in the accompanying textbook. Because of the design (e.g., background, colors, logos), students rarely have difficulty associating the web activities that are completed out of class with those done in class. Students who engage in publisher site activities may also believe that the money they spent on the textbook and ancillaries was somewhat justified.

Another advantage to publishers' sites is that they are generally well maintained. Resource sites (the sites used in the activities) are current, or alternate sites are offered to replace those that no longer work for the activity. The activity site is normally housed on a large, reliable server so that activities are available at all times and to large numbers of students simultaneously.

One difficulty with publishers' sites is the delivery of the exercises. Many sites require students to print and send their answers to their instructors. Printing can be a problem because the answers in the text boxes are often truncated and do not print in their entirety. Some publishers' sites give students the opportunity to email their assignments to their instructor by entering their instructor's email address in the appropriate box. Emailing the assignment can create problems because students may not remember their instructor's name and/or email address; students may also mistype the address or enter an incorrect address. Increasingly, publisher sites offer LMSs whereby instructors create a class site. Students enlist in the class, and then the record of student activity is accessible to the instructor (assuming students have registered in the correct class). This association may take longer to establish at the beginning of the semester (e.g., students change or drop classes), but it alleviates stress with individual assignments throughout the semester. Nonetheless, even when students' assignments are associated directly with the instructor, emailed assignments can be problematic. The instructor's email service may erroneously recognize the email as spam because the return address line indicates that the message comes from a mechanical source (the web server that houses the page) rather than from an individual user. Although most instructors are wise enough to check their spam folders, if the institution or the internet service provider (ISP) uses filters to eliminate spam, the students' emailed assignment may never be delivered to the instructor's inbox.

In recent years, almost every major textbook publisher has contracted with Quia.com or created its own proprietary software to deliver the workbook and lab manual in an online format for its introductory language textbooks. In the future, most workbooks will come in electronic form only (Mason & Rennie, 2008). To date, publishers of Spanish and French materials have led the way in the development of online ancillaries, although less commonly taught languages (LCTLs) have increasingly more materials published online. Instructors must weigh the pros and cons of the electronic workbook for their needs, purposes, and student population. Using an online workbook has many advantages. Instructors no longer need to collect homework because it is on the web. Many of the online exercises are self-correcting, so instructors do not need to grade them all. Instructors can scan homework response statistics to determine how best to spend their time in class. For example, if students have had difficulty with a concept, the instructor can spend more time or provide additional activities on it in class; if students have had no apparent problems with the homework, instructors can move on to more advanced tasks.

These advantages are offset by disadvantages. Students may have difficulty registering for the class associated with their instructor. Complications result from transferring students from one section to another or from one level to another. Although many activities are self-correcting, instructors must be mindful of a subtle return to a behavioristic mind-set. Some self-correcting activities give credit when students visit the page, regardless of whether or not they complete the assignment. In addition, giving feedback entails spending significant time on a computer. In short, instructors must decide how to use a workbook and how much trust they have that their students will use the online workbook as expected.

Dictionaries, Online Translation, and Academic Research

Online dictionaries provide an advantage over print dictionaries in a number of ways: cost, convenience, guidance, content, and additional resources. Unlike their paper counterparts, online dictionaries are generally free. A simple search for bilingual dictionaries or multilingual dictionaries will reveal a plethora of free dictionary and translation sites. These sites are generally more convenient for students if they are writing papers on a computer; rather than flipping through pages, students simply type the word and have several definitions to choose from. Online dictionaries often provide significant guidance while searching. If a learner doesn't know how to spell a word, it may take a while to locate the word in a print dictionary. If a user searches for a misspelled word, an online dictionary will often offer a list of several words with similar letter or sound patterns, including inflected forms of the word. Most online dictionaries are updated regularly (weekly, monthly, or even daily), so the definitions and uses of the terms are normally up to date and often clarify usage in a specific field. Students can also search several dictionaries at the same time to compare entries. Finally, many online dictionaries provide other services such as audio (e.g., for pronunciation), images, video, thesauruses, encyclopedias, games and puzzles, reverse dictionaries, and word-of-the-day subscription options. Activities organized around finding and using online multimedia resources may help students learn vocabulary more easily and develop their reading (Yanguas, 2009) and writing (Yoon, 2008) skills.

Even though many students are aware of the existence of online translation, they may not understand the difficulties caused by translating idiomatic expressions and homographs. Free online translation services can be found at BabelFish.Yahoo.com or Translate.Google.com. Instructors can provide activities that allow students to familiarize themselves with online translation while also discouraging them from thinking that it is the secret to success. Translation sites provide a textbox in which users enter a phrase to be translated and a selection box that allows them to choose the input language and the target output language. Learners can enter any phrase, click the *translate* button, and receive a translation. The insight for most students comes when they are asked to translate from English to the L2 and then back into English. Few sentences with idiomatic expressions or homographs will be translated back into their original form. For example, "The dog bowl got left in the yard" translated to French becomes "Le chien a été laissé bol dans la cour." which becomes "The dog was left in the court bowl." Nonetheless, recent advances in machine translation have enabled good translations of texts. A short activity using translation tools can encourage learners to use them only when the output form will be familiar to them because of their existing knowledge of the language. Instructors can also show important distinctions between translating one phrase and translating entire texts. Most online translators succeed at translating short texts, but they tend to fail miserably when it comes to translating extensive blocks of text.

Instructors who use translation activities in class can also take the opportunity to discuss the ethical issues of plagiarism by translation. Most universities have plagiarism policies that include translation, and it would be surprising if readers of this book did not have an anecdote of a student who translated an online text into the language of study and turned it in for credit. Instructors who introduce online translation services can take time to explain that translation, summary, quotes, and paraphrasing are forms of plagiarism when not properly cited.

Corpus/Concordance Activities

Concordancing means using a text to show how a word or phrase is used in context. A concordance can provide students with numerous examples (from a text or corpus of texts) of how a word or grammatical structure is used and therefore lends itself to inductive rule formation on the part of the learner. Traditional concordances are based on a text such as the one presented in Table 3.2, from which phrases are taken (in this case from *Alice in Wonderland*). Students can see each word in context. This type of presentation can help students gain a clearer understanding of nuance and usage of particular vocabulary words.

Because all of the texts on the internet can be viewed as one gigantic text (or corpus), students can create a concordance with every search on a search engine. Each results page should show the search item in context. Online concordancing activities (via search engines) tend to be more beneficial when they focus on phrases rather than on specific words (e.g., *look over, look into, listen to, listen for*), because it exposes learners to multiple uses of similar phrases which allows them to contextualize the meaning (of phrasal verbs or idiomatic expressions, for example).

Instructors can use numerous types of concordancing activities. Lamy and Klarskov Mortensen (2011) maintain a good list (www.ict4lt.org/en/en_mod2-4 .htm#sec4.1) that encourage hypothesis testing, rule formation, and contextualization of linguistic phenomena. "Guess the word" is a popular activity in which the concordance is missing the central word and students need to guess the appropriate lexical item that fits in all of the cases. This activity encourages students to test their hypotheses on how the language works. In the preceding example (Table 3.2), students would receive the table with the word *curious* missing.

Some form-focused activities encourage students to create rules for the phenomena that they encounter. For example, a concordance may have a variety of conjugated verbs to help students notice how verbs are conjugated (e.g., by person, by number, past/preterit, indicative/subjunctive). Other examples of rule-formation activities may include concordances of adjectives that agree in gender or number or grammar that may be difficult (e.g., *por/para* in Spanish, *pour/pendant* in French). *Collocation* activities help students to contextualize linguistic forms. These activities cause students to look at

---

TABLE 3.2 Partial concordance of *curious* in *Alice in Wonderland*, by Lewis Carroll

"What a	curious	feeling!" said Alice.
was playing against herself, for this	curious	child was very fond of pretending to be two
a Lory and an Eaglet, and several other	curious	creatures.
and yet—it's rather	curious	, you know, this sort of life!
She felt very	curious	to know what it was all about, and crept a little
a grin without a cat! It's the most	curious	thing I ever saw in all my life!"

how certain words are used together (e.g., "That's why" vs. "That's because") or to examine difference in varieties (American English vs. British English). This type of activity can also be used for cultural phenomena. For example, students could search *tasty* and *sweet* and compare the origin of the sites (in Europe, Australia, India, or America) with a search for *tasty* and *salty* to determine which regions seem to prefer savory desserts more than sweet desserts. Wikipedia also provides an interesting cultural corpus because students can compare different cultural perspectives on the same phenomena. For example, the French and German pages about May 8, 1945, differ considerably from the English page on the same topic, as a result of the differing cultural significance attached to that date. Similarly, the Japanese and the Chinese descriptions of the Sino-Japanese war differ considerably according to each nation's perspective on historical events.

A concordance can also show students how to improve their writing by following the most common constructions on the web. Because the web provides a huge amount of data for concordancing activities, engines such as Google or Webcorp (www.webcorp.org.uk) can show the most common way to express a concept. For example, if a learner of English is unsure whether to say "I was thinking of you" or "I was thinking about you," the learner can type each phrase into the search engine in turn to see which is the more common by comparing the number of pages that contain that expression. Concordancing activities have the advantage of providing learners with significant amounts of comprehensible input. Some evidence indicates that corpora and concordancing activities can improve students' language and critical thinking (Pérez-Llantada, 2009; St. John, 2001) as well as their writing (Yoon, 2008).

Free Surfing

Although it is not the most productive use of time for students in the computer lab, free surfing can be a relaxing way for learners to click to any site that appeals to them. One major problem with free surfing for language learning is that the majority of sites on the internet are available in English (www .internetworldstats.com, as of May 31, 2012). With a class of 25 to 30 students, it is nearly impossible for the instructor to monitor each computer to verify that the students are surfing only in the target language. Thus, free surfing is not an effective use of time, particularly if the only task is reading comprehension. If, however, the goal of the activity is to produce a five-minute presentation in the L2 about what was learned, the activity may work well regardless of the language of the pages visited; students could create the bulk of their report quickly using sites in English and then consult the target language tools to verify how to say certain expressions that they need for the presentaiton (e.g., using corpora, parallel sites, or online dictionaries). Free surfing can also provide the instructor with an indication of the abilities and preferences of the students concerning technology. The key to free surfing activities is that the students have a purpose and some structure on how they are to present what they find (see Chapter 1).

WebQuests

Dodge (1995, 1997, 2001) divides WebQuests into short-term and long-term types. The main purpose of short-term WebQuests is the acquisition of knowledge. The instructor normally provides background information concerning the topic and a set of information sources with instructions. Students then perform a particular task (such as a scavenger hunt) using the information sources to find the information on the web (i.e., sites or search engines). Finally, they report their findings to the class as an oral, written, or online multimedia presentation. Short-term WebQuests are normally designed for completion in one to three classroom periods. Long-term WebQuests are designed for completion in weeks or months and may require production of a web page for a class presentation.

Many instructors have specific ideas about what they want their classes to accomplish using the web, and these instructors can easily create their own WebQuests with an accompanying web site or handout. The following suggestions are provided for instructors to make the most of a WebQuest.

Short-term WebQuests should fit within a 50-minute class period. Instructors should begin by identifying the specific task they want their class to complete.

1. ***Task.*** Good task design starts with the end in mind. Doing so allows instructors to clearly delineate the steps of the task for the students. The most effective description of the task describes background information, sets the parameters of the search, explains the purpose of the activity, establishes the roles that each individual plays in the WebQuest, and details the expectations of the final product (e.g., presentation, tourist brochure, newscast). The tasks can be done individually, in pairs, or as a group, with a clear understanding of the role each student plays in the activity (e.g., scribe, leader, chemist, detective). One of the best ways to clarify a task is by giving the evaluation rubric or checklist to the students at the beginning of the activity. For example, instructors can list the key elements for task completion with accompanying benchmarks: Organization 1–5, Cultural relevance 1–5, Comprehensibility 1–5.

2. ***Clearly identified steps.*** The steps that the learners need to take must be clearly identified either on the web or on a handout. WebQuests are more effective when instructors present the task as a linear process with steps numbered 1 through n. When the steps are explicit, the students will be more efficient in completing the task.

3. ***Resources.*** WebQuests should be interesting, and students should have access to any information they need to complete it. The instructor should provide a variety of source URLs for the activity due to the nature of the web. Web servers can be unavailable, the location of the information has changed, or the information itself has changed; it is considered bad practice to include only one option for students. Offering only one option creates more work and risk because instructors must check the source before every class, and the server may have difficulties with that particular site during class time. Wise instructors ensure that several web addresses

are available for the activity and that any of the web sites will provide sufficient resources to complete the task. Sources do not necessarily need to be URLs; other internet sources include email exchanges and listservs, databases, online books, and chat rooms.

4. ***Follow-up and Evaluation.*** Instructors should provide guidance so that students know how to organize their presentation of the information acquired during the WebQuest. The clearer the parameters, the easier it is for learners to be critical and creative with the knowledge they have gained (Plummer, 1988).

Like short-term WebQuests, long-term WebQuests should be well defined. Instructors should clearly identify the task and the steps of collection, organization, and presentation that the learners should accomplish during the WebQuest. Longer WebQuests may also include intermediate goals and the dates by which they are due. Long-term WebQuests can be accomplished more easily if they include assignment of roles to participants, for example, reporter, detective, or spy, and simulated personae to interact with via email, such as news editor, undercover informant, or head of the Central Intelligence Agency (Gonzales, 1999). These longer WebQuests are almost always done in groups and require a considerable amount of structure and organization by the instructor.

Class Presentations

Class presentations can entail the production of a web page or web site that students work on during the semester. Using resources on the web, students create a web page, MS PowerPoint, or video that can be projected to a screen and presented to the class. The tool used to make the presentation is unimportant because a document created with PowerPoint can be saved as a slide show, a web page, or a video. Similarly, a series of web pages can be saved as a PowerPoint or video presentation. Students may also make a presentation using a blog, wiki, or a variety of online presentation tools (e.g., prezi.com, glogster.com). It would be unproductive to include a tutorial here on the use of one specific tool given the rapid changes in presentation software and the number of tutorials available online for each new version. As stated in Chapter 1, instructors should select a technology palette and use the technology they are familiar with for presentations.

Students are quick to learn the tools presented to them in class, but the instructor may need to supply a worksheet that takes students through the basics of the software. This worksheet activity is the ice-breaker task and will be discussed in more depth in Chapter 6. In short, students should be able to make short presentations following the instructor's directions before they are given free rein to create whatever they want. Student presentations are a necessary practice to allow them to display what they know, integrate new knowledge with background knowledge, and even explore what they do not yet know (Hall, 2001).

An instructor may organize the class so that the presentations take the form of an online magazine, journal, or scrapbook to which all students in the class are contributors. With enough time and talent, the class might produce several issues of its online journal. An online magazine generally takes the form of typical magazines in the target culture, so instructors will need to show examples of these to students. Most LMSs also offer the capacity for students to create online presentations.

Online Portfolios

Finally, online portfolios may be used in the same way that presentational web pages are used, except that they present a sampling of the students' work from the entire semester. Students are assigned writing tasks that are posted online to the entire class. Students are often encouraged to review and respond to one another's work. The use of online portfolios and electronic portfolios is addressed in greater detail in Chapter 10.

Suggestions for Teaching with the Web

Whatever the activity, the instructor must carefully weigh the purpose, resources, and outcomes of CALL activities to be used in or out of class. The following list provides suggestions to guide the decision of whether to use certain online materials.

1. ***Use class time effectively and assign some work for home.*** If students can accomplish the task at home, why do it in the classroom? Second language acquisition (SLA) theories emphasize, among other topics, the importance of negotiation of meaning to promote comprehensible input (e.g., Long, 1985b) and the need for socialization (Belz & Thorne, 2005; Lantolf & Appel, 1994). Whereas comprehensible input is achievable on the Web, negotiation of meaning and socialization are difficult without the use of additional computer-mediated communication (CMC). CMC includes activities such as IRCs (Internet Relay Chats), IM (Instant Messenger), bulletin boards, email, social networking platforms, microblogging, multi-user domains/dungeon/dimension (MUD), and MUD object-oriented (MOO). The latter three are discussed in greater detail in Chapters 7 and 8.

    These activities are available on the internet, but this section applies mainly to activities that use only a static web page and a browser. As a rule, the introduction to the activity should occur in a classroom to assess the ability of the students to complete the task at home. Some follow-up will be necessary depending on the resources and abilities of the students.

    Instructors should carefully evaluate the allotted classroom time and identify activities that could be accomplished at home. This is not to say that web activities should not be done in class, but rather that instructors should have a clear idea of why they want to do a particular activity in class as opposed to out of class.

2. ***Web pages change; instructors should consider multiple options.*** Every web site can be modified quickly. Pages within a site will constantly be updated, corrected, augmented, refined, abridged, moved, or eliminated. Regardless of whether the activity uses the web as a delivery medium for items such as static pages, newspapers, or literary texts or as an interactive

medium for tasks that include online grammar exercises, games, or streaming video, wise instructors always include multiple options for students. Providing alternate sites helps circumvent problems associated with access and from an instructors perspective, removing a bad link is easier and faster than finding a substitute link or creating a new activity. Nevertheless, having alternate web sites to complete an activity necessitates activities that contain more general questions rather than specific scavenger hunt activities.

3. ***Questions must be designed so that learners can respond appropriately using any web site.*** Initially, most WebQuests consisted of win–lose questions, that is, questions that required a single correct answer. If students provided the correct answer, they won; if not, they lost. More recent activities provide questions that may allow for a number of responses that are appropriate depending on the resource web site. In addition to providing win–win questions, good WebQuests will provide the opportunity for students to visit several sites to experience various perspectives on a given phenomenon.

4. ***Always reconsider the objectives for each activity.*** Once the activity has been organized and clearly delineated, instructors would be wise to reevaluate whether the activity achieves the target goals identified at its inception. Novice task designers for electronic media are often so excited about using the media that the final project departs significantly from its initial inception. Ideally, the final product will still support the initial objectives of the activity. Nevertheless, all exercise can be improved by reexamining the activity in the context of its learning objectives.

5. ***Follow-up is essential.*** Students should be able to see a direct link between work that is done at home and work that is done in class. Doering and Veletsianos (2008) show a clear relationship between the model of integrating technology in the classroom and the students' learning experience. CALL and the web are not exceptions to this rule; students should be able to perceive a distinct and unmistakable connection among work on the web, classroom activities, and their overall expectations for the course. Activities can range from short instructor-led follow-up questions to longer course presentations or even coordinated arrangements with another class. The following section discusses follow-up activities in detail.

Follow-up Activities

Follow-up activities are indispensable to remind students about what they have learned, allowing consciousness raising, and perhaps motivating them to extend their learning beyond the initial objectives of the web-based activity. Several types of follow-up or expansion activities are suggested in the following list and may be used as a template for guiding students to assess their learning:

1. ***Class discussion.*** Class discussion can be valuable for reviewing, expanding, and sharing information gained from web activities. Discussions allow students to participate in a class consensus of knowledge gained while using their speaking and listening skills in the target

language. Web activities can facilitate class discussion by helping learners prepare for them.

2. ***Class presentation.*** Class presentations allow each student to contribute to the class and practice the presentational mode of communication. Unfortunately, class presentations take much time away from other learners' opportunity to practice interpersonal modes of communication. Having students present in groups significantly reduces the time required for appropriate follow-up. Instructors can be creative with the format of the presentation using various ideas such as a travel brochure, a demonstration of how to do something, a descriptive poem, a greeting card, a web page, or even a song or play. In some cases, it may be appropriate to organize an online conference during which students' work is showcased and they vote on selected categories (e.g., best presentation, most interesting).

3. ***Course magazine.*** A course magazine creates an opportunity for project-based learning. The class is divided into groups that work on different aspects of the magazine. After a web activity is completed (e.g., a WebQuest), students contribute an article about what they learned to a class magazine. The magazine metaphor is useful because it allows small groups to discuss their discoveries and assemble knowledge into a form that others in the class or in another cooperating school can access asynchronously. A course magazine also allows students to practice all modes of communication (presentational, interpretive, and interpersonal) while concentrating mostly on the content knowledge they have gained. The major drawbacks to a course magazine are that it requires high levels of organization and structure, a significant amount of class time allotted specifically to a semester-long project, and good group dynamics in the class. However, the benefits are incomparable as far as helping students become lifelong learners of the language. Several sites also facilitate the incorporation of data from a variety of resources (e.g., Storify.com, www.Curated.by)

4. ***A class link list.*** A class link list is an enjoyable follow-up to free surfing. If learners are allowed to visit any site and read about anything they want, a few activities are better as a follow-up than just listing the sites the students found most interesting. Along with the URL for the site, students should include both a description and a critique of the site. The goals of the task should be clear to learners from the beginning: the number of sites required, the length of the description that should accompany the submission of each link, and a reiteration of the language of the submitted sites (i.e., any site or only sites in the target language). These links may be aggregated on a wiki (see Chapter 8) or as a class bookmark site (e.g., Delicious.com, Diigo.com).

The in-class follow-up is often the most rewarding aspect of the activity because students can interact with one another and verify the information they have gleaned from the web. During the follow-up exercises, instructors can also take note of the difficulties encountered by the students. Attention

to task difficulty, language difficulty, and technical difficulty should help clarify the advantages and signal methods for improvement of an activity. Often,
instructors may focus on the pedagogical aspects of the task and assume that
any technical difficulties will resolve themselves. Although this is generally the
case, most learners experience high levels of frustration with the entire course
and not just the computer when the technology fails them. To avoid learner
frustration, instructors can and should examine the web resources from various
perspectives.

ADDITIONAL USES FOR THE WEB

Two other uses of the web, although not directly related to teaching, can help
teachers. The first is class management, which is popular at the postsecondary level and includes management systems such as Blackboard, Moodle, and
NiceNet.org. The second use is for professional development, such as subscribing to and participating in conferences. Both of these uses are discussed
in greater detail throughout this book, and instructors may want to keep in
mind how each of them may complement teaching methods or detract from
instruction.

Class Management

Harrington, Gordon, and Schibik (2004) found that at the university level, nearly
90% of those surveyed use a LMS to manage their classroom. One could assume
that these numbers would be somewhat different if the subject population were
limited to language teachers alone, but LMSs are so ubiquitous that it is prob-
able that those reading this book have either taken or taught a course that used
an online LMS such as Blackboard.

LMSs have enormous benefits for instructors because they offer a wide
variety of resources for disseminating information to the class and receiving
assignments: announcement board, homework drop box, email list, quizzes
and surveys, a chat room, a grade book, and more. Rother (2005) estimates that
although 80% of instructors use technology, only 47% actually use it for teaching. In a follow-up study, CDW-G (2010) found that what most respondents
were using on a regular basis were online materials (e.g., electronic textbooks)
or LMSs. Both of these uses relate to classroom management rather than instruction. This 2010 report also found that fewer than 30% of students believed that
they were encouraged to use technology for their classes on a regular basis,
particularly for creative endeavors (e.g., presentations).

In short, most instructors are familiar with a LMS but continue to use it as
a Web 1.0 application (e.g., to post announcements, course information, and
grades and to collect comments/homework) rather than as a Web 2.0 application. They rarely use certain tools that are embedded in the LMS, for example,
wiki tools, discussion board, group sites, blogs, podcasts, online testing, portfolios, or online office hours (chat). The exceptions are teachers who use LMSs in
conjunction with an online course.

Professional Development

Professional development is a buzzword among K–12 teachers, who usually need a specific number of hours of professional development each year. Although no such requirement exists in higher education, postsecondary faculty should also take professional development seriously. Professional development related to teaching with technology should be systematic rather than ad hoc. Instructors should decide which area of their professional life they wish to develop and focus on a particular aspect within that field. The point is to develop a toolbox of options to choose from rather than to become proficient with all tools overnight.

Instructors who focus on research or assessment can use the web for surveys, quizzes, and tests (see Chapter 9). The advantages of web-based research techniques include the ability to reach larger populations (e.g., all sections of a given level or all levels of a given languages), increased participation among students both in and out of class (Van Selm & Jankowski, 2006), popularity among college students (Van Selm & Jankowski, 2006), ability to incorporate *rich* applications (e.g., video, drag-and-drop, audio), efficiency of time and cost (Wright, 2005), and ease of administration (Wright, 2005). There are several disadvantages also, such as technical difficulties, lack of control over the test setting (Ahern, 2005), and initial investment in time and resources (Van Selm & Jankowski, 2006).

Instructors interested in improving their teaching can use the web to seek out lesson plans, activities, and templates as well as to subscribe to conference newsletters and participate in state, regional, and national online forums. Many language teaching organizations have well-maintained and helpful web sites (e.g., ACTFL.org, NECTFL.org, NCLRS.org). In addition to organizational home pages, instructors can also seek out online journals and social networking sites dedicated to teaching and learning with technology. The most notable of the online journals is *Language Learning and Teaching* (llt.msu.edu), which focuses solely on research-based articles on technology and teaching. Moreover, Arnold, Ducate, and Lomicka (2007) report some important benefits of creating a community of practice among practitioners that include a supportive learning environment for novice teachers, an enlarged perspective on teaching practices, and engagement with material at a deeper level. Some social networking sites (Ning.com, Facebook.com, LinkedIn.com) have groups dedicated to teaching with technology (see Chapter 6 for more information). Instructors can also follow other like-minded colleagues on Twitter (Twitter.com) to keep up with the latest trends in language teaching.

The keys to using the web for professional development are temperance and consistency. It is generally of little value to join every group online and then never have enough time to participate fully in the groups. Most instructors find it more rewarding to choose small research projects and follow through completely or join a few groups online and participate fully rather than attempt a cursory overview of everything available. The Web 1.0 model was to acquire as much information as possible; the Web 2.0 model is to establish the appropriate links to locate useful information to access on an as-needed basis.

TECHNICAL CONSIDERATIONS

One of the most important questions that instructors can ask in evaluating the technical aspects of web site use in a language learning activity is what resources do learners need in order to interact with a page, for Web 1.0 purposes or some of the Web 2.0 purposes discussed later in this book. To accurately answer this question, instructors must identify the in-class and out-of-class resources of their students. These resources relate to hardware, peripherals, and software.

Bandwidth, processor speed, and memory are the three considerations for hardware. Bandwidth refers to the amount of information that can travel from the internet to a computer. Bandwidth for dial-up connections is low (56 Kb/sec), whereas broadband connections (cable/DSL) tend to have much higher bandwidth (700 Kb/sec–12Mb/sec). *Processor speed* refers to the speed at which a computer can make sense of the information it has downloaded (for example, a computer downloads an image as a stream of bits; even if the connection speed is high, a slow processor will take more time to render the image on the screen). Memory is the ability to render the page with all the images, fonts, and interactive code while everything else in a computer is running. Web pages that are heavy on graphic images, digitized video, and/or audio may not be easily downloadable or usable by students unless they have reliable access to a high-speed internet connection.

Instructors must also consider whether or not a web page requires peripherals, such as a microphone, headphones, printer, speakers, or video card. The fact that a web site performs well on one computer does not mean that it will function on a computer that is similar but lacks certain hardware or software. Notwithstanding, most professional web sites are designed to function on a variety of hardware and software platforms (including alternate sites for mobile devices—for example Google.docs will recognize if users access the site using an iPad or iPhone and automatically forward the user to a site tailored to the device). Instructors should still be aware of what technology is available to the student population. For instructors beginning a new job, the best resource for this information is the school or university librarian.

Software is the final technical consideration that will be mentioned here. The first consideration is the browser that students are using. Some amateur sites do not look or perform as well in one browser as they do in another. Instructors would be wise to view the page from at least two browsers such as Firefox, Chrome, Safari, or Internet Explorer to ensure that the site has no significant problems in the most popular browsers (e.g., text boxes covering portions of the page in one browser but not another). In addition to browsers, some sites make use of plug-ins or helper applications such as Adobe Acrobat, Java applets, Macromedia Flash or Shockwave, Authorware, Director, RealAudio, or additional forms of video or audio that would need a player—some of which may be unavailable on a mobile device. Some students may be unable to download the needed plug-in because of lack of knowledge or because they are using a public computer. Instructors who are concerned about this should ensure that students have a resource that they can easily contact for assistance (i.e., help desk, librarian, or the instructor).

If instructors assign material that uses non-roman fonts, they need to ensure that the fonts are installed on departmental computers and that browsers automatically default to the appropriate alphabet or syllabary (Cyrillic, Japanese, etc.). Fonts are image files of alphabets, syllabaries, or icons that a computer uses to portray written texts on the screen. If the desired fonts do not exist on the computer being used to view the page, then the text will not appear correctly on the screen. Rather than seeing the required font, web surfers will see only the default font (i.e., Times New Roman or Helvetica in most cases) and it will be rendered as a series of meaningless letters. Many users are unaware of how non-roman fonts work on a computer, and they are often unable to load them appropriately without technical assistance. Instructors teaching non-roman languages may consider creating an instruction sheet for their students or using one available on the web.

Although the concept of the web is no longer new, the content on the web is constantly changing. When instructors configure activities appropriately, students can concentrate more fully on content and their ability to use the information they glean from the web. Because of the changing nature of the web, the exercises in the following section give general guidelines concerning activities that will help familiarize instructors with some of the technologies mentioned in this chapter, rather than offering specific tutorials on particular sites.

Practical Work

This section is designed to expand your technological tools palette. The following activities should help you design activities that use the web and gain a web presence for yourself.

1. Design a WebQuest.[2]
    a. Decide on a task that is interesting and able to be completed.
    b. Write an introduction that provides background information, puts the task in context, makes clear what the final project should be (worksheet, PowerPoint presentation, song, etc.), and how the final product will be graded.
    c. Decide on the web site sources needed to complete the task. Each site should be identified precisely by its URL.
    d. Write a detailed description including the purpose of the activity and each step learners should undertake to accomplish the task.
    e. Provide guidance on how to organize the information acquired during the activity. Examples include a questionnaire, a timeline, tables, or check boxes of applicable concepts.
    f. Restate what the final product should be (class presentation, collage, one-act-play, etc.).

---

[2]Examples can be found at WebQuest.org/.

2. Acquire a web space of your own if you don't already have one.

   a. Open your browser.

   b. Go to one of the following sites (your university help desk, Sites.Google.com, Yahoo.com, NiceNet.org, Moodle.org).

   c. Fill in the appropriate information.

   d. Wait for a response that provides you with a web address with some additional help information.

   e. Find and follow the instructions for uploading documents.

3. Introduction to a web portfolio.

   a. Begin by using a text editor (e.g., MS Word) to write an introduction page for your electronic portfolio.

   b. If the text can be saved as web page or html, save it in a folder just for your web pages. For more information on how to do this, click on the *Help* menu and type *Web page* or *html*.

   c. If you have not already received it, ask your instructor for a worksheet that lists the instructions for each of the items to be included in your ePortfolio.

4. Begin a weblog (blog).

   a. Open your browser.

   b. Go to one of the following sites (your Blackboard, www.Blogger.com, WordPress.com, TypePad.com)

   c. Follow the online directions for registration.

   d. Post a journal entry that discusses your response to what you've learned so far in this class.

Suggestions for Further Reading

Arnold, N., Ducate, L., & Lomicka, L. (2007). Virtual communities of practice in teacher education. In M. A. Kassen, R. Z. Lavine, K. Murphy-Judy, & M. Peters (Eds.), *Preparing and developing technology-proficient L2 teachers: CALICO Monograph Series Volume 6* (pp. 103–132). San Marcos, TX: CALICO.

Dodge, B. (2001). FOCUS—Five rules for writing a great WebQuest. *Learning & Leading with Technology, 28*(8), 6–9, 58.

Gonglewski, M., & DuBravac, S. (2006). Multiliteracy: Second language literacy in the multimedia environment. In L. Ducate & N. Arnold (Eds.). *Calling on CALL: From theory and research to new directions in foreign language teaching* (pp. 43–68). San Marcos, TX: CALICO.

Son, J.-B. (2008). Using web-based language learning activities in the ESL classroom. *International Journal of Pedagogies and Learning, 4*(4), 34–43.

Taylor, R., & Gitsaki, C. (2004). Teaching WELL and loving IT. In S. Fotos & C. Browne (Eds.), *New perspectives on CALL for second language classrooms* (pp. 131–147). Mahwah, NJ: Lawrence Erlbaum Associates.

Walker R., & Davies, G. (2012). Exploiting World Wide Web resources online and offline. Module 2.3 in G. Davies (Ed.), *Information and communications technology for language teachers (ICT4LT)*. Slough, England. Thames Valley University [Online]. Retrieved 2012, from www.ict4lt.org/en/en_mod2-3.htm.

CHAPTER 4

Theories of Second Language Acquisition

OVERVIEW

Pedagogy, not technology, should be the driving force behind computer-assisted language learning (CALL) use. Effective second language (L2) pedagogy is informed by second language acquisition (SLA) research. This chapter offers an overview of key concepts in SLA and identifies the relationship between various theories of SLA and optimal teaching guidelines using electronic media. As Salaberry (1996) states, "the potential pedagogic effect of the technological tools used in second language instruction...is inherently dependent on the particular theoretical or methodological approach that guides its application" (p. 7). An understanding of SLA theories is essential to good decision making concerning the use of CALL.

In addition to introducing SLA theories, this chapter discusses how those theories inform task design, evaluation, and syllabus design for the technology-enhanced classroom. Indeed, by its own definition, CALL is designed to assist language learning, not direct the methods used for language acquisition; effective teaching methods rely on pedagogy that is informed by SLA research (Curtain & Dahlberg, 2010; Horwitz, 2008; Shrum & Glisan, 2010). This chapter begins by looking at how SLA theories address what it means to know a language, how students learn, and why some students are more successful than others. The discussion aims to clarify what we believe and know about SLA and what we cannot know for sure. We then present a brief history of SLA and CALL to examine how the two interact.

SLA THEORIES

The broad scope of the SLA field includes theories that explain various phenomena from numerous perspectives. An in-depth explanation of the mechanisms involved in SLA is beyond the scope of this chapter. In fact, Ellis's (2008) 1,000-plus page treatise is evidence of the extent of SLA, yet Doughty and Long's (2003) edited *Handbook of Second Language Acquisition* makes a clear case that SLA is still in its infancy. To date, most of the widely accepted theories are incomplete. They focus on varying specific aspects but do not address the entire scope of SLA.

SLA theories consider a variety of contexts such as natural or instructed; children and adults; individuals and groups; and foreign, second, and *lingua franca* settings. SLA studies also include second, third, and subsequent language acquisition as well as second language attrition and loss. The field is laden with theories that extend beyond the scope of this chapter. Here, SLA will generally refer to instructed SLA (which occurs in a classroom or similar formal setting) and will exclude naturalistic SLA, attrition, and loss.

SLA theories address what it means to know a language (properties theories), what it means to learn a language (transition theories), and why some learners are more successful than others in learning a language (environmental theories; see Doughty & Long, 2003; Ellis, 2008; Mitchell & Myles, 2004; Ortega, 2009; Robinson & Ellis, 2008). Language instructors should be aware of all three areas. Indeed, many of the sources of the disparate approaches to learning language are found in differing views on language and language acquisition (Tyler, 2008).

Property theories concentrate on the state of the language in the learners' mind. An understanding of the properties of language acquisition enables instructors to posit what students are to learn (known as *targets*) and what the language system should look like at various points in the development of the learner (called *benchmarks*). For example, language representation in the brain is highly organized and tends to be acquired systematically, so researchers and instructors can. Knowledge about the properties of the developing language system is important for assessment and feedback purposes because they deal with the language characteristics and not directly with how the language is acquired or learned.

Transition theories seek to explain why and how students progress in the language. They can help guide instructors to provide appropriate learning opportunities for students to develop their linguistic systems. Swain's (2005) output hypothesis is a good example of how transition theories can guide classroom practice; meaningful output aids acquisition, so instructors should create opportunities for students to produce the language in meaningful ways.

Environmental theories tend to address motivation and affective concerns (e.g., attitude, anxiety, self-confidence), and how extracurricular activities impact language development. They can help instructors identify methods for creating lifelong learners, such as language clubs, study abroad experiences, and links with speakers of the target language.

These three theory types are described in the following sections; in reality, however, the distinction among theories is not clear—most theories overlap with others or do not attempt to describe all aspects related to SLA from a single perspective. The following discussion draws on various principles that stem from current models, theories, or hypotheses.

Property Theories

Property theories deal mainly with models of what the language learner acquires, learns, or internalizes. The fields of linguistics, neurolinguistics, and cognitive science concentrate on the aspects of language that are acquired. Most property theories are essentially versions of Universal Grammar (UG). The fundamental disagreement among the models in this area is whether the system of knowledge is rule driven or pattern driven or whether it is a tool for structuring information. The constructs generally include universal grammar (and grammaticality), interlanguage, and linguistic competence. The average teacher tends not to dwell on the properties of the L2 system because the benchmarks and standards from professional organizations such as ACTFL (The American Council on the Teaching of Foreign Languages) can more easily be applied to the classroom setting and the types of language that learners produce (see National Standards in Foreign Language Education Project, 1999). Nonetheless, knowledge of the patterns of development and specific linguistic paths that learners follow can guide instructors to efficient assessment and feedback on learner language. Although these concepts may seem intuitive to seasoned instructors, an explicit review of them can help teachers at all levels to make sense of learners' utterances, as well as their errors. Moreover, these accepted observations about SLA can be useful even if researchers disagree on a specific mental representation of the language.

First, it is clear that the L2 system acquired by learners goes well beyond what is taught. Learners maintain an intermediary linguistic system that Selinker (1972) dubbed *interlanguage* (IL). IL characteristics include some aspects of the first language (L1) and some aspects of the L2. More important, IL is always governed by rules, principles, or constraints such that it does not manifest wild or rogue (i.e., random) grammar characteristics. This IL system is not identical to the L1 system nor is it the same as the system of monolingual native speakers of the target language, but rather it has a third place between the two. In additional, the IL system extends beyond what instructors focus on in class. This notion of IL affects the technology needed for accurately identifying appropriate characteristics of an acceptable IL. For example, speech recognition systems continue to have difficulty with variability (e.g., speaker variation, style variation). Many of the systems currently control for variability by limiting input available to the computer, by restricting the vocabulary, speed, volume (i.e., microphones and headsets), and/or learner (i.e., requiring calibration for the program, customizing the application for dialect, or adapting the program to the level of the learner). With the IL as the referent (a system in which errors are expected) rather than the native speaker (a theoretically ideal system that does not account for error), more appropriate guidance could be given concerning the target forms of the IL. The previous example would extend to areas beyond pronunciation (e.g., grammar, lexical choice) and the use of the IL as the target would theoretically provide more efficient feedback for improving acquisition (see transition theories later in the chapter).

Second, the language acquired by learners varies considerably. They may develop oral competencies such as speaking and listening, and they may develop written competencies such as writing and reading. Generally, however, most teachers aim to help students develop both oral and literacy skills concurrently because the two often complement and reinforce each other. Despite instructors' efforts, learners' IL may develop with considerable variability among the various modes of communication. Trends in computer-mediated communication (CMC) have blurred the distinction between written and spoken text (Crystal, 2001). Chat, although it is written, may not be considered written discourse but rather oral discourse in written form. The same can be said for short messaging services (SMSs), texting, blog comments, PowerPoint presentations, status updates, or wall posts. Part of this acquisition of knowledge entails learners' association of forms in the language (i.e., vocabulary, morphology, phonology, syntax, discourse) with particular meanings. These form–meaning links constitute acquired knowledge on how to use the language. Some form–meaning associations such as intonation or vocabulary (i.e., cognates) transfer from the L1 if the L1 and L2 have a close genetic relationship. Learners may also create or reinforce associations through participation in communicative activities.

Third, in addition to developing IL and form–meaning associations for performing tasks in the language, learners develop both learning strategies (approaches to studying and learning) and communicative strategies (techniques for completing linguistic tasks). These strategies included specific techniques such as avoidance, circumlocution, and repair, as well as larger rhetorical devices of linking ideas, appropriateness of utterances, and nonverbal factors, such as gestures or appeals for assistance.

For most language teachers, these concepts have been operationalized under the label of *communicative competence*. Communicative competence refers to what a learner needs to know to communicate in a language community. For most teachers, it clarifies what students learn when they learn a language (Bachman, 1990; Campbell & Wales, 1970; Canale 1983; Canale & Swain, 1980; Chomsky 1965; Hymes, 1972; Savignon, 1972). Celce-Murcie, Dörnyei, and Thurrell (1995) provide a model that depicts what language learners learn as five interconnected aspects visualized as a triangle. At the center is *discourse competence*, which refers to how morphemes, words, and phrases are connected to express meaningful ideas. On the corners of the triangle, *sociocultural, linguistic*, and *actional competences* provide the bases for appropriate (sociocultural), well-formed (linguistic), and functional (actional) utterances. The preceding competences are supported by *strategic competence*, which surrounds and connects the other competencies. Strategic competence compensates for deficiencies in the other competencies and provides time and resources that may be lacking in the rest of the developing linguistic, social, or pragmatic systems.

The role of technology becomes apparent when competencies are related to online behavior. Discourse competence signals not only how morphemes, words, and phrases are connected but also how abbreviations, emoticons, and numbers can express meaning. Appropriate, well-formed, functional utterances may depend on length (because wall or Twitter posts require short interchanges), response-time, and reported actions (that is, comments that indicate what the user is doing, such as *shrugs, *facepalm, *hugs, or laugh out loud [lol]). Strategic competence is also expanded to include friending/blacklisting, technological skill, or hiding one's status.

An important theoretical benefit of this model of communicative competence is that it implies that students learn more than they are taught and that they must learn more than just the linguistic system–they also need to acquire language that is not the focus of their learning (Doughty & Long, 2003; Ellis, 2008; VanPatten, 2007).

Property theories study what is acquired and have revealed the following:

- Learners acquire language that is not taught (Hellermann & Vergun, 2007; Pulido, 2007). Learners can identify syntactic or morphological patterns that are not part of the instructional sequence simply because they want to perform specific functions in the language.
- Learners maintain an intermediary language, an IL, that is neither the L1 nor the L2 (but rather an interim grammar; Selinker, 1972).
- The language learned is variable (i.e., learners may develop syntactic systems at different rates; Gass & Selinker, 2008; Schwartz, Kozminski, & Leikin, 2010).
- Learners make connections between form and meaning in the language (Chen, 2005; Lee & Valdman, 1999; Midgley, Holcomb, & Grainger, 2009). In other words, students associate structures that they encounter in the language (syntax, phonology, etc.) with experiences that they have in the world.
- Learners acquire strategies for learning the language (e.g., how to study or how to make connections among functions or forms) and strategies for using the language, such as avoidance or circumlocution (Peters, Hulstijn, Sercu, & Lutjeharms, 2009).
- Learners acquire language that is not the focus of their learning (Bell & Collins, 2009). For example, learners can acquire new syntactic structures while focusing on morphology or lexical items.

The characteristics of the language that are acquired change significantly through the use of technology, and particularly CMC. IL plays an important role in operationalizing the type of language spoken by an L2 learner, yet it is rarely, if ever, used in CALL as the target form for assessing utterances because of the variability of forms involved in an IL. Technology has also added to the variability in the development of language systems by blurring distinctions between written and spoken texts. Additionally, strategies for gaining competence in the language have changed to include online behaviors. The inclusion of technology into SLA allows new threads of research for property theories to define what language is acquired by the learners.

TASK 4.1

Examine the type of language that you use to communicate via email (which is, to a large extent, standardized). Compare that with language that you find online in a chat room, forum, or SMS text messages. What are the main differences (i.e., variability) that you can identify?

Transition Theories

Transition theories focus on how the language is acquired. These approaches to SLA are often more important to language teachers because they emphasize how acquisition takes place and can often provide guidelines for activities that aid the acquisition process. Transition theories are learning theories and can be specific to language learning as they describe input, output, and interaction. These theories are generally cognitive in nature and propose constraint-based models (built upon hierarchal structuring linguistic constraints), rule-based models (founded upon formalist, generative linguistics), or processing-based or computational models, which emphasize general cognition over language-specific modularity (Ellis, 2008). As with property theories, transition theories disagree about how learning occurs and how this process manifests itself in the learner. Nonetheless, most researchers agree on a few principles concerning input, output, and interaction.

Researchers agree that comprehensible input is essential for acquisition, even if it is not sufficient. Most instructors are familiar with Krashen's (1982, 1985) Input Hypothesis that articulated the idea that students should be exposed to input that is just above their capabilities. This concept is represented as $i + 1$, where i is the input and +1 represents the next level beyond the learner's current level of competence.

The notion of comprehensible input has been well received by many practitioners, yet two major criticisms exist. First, little empirical evidence supports the claim, and it is not easily testable because the concept of *understanding* is not easily or consistently operationalized (McLaughlin, 1987; Pienemann, 2003). In short, there is no valid and reliable way to characterize a learner's current level (i) or the target form (+1) because of the complexity of language as it relates to the learners' abilities in phonology, syntax, and other components of a linguistic system. The problem of definition is exacerbated with the facets of competence mentioned earlier, such as sociolinguistic and strategic communicative competence. A second major criticism is Krashen's claim that exposure to comprehensible input is sufficient for language learning to occur. Canadian researchers, for example, studied French immersion programs for English L1 learners and identified fossilization in oral production, that is, the inability to progress beyond a certain point and thereby the failure to achieve productive control of certain aspects of the language (Swain, 1985; Swain & Lapkin, 1998). The purist notion of comprehensible input would argue that reading online journals or web sites (all Web 1.0 applications) should be sufficient to acquire a language. Although conclusive research to prove or disprove the sufficiency of input is lacking, most instructors would agree that extensive reading (online or offline) may not be the most engaging learning activity for students.

Some researchers developed the idea of comprehensible input within the field of Input Processing (VanPatten, 2007). Property theories argue that learners connect grammatical forms with their meanings as part of the acquisition process. Input Processing investigates how, when, and why learners make and strengthen these connections. The following are three important tenets of Input Processing:

- Learners process content words before anything else.
- Learners process nonredundant meaningful grammatical markers before nonmeaningful markers.
- Effortful comprehension is necessary.

Input Processing makes a distinction between comprehensible input and intake. *Intake* refers to language that is comprehended and processed for use in the developing linguistic system. Thus, according to Input Processing, it is not enough for the language to be comprehensible; it must also be meaningful and useful to the individual.

Although Input Processing is not a SLA theory per se (VanPatten, 2007), it avoids a focus on comprehensible input and concentrates rather on how any input become intake (which has led to a model of pedagogy called *processing instruction*). It also improves on Krashen's hypotheses by admitting the crucial nature of output and interaction in the language acquisition process, even if it doesn't describe the precise role that output and interaction play.

Indeed, learner output has also been shown to be essential in the language acquisition process. The Output Hypothesis (Swain 1985, 1998, 2005; Swain & Lapkin 1995) states that L2 learners acquire new forms as they are forced to form new hypotheses about target language structures and to attempt them in spoken form. Swain (1998) states that "learners may use their output as a way of trying out new language forms and structures as they stretch their interlanguage to meet communicative needs; they may use output just to see what works and what does not" (p. 68). The need for output is a call for Web 2.0 applications that require students not only to read but also to write on the web and contribute to the development of some body of knowledge. Today's applications easily allow for output in a technological environment (e.g., discussion boards, email, video production, podcasting).

Swain (2005) posits that the additional processing encourages acquisition of the language beyond what Input Processing allows. Relatively little research supports the output hypothesis as far as grammatical structures are concerned, but the advantages in vocabulary acquisition are well documented (see Swain, 2005). Ortega (2009) makes the interesting argument that Swain has moved closer to the sociocultural perspective on language learning (see environmental theories later in the chapter).

The need for both output and input provided a natural progression to the argument for the importance of interaction. Gass and Mackey (2007) further articulated Long's (1996) reformulation of the Interaction Hypothesis. They explain that a learner's acquisition process is mediated by two concepts: processing capacity and selective attention to input. This mediation happens most productively during the negotiation of meaning. Negotiation of meaning happens when interlocutors identify problems in the conversation and attempt to repair them to maximize comprehension. The feedback during negotiation of meaning is characterized by confirmation checks, comprehension checks, elaboration and clarification requests, and recasts. Long (1996) explains that this interaction facilitates acquisition because it "connects input, internal learner capacities, particularly selective attention, and output in productive ways" (pp. 451–452). In short, negotiation provides opportunities for learners to notice distinctions between their language and that of other speakers, identify deficiencies in their IL, and consciously attend to new forms (e.g., lexical items, pronunciation, constructions) to contribute to the developing L2. The time span between the interchanges is not specified by the research. Negotiation of meaning could take place over a series of months (a blog or podcast), weeks (email or a discussion board), days (a wiki or knowledge base), minutes (Twitter or status updates), or in real time (SMS, IM, chat, videoconference).

Another important perspective on how languages are acquired has come to light in Lantolf and Appel's (1994) and Lantolf's (2000) rereading of Vygotsky's (1978) sociocultural theory. Sociocultural theory does not directly dispute the importance of input, output, and interaction; rather, it reassigns the role of these activities into a social context. For example, comprehensible input (and intake) as described earlier rely solely on how the learner attends to and processes input without direct consideration of the source of the input or the nature of the communicative activity. Within the framework of sociocultural theory, all input and intake are dialogic in nature. The benefit accorded to the learner depends on how he or she participates in and regulates a communicative activity. A final and seemingly critical difference is that Gass and Mackey's (2007) formulation of the Interaction Hypothesis posits interaction as beneficial for acquisition, whereas sociocultural theory views interaction as essential to the language learning process. This distinction may be key in determining if CALL environments are necessary for contemporary learners or merely beneficial. The use of technological tools (such as blogs or social networking sites) to facilitate participation in scaffolded activities (i.e., with others learning the language) is not uncommon (see, e.g., Italki.com, LiveMocha.com, MyLanguageExchange .com). To date, however, no significant studies show the efficacy of individual participation in these types of online communication groups.

Sociocultural theory is founded on the idea that individuals need both interpersonal and intrapersonal communication. Intrapersonal communication is often called *private speech*. Interpersonal communication occurs between two or more individuals. It can be in oral, print, or multimedia format, and various technologies may be used for this purpose, such as chat, email, and videoconference. From a sociocultural standpoint, it is important that language activities fall within the Zone of Proximal Development (ZPD). The ZPD is the area of potential development, and it differs from $i + 1$ (Kinginger, 2002). Whereas $i + 1$ signifies the input that is just beyond a learner's capability to comprehend individually, the ZPD indicates a field of potential ability that a learner has with the appropriate assistance. As indicated earlier, there is no way to determine what $i + 1$ is for any given learner, but the ZPD can easily be determined by a learner's responsiveness to the assistance provided. For example, a learner may be unable to say what she did over the weekend without vocabulary help or additional prompting. Given the appropriate help, she may accomplish the task. This additional help is called scaffolding, which is any verbal or non-verbal help provided to the learner that enables him to complete a task that may be too difficult to accomplish alone. Lantolf and Appel (1994) provide a regulatory scale that lists 12 levels of regulation or scaffolding beginning with "no help" and passing to the last level of "providing examples" when other forms of help fail to produce an appropriate response. The level of scaffolding needed to accomplish a task depends on the learner and the task.

Aljaafreh and Lantolf (1994) make important claims about the nature of the scaffolding that apply to the use of technology: It must be graduated and contingent. Graduated feedback provides exactly the support necessary. Providing too much assistance hinders the learner's ability to become self-regulated (i.e., determine for themselves which actions to take), and too little hinders the learner's ability to perform the task. This notion of graduated feedback relates to VanPatten's (2007) idea of effortful comprehension because students benefit when they work to comprehend the language for performing a task. Contingent feedback is based on actual need; when the learner demonstrates the ability to function independently, the assistance should be removed to encourage the learner to self-regulate.

Several major distinctions can be drawn between the cognitivist constructs of input, output, and interaction and the sociocultural constructs of ZPD, private speech, and mediation. First, cognitivists are interested in constructs of the mind. The terms *input, output,* and *interaction* are based on the general notion that learning occurs in hypothesis testing whereby new forms are acquired through inductive learning (some call this process rule formation; others call it connections), and this process occurs in the learner's mind. Sociocultural concepts are based on the notion that learning occurs through guided participation structures that encourage self-regulation. Socioculturalists are interested in the processes of internalization and externalization in social relationships that help learners understand the uses of language.

Second, cognitivists generally take the individual as their starting and ending point. The individual acquires language by moving toward a state of automatization or full control through internal processes (Mitchell & Myles, 2004; Saville-Troike, 2006). Socioculturalists tend to see the acquisition process as dialogic whereby learners acquire mediational tools (e.g., rules, goals, private speech, note cards, gestures) to regulate their activity through scaffolded internships with other users of the language (Lantolf & Thorne, 2006).

Some generally accepted facts about SLA support these theories, whereas others call into question their premises. The following discussion examines some important points of clarification for teachers.

First, exposure to comprehensible input is necessary for acquisition to take place. There is disagreement on whether it is *sufficient* for language acquisition. Many researchers believe that although it is necessary, many other aspects also come into play (see VanPatten, 2007). Both Web 1.0 and Web 2.0 applications can provide ample amounts of comprehensible input in a variety of modes (e.g., visual, textual, audio, audiovisual).

Second, learners seem to acquire forms in a regular order called *developmental sequences* (Bailey, Madden, & Krashen, 1974). For example, learners first acquire negation with respect to phrases (e.g., he no go to school). They later attach them to modal verbs (can't, won't, doesn't—he doesn't go to school). Instruction seems to have no effect on the order of the stages through which learners pass in their IL. Learners must pass through each stage of acquisition, whether or not their control over grammatical forms (e.g., accuracy, fluency, function) is overt (Bardovi-Harlig & Comajoan, 2008).

Third, formal instruction has been shown to have no effect, some effect, or a significant effect on acquisition (Doughty, 2003; Ellis, 2008). For example, instruction does not change the order of acquisition or enable learners to skip sequences in the natural order. Instruction can, however, be detrimental and slow the acquisition process. Instruction has been shown to influence the rate at which learners pass through the developmental sequence and what the final acquisition may be. In short, instruction may be beneficial, but the relationship between acquisition and instruction is, at best, indirect and by no means settled among researchers.

Fourth, much disagreement exists about the form and role of interaction. We are unsure if interaction is causative or merely facilitative. It is also unclear what can be considered interaction. Sociocultural theory, for example, can argue that private speech is a form of social interaction. Likewise, students' interaction with texts and audio, video, and multimedia applications can theoretically count as interaction, and scaffolding would take the form of support mechanisms such as online glosses (textual or graphic), supplementary examples, or even corrective feedback (e.g., "Did you mean: X?" "Check for agreement."). Currently, however, no widely available software is sophisticated enough to supplant face-to-face interaction as far as graduated and contingent assistance is concerned. A few have investigated the capabilities of computer-generated feedback (e.g., Dickinson, Eom, Kang, Lee, & Sachs, 2008), but it appears to be in its nascent stages.

Fifth, the form-to-meaning mapping addressed by property theories progresses from an initial focus on context and lexicon to increasing reliance on syntax and morphology. As learners need more sophisticated forms to communicate a meaning, they rely increasingly on grammatical forms to represent those meanings. In short, beginning learners focus on context and vocabulary to derive meaning (i.e., make input meaningful) from what they hear. As their language skills progress, they rely more on the grammar. For example, students pay attention first to terms such as *yesterday*, *tomorrow*, and *today* to determine the time reference for a sentence. As their proficiency increases, they rely more on verb conjugations. Context also plays a part; sentences such as "I left after him" are more frequently misunderstood than "I left before him" because the sentence order is parallel to the semantic meaning in the "I left before him," but it is the opposite in "I left after him." Attending to more syntacticized forms (e.g., I went [past indicated only in the verb]) rather than their paratactic counterparts (e.g., yesterday[past indicated outside the verb], I went) is also facilitated using CMC. As shown in more detail in Chapter 7, students tend to use more syntactically complex language in email, online discussion boards, and wikis (Hirotani, 2005).

Sixth, acquisition in language happens progressively; however, the L2 system does not show steady improvement over time but rather abrupt changes and plateaus. This characteristic of development is often used to justify the view that some steps of the acquisition process entail a certain amount of restructuring of the developing linguistic system to permit further progress. Interactive CALL systems can recognize when students make abrupt advancements in the language or provide additional resources for those who stagnate at various points.

In short, transition theories prove to be useful to instructors because they explain much of how learners acquire an L2. CALL methodology has relied to a large extent on transition theories to drive its implementation. Transition theories posit the following six points:

- Exposure to comprehensible input is necessary.
- Learners acquire forms in a regular order or developmental sequence.
- Formal instruction may have none, some, or a significant effect.
- Disagreement exists about what constitutes interaction and what the benefit of interaction is for the learner.
- Initially, learners use context and lexicon to infer meaning with increasing reliance on syntax and morphology as proficiency increases.
- L2 acquisition happens progressively but marked improvement is not regular.

TASK 4.2

Transition theories focus on how language develops. The focus on development and learning lends itself to identifying sound classroom practices or guidelines. Identify five practices of using technology that you can justify by using principles of transition theories.

Environmental Theories

Whereas property theories focus on what language is acquired and transition theories focus on how second languages are acquired, environmental theories focus on why learners have more or less success in learning an L2. These theories tend to be conceptually useful for teachers but not so much in practice because teachers have only indirect control over the acquisition process. Many of these models focus on motivation and thereby have important implications for extracurricular activities such as study abroad and language clubs, as well as in-class activities such as keypals, videoconferencing with native speakers, and virtual visits to the target culture. The term *environmental* is used here to denote characteristics of the language acquisition process that fall outside the linguistic realm (e.g., not syntax, phonology, phonetics).

Environmental theories concern the role of society but include a number of variables that fall well outside of what one would consider social. These variables are important because of their impact on why language acquisition occurs. This section discusses the relationship between acquisition and age, individual differences, social context, cross-linguistic influence, motivation, and context.

Age is anecdotally considered one of the main reasons that adults do not acquire languages as well as children (as far as ultimate attainment is concerned). Penfield and Roberts (1959) popularized the idea of a critical age for language learning, and Wiesel and Hubel's (1963, 1965) famous blind kitten study gave strong support to the concept of a critical period for language acquisition. Wiesel and Hubel (1963, 1965) monitored new-born kittens and discovered that light deprivation to the visual cortex during the first three months of life leads to virtual blindness. Cats were monitored for an additional 15 months and demonstrated limited (yet abnormal) recovery even after light was restored to the visual cortex. The loss was both behavioral (cats did not use visual cues for movement) and biological (the cells in the eye and brain did not respond normally to visual stimuli). Yet even though the notion has been hotly debated for decades, the existence of a critical period for SLA is still an intensely controversial topic for many researchers (see Birdsong, 1999; Birdsong and Paik, 2008; Hyltenstam & Abrahamsson, 2003). For example, the adage that younger learners are better may not hold. Older learners tend to learn language at a faster rate (Krashen, Long, & Scarcella, 1979; Muñoz, 2006), but younger learners tend to attain greater ultimate success (Birdsong, 2006; Johnson & Newport, 1989; Krashen et al., 1979). It is clear, nonetheless, that these tendencies are far from absolute, and the issue is not approaching a resolution. The most we can say for sure is that a difference exists between older and younger learners, but we cannot attribute that difference solely to biological constraints (e.g., brain plasticity), psychological constraints (e.g., quality of input), or social constraints (e.g., motivation, opportunities for interaction).

Individual differences is a term that often refers to aptitude. Aptitude can be signaled by a learner's ability to process input efficiently and make hypotheses and generalizations. Aptitude has traditionally included attention and memory constraints. Individual differences can also refer to general tendencies and strategies for learning and communicating in an L2. Robinson (2002, 2005) offers a threefold definition of aptitude: (1) It is made up of a variety of aptitude complexes, (2) is intertwined with context and environment, and (3) must recognize motivational and affective influences. Aptitude complexes are groups or sets of cognitive abilities that function together to facilitate language acquisition (e.g., phonological awareness and short-term memory may facilitate intake). The context refers mainly to the instructional setting and how much and what kind of attention is given to implicit or explicit feedback in conjunction with attention to form or meaning. The third category, motivational and affective influences, ties together the other two categories, complexes and contexts, by influencing how well the individual exploits them. For example, one could suspect that an individual who views each interchange as a learning opportunity or as an opportunity for induction into the target language society is more likely to use resources to attend to incoming messages and thereby show more aptitude. However, the relationship between these influences is not well articulated or explored, and future research will need to investigate them more fully (Ortega, 2009).

Studies that focus on social context have generally addressed ultimate acquisition more than on rate or developmental patterns. The variables and conditions that can be considered in social contexts are innumerable but often include comparisons such as between naturalistic or instructional settings; social status of the L1 and L2; formal or informal settings; institutional and individual boundaries; social and individual identity; and majority, minority, or heritage language contexts. Social context plays a role in how much and what type of input a learner receives and often relates to motivation and continuation of language learning. The sheer number of variables and researchers' inability to control for these variables tend to render little experimental evidence to support strong claims in this arena. Even more naturalistic and ethnographic studies are needed to provide convincing evidence concerning the importance of social context (see Siegel, 2003).

The importance of cross-linguistic influence (also known as language transfer) is, for the most part, undisputed, but the nature of cross-linguistic influence is controversial (Ellis, 2008; Gass & Selinker, 2008; Odlin, 2003, 2005; Ortega, 2009). It is explored from so many diverse perspectives that as Odlin (2003) states, "the highly diverse evidence for transfer has impeded attempts to develop truly comprehensive theories of cross-linguistic influence" (p. 437). It does seem that languages that are close typologically tend to be easier to acquire. For example, a Spanish speaker would theoretically have an easier time learning Portuguese than Russian. Likewise, an English speaker would theoretically learn German at a faster rate than she would learn Korean. Beyond these seemingly obvious statements, it is difficult to posit any cross-linguistic effects with any confidence. Other studies have found interesting correlations with speakers' location (Pavlenko, 1999), social class (Schmidt, 1987), urban versus rural environment (Chumbow, 1981), pragmatics (Yu, 2004), and culture (Schumann, 1978), to name only a few.

Shumann (1978) uses the term *distance* to describe differentials between social and psychological standards in the L1 and L2. Cultures with less social and psychological distance between the L1 and the L2 create conditions that are favorable for acquiring the L2. These social factors focus on how learners achieve and maintain contact with the target group. They include concepts such as social dominance, integration patterns, enclosure, cohesiveness, size, congruence, attitude, and intended length of residence. The psychological factors concentrate more on the individual's attitudes about the target culture and include language shock, culture shock, motivation, and ego permeability. These factors affect both the quantity and quality of input that learners encounter.

The concept of *motivation* in language learning has received more attention than any other single individual difference (Ellis, 2008). Dörnyei (2005) states that almost 100 studies on motivation were published during the 1990s alone. The concept of motivation is well articulated and theoretically operationalized, so researchers have managed to develop studies on student motivation. Motivation determines the effort and time that learners put toward acquiring the language, including seeking out opportunities for use, negotiating and processing input, and appropriating a linguistic identity (e.g., maintaining a target language identity that is different from a L1 identity). Motivation receives considerable attention because it is key in the ultimate attainment of proficiency as well as rate of acquisition. The only problem is that we cannot establish whether motivation is a cause or a result. In other words, high motivation may stimulate learning, but high success in learning may also stimulate motivation. Moreover, it is unclear if pedagogical procedures have a significant influence on motivation. However, many have indicated positive motivational effects of using technology in class (Belz, 2002; Blake, 2008; Fitze, 2006; Mullen, Appel, & Shanklin, 2009; Tian & Wang, 2010).

Historically, little research has focused on the environmental (i.e., social and contextual) aspects of L2 acquisition (Ortega, 2009), yet since the beginning of the twenty-first century, researchers have turned their attention to a social understanding of cognitive characteristics, paying particular attention to the relationship between the cognitive dimensions of language acquisition and the social ones (Block, 2003; Lantolf & Thorne, 2006). These theories argue that cognition is social (Lantolf & Appel, 1994), language is a process of socialization (Duff, 2007), and identity plays a major role (Norton, 2000) in determining why some individuals are more successful than others. These arguments are salient considerations for using social networking technology such as Facebook, Twitter, or Flickr. Studies have showcased these technologies and highlighted the need for more SLA research related to these tools (Levy & Stockwell, 2006; Lomicka & Lord, 2009). A significant gap remains in the available research concerning these concepts, particularly in regard to the use of technology. Most of the prominent research in CMC has relied on the version of sociocultural theory posited by Lantolf and others (Lantolf, 2006; Lantolf & Appel, 1994; Lantolf & Pavlenko, 1995; Lantolf & Thorne, 2006).

TASK 4.3

Using the concepts presented in this chapter, write your philosophy of teaching. Make sure to be clear on your beliefs about the learner, the instructor, social relations, and language acquisition.

TECHNOLOGY AND SECOND LANGUAGE ACQUISITION

The initial combination of technology with second language learning and instruction was tightly bound to a behaviorist model of language learning (Blake, 2000; Warschauer, 2004). Once viewed as nearly unbreakable, this link has dissolved with the arrival of more advanced technologies and with developments in SLA theory. Hardware and software developed from being large, expensive, often complicated, and text based to being small, ubiquitous, easily networked, and multimedia. In its own field, SLA research has made important contributions to both theoretical and pedagogical practices. These practices are merely different perspectives on the same phenomena; alone, each can justify its positions only with great difficulty. Hence, this section is designed to enhance not only a theoretical understanding of the variables involved in SLA (such as input, output, and interaction) but also the practical application of the interaction among those variables for design and evaluation of CALL activities.

We begin by reexamining the historical development of CALL and investigating the concepts of input, output, and interaction. From these mainly cognitive notions, the orientation turns to social theories that examine how today's learners approach learning and emphasize how technological innovations can promote activities to enhance their progress.

A Brief History of SLA and Typology of CALL

A considerable amount has been written tracing the history of CALL and SLA theories or methodological orientations (Chappelle, 2001, Kern & Warschauer, 2000; Levy 1997; Liu, Moore, Graham, & Lee, 2002; Luke, 2006; Warschauer, 1996b, 2004). This section offers an overview of basic concepts leading to the current pedagogical orientations. It also describes these concepts in a historical fashion to show the development of thought. Readers should not be misled into believing that each new wave was successful at eliminating the previous methodological perspective. For example, it would be unrealistic to assume that all language teachers avoid grammar–translation or audiolingual methods—translations and flashcards are not uncommon practices in language learning. The point of the discussion is to demonstrate consistency in the governing metaphor across learning theories, language theories, language teaching methodologies, and available technologies.

In the 1970s, learning theories based on behaviorism allowed the audiolingual method to flourish and mainframe computing to guide the stimulus–response drills for the structure of the language such as grammar, vocabulary, and pronunciation. Stimulus–response drills worked extremely well with the input–output model of computing at the time.

The advent of the personal computer (PC) gave way to instructional technology that targeted the tutor–student relationship and aimed at guiding learners to communicate. This development in instructional technology enabled a departure from stimulus–response models. At the same time, advances in language acquisition were influenced by cognitivism; both language learning and computers integrated easily with cognitivistic principles. Computers (specifically PCs) enabled students to follow a meaningful path of study leading from conceptual awareness to partial control to full control. The path could be monitored; if certain modules were not mastered, the learner could be forced to review or retake a test before continuing to the next learning module. Although he does not apply it to CALL, Krashen's (1982) Input Hypothesis typifies this orientation; the computer's role and the goal of the accompanying software were to guide students to acquire the language implicitly by giving them the next comprehensible step ($i + 1$) in the language.

As personal computers and software became more sophisticated and ubiquitous, many teachers shifted to embrace constructivism as their implicit theoretical framework for using CALL. Although constructivism has its roots with Dewey (1916) and Piaget (1970), this orientation saw a significant rise in popularity in the late 1990s and early twenty-first century. The basic premise of constructivism is that learners must construct knowledge and that the learner, the task, and the instructor are equally involved in the construction of that knowledge. Instructors who embrace constructivism tend to prefer project-based instruction in which students produce presentations, perform, or solve real-world problems. Computers have been able to facilitate these tasks using presentational software, video and audio recordings, and prominent web technologies (see Chapters 7 and 8).

Lantolf and Appel's (1994) edited volume brought the most recent wave of interest to social constructivism as Vygotsky's (1978) ideas were applied to language learning. From a sociocultural perspective, both the computer and the language are mediational tools that work together to accomplish goal-oriented activities. In the context of CALL, Warschauer (2004) calls this *integrative CALL* and makes a clear case for the use of the internet and multimedia as a means to what he calls agency (p. 23). Lantolf (2000) indicates that the computer and the language are merely tools for self-regulation (p. 80) and what Vygotsky refers to as self-mediation. Table 4.1 shows the progression of SLA theories and how they relate to CALL with examples of language learning methodologies; we will examine CALL methodologies more fully in Chapter 5.

Table 4.1 lists samples of each category and is not meant to be exhaustive. The dominant theories in SLA and technology today are social constructivism and sociocultural theory (SCT). Although many researchers still focus on functionalist and cognitivist theories, the general trend in technology and SLA is to

TABLE 4.1 Perspectives on learning, language, and CALL

Theories of learning	Theories of language	Methodological orientation	Applications and computer tools
Behaviorism	Structuralist	Grammar–translation method, audiolingual method	Translation, drills, computer flashcards
Cognitivism	Cognitivist	Communicative Language Teaching (CLT)	Tutorials, guided instruction, WebQuests, email
Constructivism	Functionalist	Project-based learning, content-based learning, task-based learning	Word processors, spreadsheets, PowerPoint, web site construction, blogs, podcasting
Social Constructivism	Sociocultural	Situated practice, overt instruction, critical framing, transformed practice	Collaborative software, email/bulletin boards, wikis, other Web 2.0 applications

underscore the importance of social concerns (see Kassen, Lavine, Murphy-Judy, & Peters, 2007; Lomicka & Lord, 2009; Thomas, 2009). SCT has been able to marry social concerns with language acquisition.

A few trends seen in Table 4.1 are worth noting. The most notable one is a shift from a focus on the individual to a focus on the society. Early theories and methods focused on the individual as the main component of learning a language. Later theories and methods increasingly incorporated the society and its role in the learner's language development, including how the learner constructs his or her identity in the target language community. The growing importance of society can be seen in a number of other fields outside of language learning and the technological tools that have facilitated these developments. The most prominent example is open-source software design for which specialists (e.g., computer programmers, graphic designers, content experts) contribute to the development of software. Similarly, crowdsourcing involves a variety of individuals who contribute to a product (e.g., Wikipedia, social bookmarking). The most commonly used social tool is probably online reviews of products (e.g., at Amazon.com and UrbanSpoon.com) or selling (e.g., Ebay.com).

The trend toward societal inclusion also involves education and learning theories (Sharpe, Beetham, & de Freitas, 2010), literacy theories (Van Waes, Leijten, & Neuwirth, 2006), and distance education (Mason & Rennie, 2008). Much has been written about social characteristics such as the attitudes, approaches, and learning styles of the Net generation (Baron, 2008; Collins & Halverson, 2009; Lomicka & Lord, 2009, Oblinger & Oblinger, 2005). Although it may be unreasonable to describe a whole generation of learners in simple terms, those individuals in a technologically rich learning environment tend to move toward the following behaviors:

- They are active participants in their learning and shape their own learning environment (Sharpe et al., 2010).
- They learn more by doing than by examining (McNeely, 2005).
- They view technology as embedded rather than additional tools (Oblinger & Oblinger, 2005).
- They expect self-directed, meaningful social interaction (Glenn, 2000).
- They prefer running commentary to reflective synopsis (Baron, 2008).
- They feel the need for immediacy (McNeely, 2005).

These behavioral characteristics guide learners in technologically rich environments to seek opportunities for learning that are both immediate and social. The technologies that support these are mobile (e.g., iPhones/iPads/iPods, instant messenger/SMS texts, videoconferencing), always accessible and current (e.g., blogs, microblogs, wikis), and socially oriented (e.g., social networking sites, collaborative software, friend lists). Not surprisingly, the dominant theories of learning and language acquisition have emphasized these practices, and future research will investigate further the coordination of these practices with their results (Levy, 2007; Lomicka & Lord, 2009).

The second trend is the shift from a focus on the language to a focus on the learner. Warschauer (2004) argues that earlier methods and theories concentrated on accuracy and fluency in the language; later methods target agency of learners to use those tools for their own purposes. Gonglewski and DuBravac (2006) also show the increasing importance of encouraging learners to develop multiliteracy skills to function in the language using the available technology to connect themselves to others and communicate the appropriate message for the context. As mentioned previously, tech-heavy learners tend to pursue learning for their own purposes and numerous technologies support a more independent style of learning (Schwienhorst, 2008). The most prominent technological innovations are Web 2.0 developments, or the read–write web. Using blogs, Wikipedia, YouTube, or social networks, learners can autonomously deepen discussions about any topic that interests them. They solicit feedback from others and improve their understanding of the topic they choose. Learners can also subscribe to a variety of RSS feeds depending on their interests, preference (audio/video/print, comic/serious), and time constraints. With today's technological innovations, learners have control over how, when, where, and what they learn.

The third trend is for instructors to view the language as a tool rather than as the goal. Early theories saw language as the goal of instruction. For example, the audiolingual method encouraged learners to speak accurately without necessarily being able to accomplish any tasks. The proficiency movement did much to improve this, but the focus tended toward accomplishing researcher-defined linguistic tasks such as narrating, describing, or asking questions. Later perspectives on language learning underscore that language is a resource for accomplishing authentic tasks such as making friends, producing a radio show, or realizing learners' identity in the foreign culture. This view of language as a tool also extends to viewing technology as a tool. It bears reemphasizing that use of blogs, wikis, or other Web 2.0 technologies will not necessarily help students acquire the language at a faster rate, nor will it inevitably improve motivation. Rather, when the technology is used to facilitate the task, learners can take advantage of opportunities for interaction in the target language. The technology can satisfy the need for immediacy (e.g., IM, video collaboration), the preference for running commentary (e.g., Twitter, status updates), and the expectation of meaningful social interaction (e.g., texting, photo sharing, social networking), but using the technology cannot be the final goal for class activities.

Finally, there is a trend to view learners as larger contributors to the language learning process and the instructor as less and less prominent. Early theories tended to put the teacher in front and allow the instructor to govern almost all of the class activity. The focus on the instructor has gradually shifted to the learner. Today's language learners have much more control over what, how, and when they study. This shift also enables the computer to play the role of assistant or tool rather than instructor. This shift is related to the initial point mentioned previously, the trend toward larger social inclusion, because the computer can be a tool for communication with any qualified individual (e.g., guest lecturers, crowdsourcing, peer-exchanges). As the prominence of the instructor has diminished, collaboration with others has become increasingly important to help learners direct their own learning and assess their own performance. This need for collaboration fits directly into sociocultural and social constructivist theories that describe a collaborative, negotiated relationship rather than a leader–follower relationship.

SLA has developed considerably in the past 30 years. Although researchers are confident about a number of concepts, we are more knowledgeable about the limitations of instruction than we are about the most appropriate methods for the tools we have. This chapter has attempted to describe some of the major aspects of SLA theories. Despite the lack of an overarching, unifying theory, we have attempted to discuss the what, how, and why of SLA. Readers should be aware that a unifying theory of SLA is not forthcoming. This lack of consensus may be frustrating to new instructors because each theory takes a different perspective on the language learning process. Nonetheless, the various aspects presented in this chapter aim to provide a foundation for guidelines in teaching world languages and for identifying appropriate expectations from students and teachers, particularly in respect to the use of technology and technological resources in and out of class.

The emphasis given to socially constructed meaning, activity theory, and the appropriation of new language forms in sociocultural theory makes it a solid base for defining a teaching methodology. Moreover, sociocultural theory appears to feed directly into task-based language teaching as a methodology for the technology enhanced classroom. Task-based teaching emphasizes the accomplishment of specific tasks and appears to meet the needs of the learners described earlier because it (1) allows learners to be active participants in their learning, (2) allows them to do in order to learn, (3) embeds technology, (4) encourages meaningful social interaction, and (5) satisfies the need for immediacy.

The next chapter focuses on teaching methods and principles for using technology in the classroom; this chapter has stressed the importance of understanding the theory behind how and why these tasks work in order to create, adapt, and maintain activities that support language learning.

Practical Work

1. Identify several types of software applications that promote social links among individuals (e.g., Facebook.com). A well-maintained list of social networking sites is available at www.go2web20.net/. How do you suppose college students use these applications? Design a questionnaire or interview protocol, and gather data from several students to verify your suppositions.

2. Use presentational software such as PowerPoint to summarize what you have learned in this chapter. Numerous online sites support activities of this nature: show.zoho .com, animoto.com, www.voicethread.com, www.glogster.com, slidesix.com

3. This chapter identifies numerous concepts that influence SLA. Make a list of items that you would have expected to see in a list of known variables about SLA. Which concepts are new to you? Which of the theories influences your teaching the most (property, transition, or social)? Post your teaching philosophy to your blog, Twitter, or wiki account.

Suggestions for Further Reading

Doughty, C. J., & Long, M. H. (Eds.). (2003). *The handbook of second language acquisition*. Oxford, Eng.: Blackwell Publishing.

Kern, R., & Warschauer, M. (2000). Theory and practice of network-based language teaching. In M. Warschauer & R. Kern (Eds.), *Network-based language teaching: Concepts and practice* (pp. 1–19). New York: Cambridge University Press.

Lantolf, J. P., & Thorne, S. (2006). *Sociocultural theory and the genesis of second language development*. Oxford, Eng.: Oxford University Press.

Ortega, L. (2009). *Understanding second language acquisition*. London: Hodder.

VanPatten, B., & Williams J. (Eds.). (2007). *Theories in second language acquisition: An introduction*. Mahwah, NJ: Lawrence Erlbaum.

Warschauer, M. (2004). Technological change. In S. Fotos & C. M. Browne (Eds.), *New perspectives on CALL for second language classrooms* (pp. 15–26). Mahwah, NJ: Lawrence Erlbaum.

CHAPTER 5

Activity- and Task-Based Teaching for Technologically Enhanced Classrooms

OVERVIEW

Years ago, many instructors sought to implement technology in their classes simply because computers were new and exciting (Bush, 1997). Today's students are not as intrigued by technology because they have grown up with it (Sharpe, Beetham, & de Freitas, 2010). Tasks now take precedence over technology in computer-assisted language learning (CALL) activities. This chapter uses task-based instruction as the framework for language pedagogy and technology. Numerous types of tasks are available in computer-assisted instruction (CAI) or computer-based instruction (CBI). We begin with some theoretical justifications for a task-based framework to provide a basis for designing and using various types of tasks while considering curricular structures to support those tasks. Sociocultural theory presents a clear framework for identifying principal parts of task design for the language classroom. Activity theory, one aspect of sociocultural theory, offers the main basis for task design, facilitation, and evaluation.

We begin with a short overview of sociocultural theory as it relates to CALL. We then consider the distinctions among *activity, task,* and *exercise* and examine the implications of the five basic principles of activity theory (hierarchical structure, object-orientedness, internalization/ externalization, development, and mediation). Activity theory calls for variety and routine, encourages both individual and group tasks, posits open tasks over closed tasks, and fosters a positive sense of community among learners. A taxonomic presentation of various types of tasks that are common in instructional software clarifies options for instructors who anticipate increased use of technology in their classes. Finally, we reflect on participation structures and how technology supports a variety of interaction levels in class.

SOCIOCULTURAL THEORY AND CALL

As explained in the previous chapter, sociocultural theory provides a solid basis for using tasks and technology in language teaching. More important, sociocultural theory lends itself to both the study and the teaching of a second language (L2) in ways that are not available from other theoretical perspectives (e.g., interactionist, cognitivist, linguistic). The main advantage to sociocultural theory is that it "offers a framework through which cognition can be systematically investigated without isolating it from the social context" (Lantolf & Thorne, 2006, p. 1). Warschauer (2005) notes two important characteristics of sociocultural theory in regard to CALL. First, it perceives tools (e.g., language, computers) as mediational means and considers how these tools fundamentally change the way humans think. Rather than looking at how tools facilitate tasks, sociocultural theory, through the lens of activity theory, investigates how tools actually transform tasks. Second, sociocultural theory emphasizes the need for social learning. Whereas interactionist and cognitivist perspectives analyze individual progress manifested by performance, sociocultural approaches focus on developmental potential observed in interactions with other speakers that occur within the zone of proximal development, or ZPD. As discussed in the previous chapter, the ZPD is simply a theoretical construct that describes the distance between current development level as determined by independent problem solving skills (i.e., no help or guidance) and potential development level as determined by what can be accomplished in collaboration with more capable peers. The ZPD differs considerably from Krashens (1985) version of $i + 1$ because $i + 1$ is an individual construct that depends on only the individual ability (i), whereas the ZPD is social because it depends on both the learner and the expert speaker involved in the collaborative act.

These characteristics of sociocultural theory provide a solid theoretical foundation for developing tasks for a variety of levels using a variety of technological innovations. Other theoretical orientations (cognitive, social, linguistic) support the task-oriented position presented in this chapter, but the discussion that follows relies principally on sociocultural theory, focusing mainly on the distinctions among activity, task, and exercises; task types for CALL; and participation structures.

Activity, Task, and Exercise

The main distinction among activity, task, and exercise concerns scope and intent. *Activity* is everything that occurs in a class (e.g., instruction, management, socialization). Activities are generally carried out by the society or community (e.g., class). Activity, in this sense, is the overall concept of why something happens and it accounts for the context, the participants, and the actions. It refers to recurrent or long-term developments in class. *Tasks* are smaller in scope and more precise in intent than activities. Tasks are used to promote linguistic performance in goal-oriented activity. They are blueprints for linguistic activity that is oriented toward a nonlinguistic goal; that is, students performing tasks focus on accomplishing a goal rather than producing forms in the language. *Exercises* are blueprints for linguistic activity toward a linguistic goal—the purpose of exercises is to cause learners to produce forms in the language, and not necessarily to do anything with the language they produce (Lee & VanPatten, 2003). One major distinction between tasks and exercises is that tasks are completed when participants have performed a function (e.g., gained information by asking a question, bought a present, ordered some food); exercises are completed when participants have supplied the correct language forms (e.g., conjugated a verb, produced the appropriate preposition, repeated *est-ce que*). Tasks push students to accomplish a real life goal using the language; examples of tasks include explaining the location of a park on a map or agreeing with a partner on where to eat or which movie to see. Some examples of exercises are fill-in-the-blank worksheets or oral questions. On a written worksheet, students fill in the appropriate number of spaces to complete the exercise. In an oral question–answer exchange, students often give a single response; instructors may give the student credit for having answered rather than having maintained an authentic conversation.

According to the sociocultural perspective, the concept of activity is essential to cognitive development. Activity that occurs as assisted interaction within the ZPD and promotes mediation is particularly valuable for L2 development. One building block for the type of activity that promotes mediation is a task. The use of tasks is supported from perspectives other than sociocultural theory. For instance, Doughty and Long (2003) and Pica (2008) demonstrate how second language acquisition (SLA) theory from cognitivist and interactional orientations argues for the use of tasks for language learning and teaching. Mohan and Luo (2005) likewise make a clear case for CALL tasks from the perspective of systemic functional linguistics.

The notion of a ZPD rejects Piaget's (1979) claim that learning does not affect the course of development. Piaget (1979) asserted that learning depends on the maturity of the individual; the learner will learn when he or she has reached a certain level of maturation. Vygotsky's (1978) sociocultural view posits that learning and maturity interact within the ZPD, whereby a learner's performance with other participants exceeds his or her performance alone. The ZPD requires researchers to focus on a learner's potential development (a Vygotskyian concept) rather than his or her actual development (a Piagetian concept). The realization of this potential is achieved through assistance from a more capable speaker, a process called *scaffolding* (as discussed in Chapter 4). During scaffolded interaction, the more competent speaker manages the portions of the task that extend beyond the learner's capacity. This assistance allows the learner to focus on the portions that are within his or her range of competence. Donato's (1994) work indicates that learners at the same level of competence in an L2 can provide scaffolding support even though they are not expert speakers. Thus, in a sociocultural framework, peers are able to provide sufficient structured support for one another. Donato's (1994) results are also important because they show that language development is a social process. That is, L2 acquisition is not represented by the attainment of structures and the processing of input, but rather is characterized by the co-construction and internalization of knowledge made in a social activity.

Activity theory should lead to "transforming practice in ways that might potentially ameliorate the everyday conditions and outcomes of teaching and learning" (Lantolf & Thorne, 2006, p. 260). To be precise, activity theory makes no specific case for the role of the teacher, the student, or the technology, but rather situates them in a structure that can then be used to transform the practice of L2 pedagogy in beneficial ways. CALL technology increasingly includes computer-mediated communication (CMC), social networking, and social presence—arenas in which instructors have less control over the activity associated with the tasks assigned. Activity theory posits five main principles: hierarchical structure, object-orientedness, internalization/externalization, development, and mediation. Each of these principles is important for designing appropriate tasks and understanding how the tasks can help drive the activity in class.

The *hierarchical structure* of activity is best shown by Leont'ev's (1978) three levels: activity, action, and operation. These levels should not be confused with the earlier discussion of activity, task, and exercise—all of which would correspond to Leont'ev's top-level category of activity. The hierarchal structure of activity is similar to long-term, short-term, and immediate goals. In brief, *activities* are goal-directed pursuits motivated by conscious effort, *actions* are the stepping stones/short-term goals used to accomplish those activities, and *operations* are the methods for accomplishing actions in specific contexts. Although this trichotomy is not particularly insightful for CALL and L2 learning, it should be noted that different actions may accomplish the same activity, and operations vary according to the context. These distinctions are explored further in the discussion on task design for CALL.

Object-orientedness refers to the idea that the things that create our reality have specific objective properties on various levels, including biological, cultural, or social. All activity is oriented toward an object. Objects can include the solution to a problem, a goal, or the intent that drives action. For the purposes of CALL, then, the tasks designed for class should have a clear purpose and goal. This goal should have a functional, communicative purpose; it should not be merely to practice or review language structures. Ellis (2012) reviewed a number of studies in task-based language teaching (TBLT) and examines the claims of the updated Interaction Hypothesis (Long, 1996). He argues that both theoretical perspectives (interactionist-cognitive or sociocultural) strongly support a tasked-based methodology. Both theoretical orientations emphasize tasks that direct talk to focus on understanding and develop attention to linguistic features. Both perspectives also acknowledge the value of feedback because tasks allow for direct, real-time, and understandable feedback on both the developing linguistic system and learner control over the functions involved in the task.

Internalization and *externalization* are related processes that enable both learning and action in society. Activity theory distinguishes between external and internal activities but maintains that internal activities cannot be understood in isolation from their external realization; both activities are ontologically inseparable because they transform into each other. Internal activities reflect the traditional understanding of mental processes. Internalization is the mechanism by which external activities become internal activities. Internalization includes practices such as visualizing, imagining, simulating, and planning. It provides an opportunity for interaction whereby individuals can try potential interactions without working with external objects (e.g., other people, books). Externalization is the process by which internal activities become external ones; it is the physical expression of a mental model. Externalization is a necessary component when internal activities require repair (as in the negotiation of meaning) or coordination among participants (for group work). Language play, pastiche, and copying others' speech are some ways that learners engage in the internalization/externalization dialectic.

The shift between internal activity and external activity is dialogic and is often referred to as *self-regulation*. Regulation occurs on three levels: object-regulation, other-regulation, and self-regulation. Children are largely object-regulated because they depend on the environment to accomplish tasks. For example, if a child wants milk, the child will normally simply say "milk" or point directly at the milk. As children grow, they learn to be other-regulated, relying on others (e.g., parent, teacher, peer) to scaffold their performance to accomplish certain tasks. To revisit the previous example, when an older child wants milk, he or she will talk in a demanding way to the caregiver or other individual who can get the milk (e.g., "Mom, get milk!"). The child in this instance is focusing on using the caregiver to get the milk and not simply on the milk. The important issue in other-regulation is that the child identifies that the caregiver is a means of accomplishing the task, whereas in the first example, the child is merely focusing on the object. Finally, humans learn to be self-regulated when they have control over their environment and are able to initiate change. If, for example, a child who is self-regulated wishes to have milk, he or she can pull a chair to the refrigerator, open the door, and attempt to pour the milk. That is not to say that the person has complete control over all tasks, but rather that he or she is able to use a number of tools (e.g., lists, private speech, mnemonic devices, self-assessment) to mediate activity.

Development within activity theory is dialectic and dialogic in nature. Activity is situated in a context and can be understood only by looking at its developmental transformations. These developmental changes are dialectic— they are constantly in flux and specific to the individual and the society together. Development is dialogic because society, the tools being used, and the purpose of those tools are in a constant state of change as activity continues. As such, we use tools to accomplish goals with others, and the tools change our way of thinking, thereby modifying the activity depending on context, society, and personal choice. All interactions (e.g., feedback from others, self-assessment) aim to modify the entire activity (e.g. student participation, final project, pronunciation).

Mediation plays a central role in representing how humans accomplish activity. The activity between humans and object or others is mediated through the use of tools. Tools are created and used during the activity and carry with them traces of the cultural development of their creation. The term *tool* is used here in its broadest sense; some examples are language, computers, textbooks, chalkboards, checklists, digital photos, and mobile devices.

The idea of language as a tool for mediation has become particularly significant in SLA studies because of the importance given to private or inner speech (Lantolf & Thorne, 2006). During language learning, many learners will use language to regulate the object; in other words, learners talk to mediate the parameters of the task. Some of these comments include statements such as "What do we do now?" and "Are we supposed to write this down?" Further statements from students can signal other-regulation: "So, do you want to start?" or "It's your turn." In addition, private or inner speech may signal self-regulation when students practice the correct forms internally before speaking. Mediation may also take the form of self-assessment whereby students determine if they are appropriately accomplishing the task. Encouragement for self-assessment may help move students beyond object-regulation (the task) or other-regulation (feedback) toward self-regulation.

Many of the concepts we have discussed thus far fit into contemporary views of communicative language teaching (CLT). Traditionally, CLT proposed the use of a variety of activities targeting the acquisition of skills (i.e., reading, writing, listening, speaking, plus culture) or the acquisition of functions (e.g., inviting, describing, introducing someone, expressing likes and dislikes; Richards, 2006). Much has been written about CLT, and in the past 30 years, it has incorporated many new insights drawn from changes in our understanding of the nature of language, the nature of learning, and the nature of teaching. CLT has, in many cases, become an umbrella term—indeed, who would claim to teach language that wasn't communicative?—and with the rise of sociocultural theory, CLT has also integrated the concepts mentioned previously. Nunan (2004) states that "learning as a social process is increasingly emphasized, and sociocultural theories are beginning to be drawn on in addition to (or even in preference to) cognitive theories" (p. 7).

Nevertheless, the inclusion of sociocultural concepts into CLT has caused some instructors confusion and this confusion has polluted some important sociocultural notions on a number of levels (e.g., the mixing of $i + 1$ and the ZPD, the confusion between scaffolding and interaction, misunderstandings concerning internalization and copying). The major differences between sociocultural theory and interactionist-cognitive theories lie in the conceptualization of the nature of language and the nature of learning. For socioculturalists, language is a tool for accomplishing the task, whereas interactionists tend to view language as the object of study (and thereby seek more often to explore explicit knowledge). The nature of learning also differs considerably; interactionists target the acquisition of language by allowing the individual ample input and opportunitiy to acquire the features from the input—tasks to an excellent job of providing input, opportunity, and motive. For sociocultural theorists, the development of language occurs only during interaction that mediates its own construction—tasks provide excellent support for mediated development. In short, for interactionists, the learners acquire target language features from the input that is afforded by the interaction; for socioculturalists, the learner develops language ability from the interaction that uses the target language features.

This distinction manifests itself in the use of L1 in the target language: interactions argue for maximal input, whereas socioculturalists concede the value of a shared L1 as a useful tool for communication.

Sociocultural theory conceptualizes language as a tool that develops from the activity required to accomplish a task or goal and not merely as a system to be implemented after acquisition. Moreover, sociocultural theory assumes that all tools develop through use. Hence, language is a dynamic system that is constantly changing as it is used. Development of the tool (language), then, occurs best through use or activity.

Whereas other theories point to the association of form and meaning, sociocultural theory regards learning as socialization and acculturation into a specific group through shared, scaffolded activity. In the classroom context, the notion of activity extends beyond the concepts of noticing (Schmidt & Frota, 1986), negotiating meaning (Long, 1985a), and deriving intake from input (Lee & VanPatten, 2003). Activity includes participation in the classroom society as well as any classroom tasks. Even though participation in the classroom society may be achieved in numerous ways, tasks designed for the classroom should ideally maintain the five tenets of activity theory:

1. *Hierarchical structure.* Students should be able to clearly identify a hierarchical structure of actions (step 1, step 2, etc.) to accomplish a goal. The focus should be on the completion of the task and the actions needed to satisfy that end.
2. *Object-oriented.* Tasks should be goal oriented, and learners must be able to complete the task and show that they have a finished product. A finished product is not a completed worksheet or exercise; it is a presentation or product with real-world consequences that are relevant to the learners.
3. *Internalization/externalization.* Tasks should produce the need for shared attention among participants and generate opportunities for learners to focus on forms (e.g., imitation, dialogues). Also, students should have the opportunity for language play, and classroom activity should allow for regulation (i.e., scaffolding support should be available) and encourage episodes for recurrent self-assessment.
4. *Development.* The tasks not only guide activity in the classroom but also drive assessment; assessment focuses on formative evaluation. Activities can span short periods of time or extend over the course of the semester, but the feedback given on any of the tasks aims to improve the overall performance of the individuals.
5. *Mediation.* Activities should require mediation using the tool (i.e., language) that may occur as private speech and written or oral communication to others (e.g., negotiation). The activity cannot be efficiently completed without using the tool.

These five characteristics are central to task design for any foreign language class but are particularly useful for technology-enhanced tasks. Not surprisingly, these five requirements appear widely in the literature despite disparate theoretical orientations and differing positions on task definition (Breen, 1987; Candlin, 1987; Chapelle, 1999; Crookes & Gass, 1993; Ellis, 2003; Hall, 2001; Lee, 2000; Lee & VanPatten, 2003; Long, 1985a, 1996; Nunan, 1989, 1999; Skehan, 1996). One notable advantage of a sociocultural perspective involves the notion of agency; sociocultural theory inherently accounts for the agency of those involved in the activity, whereas other perspectives generally regard the task as distinct from other learner factors. Ellis (2003) states that "such an [interactionist] approach views tasks deterministically and runs the risk of trivializing the contribution that learners make to the co-construction of the social reality of tasks" (p. 100).

Activity theory drives the need for routinized, well-structured tasks that elicit creative language use, that is, language that "involves the recombination of familiar elements (words, structures, and prefabricated patterns) in new ways to provide utterances that have never been produced before" (Nunan, 1999, p. 77). Routinization is a key concept in that it encourages learners to take a certain stance toward classroom tasks. Specifically, the learner controls the task by his or her orientation that determines what and how something is to be done. For example, if students are accustomed to display activities or form-focused activities, their goal is to display knowledge. Ellis and He (1999) argue that the type of discourse that results from display behavior is not beneficial for acquisition. On the other hand, if students are accustomed to problem solving, information exchange, or jigsaw tasks, they begin the task with an entirely different goal and produce significantly different discourse (Ortega, 2005).

Well-structured tasks lead learners to focus on certain structures and concepts that may be used as comprehensible input. This type of task with clear (and strict) parameters allowing for efficient execution is preferable to poorly structured tasks that cause learners to spend more time on definition than on performance. In addition, well-structured tasks demonstrate a method for determining the extent to which the task is completed.

Finally, Hall and Verplaetse (2000) give additional advice for tasks from a sociocultural perspective. First, tasks should be interesting so that learners are encouraged to make connections to their own lives. Second, interactions must foster a sense of community by being cognitively appropriate and affectively encouraging. Third, everyone must be active in the learning process, which is to say that tasks must create opportunities to show both the knowledge learned and the process of learning. Fourth, learner development and student development are inseparable, which is represented in tasks that enable the individuals in the classroom to learn to be social human beings as much as they are learning to use the language.

TASK 5.1

Think of a successful activity that you have seen (or done) in a language class. Why was this activity particularly beneficial? Explain how the activity you have chosen satisfies (or does not satisfy) each of the five tenets of activity theory.

TABLE 5.1 Examples of task types
Tutorial
Drills, educational games, and quizzes
Simulations
Information-gap
Consensus activity
Discussion (teacher led, student led, entire class vs. group vs. pair)

Types of Tasks in a CALL Environment

To this point, we have discussed tasks for language learning and the theory underlying their design and implementation in class. Tasks using computers should adhere to the same standards as non–computer-based tasks. This section discusses various types of tasks that focus on form and meaning that are part of stand-alone applications, hybrid environments, and fully supported CMC. Some sample activities are described next and displayed in Table 5.1. The point of this taxonomy is not to argue for the advantages of one task type over another, but rather to provide a palette of task types for instructors to draw on for their classes. Using one type consistently will provide routinization, but lack of variety can cause boredom or frustration among students and instructors.

One of the most popular types of software in instructional technology is *tutorial* software (Grabe & Grabe, 2001). Tutorials typically consist of a series of short learning segments, each one followed by a short exercise to measure how well the student has mastered the new concept, knowledge, or skill. However, tutorials are not used extensively in SLA despite the growing popularity of commercial programs such as Rosetta Stone® and Tell Me More®. Tutorials are of little help for the acquisition of language for a number of reasons. First, language acquisition tends to take place over a long period of time, and it is unlikely that any single tutorial will contribute significantly to acquisition. Second, tutorials, in general, fall short on satisfying many of the demands of activity theory. For example, most tutorials do not allow for induction into a social group through shared, scaffolded activity. As stated previously, focus on language manipulations may have negative effects on the type of language produced and elicited.

Drill-and-practice exercises focus on manipulation of language structures in a repetitive manner. Many of the online language games could easily fall under this category because they encourage a focus on form and often instant recasts or feedback that has arguably been shown to help learners acquire certain syntactic forms (Ayoun, 2001). These types of exercises were popular in the 1980s with a short resurgence in the 1990s (Davies, Walker, Rendall, & Hewer, 2011), but today many of these activities have been eliminated from most classrooms and from the curriculum or simply moved to an online homework component, due to the rise of CLT that rejected these types of activities.

Educational games and quizzes are similar to drills. Educational games are often quizzes that have no global grading mechanism, although they may give points, badges, or other recognition for each specific game or quiz. In general, they focus on language structures and can give rewards for grammatically correct responses. The standard written test options (true/false, multiple choice, matching, short answer) are available on the computer with a few advantages, because multimedia support may include reading, writing, and listening. Matching can be enhanced through drag-and-drop procedures and can even be extended to classifying so that several objects can be paired with other objects without adherence to a 1:1 matching schema. As with the previously described types of tasks, a major drawback to quizzes and games is that they do not necessarily inspire social interaction unless the quiz can be taken with partners or unless learners create it for other learners in the class. Students can easily design short tests, surveys, polls, and questionnaires for one another using Quia.com, Blackboard, or a number of other online resources.

Simulations became popular in the 1990s and have maintained their popularity in foreign language media centers and classrooms. The most popular of the stand-alone simulations is *A la rencontre de Philippe*, created at the Massachusetts Institute of Technology (MIT; Furstenberg, 1994). In this video-disc-supported software, the student must watch and listen to help Philippe accomplish certain tasks around town (listen to his answering machine, pay the plumber, catch the metro, make up with his girlfriend, etc.). Multiple endings are available depending on the user's completion of certain tasks. Some language resource centers have examined the use of popular gaming and simulation software often including role-play simulations such as the Sims (EA Games, 2007) in the target language. Similar to the popular game How to Host a Murder, Misterio en Toluca was an early example of an online role-playing simulation but is no longer supported due to the dark nature of the storyline (a murder). The instructor assigned students to different groups in which each student would take a role. The supporting web site offered a map of the town and some global clues including links to various sites around the Internet. Each role player received information that he or she was to share with the rest of the group in order to solve the mystery. The task entailed exchanging information in the target language using email.

Information-gap activities rely on the co-construction of meaning from at least two participants, each of them knowing only a part of the information needed to perform the activity. It can be one-way, whereby learner A must provide information to learner B to solve a given problem, or multidirectional, whereby both learner A and learner B (or learners C, D, and E) must share information to complete the task. Neither learner has access to the other's information beyond what each is able to communicate. Trotta (2004) provides an example of information-gap tasks (www.eslgo.com/resources/sa/ig_tiger.html) whereby learners exchange information about tigers and then seek new information on the web. These types of activities can occur through face-to-face or CMC.

Consensus activities are similar to information-gap activities in that members of a group must communicate to solve a problem. However, here all learners in the group have access to all of the information, and they must negotiate to arrive at an acceptable solution for the entire group. An example is a vacation-planning activity whereby students must decide as a group which monuments to see and which activities to do in Paris for the day. They log into a chat room while also reading information from a web site. The web site provides the information that they need to communicate via the computer and to organize times and activities. Learners must also come to a consensus concerning which activities are done at which times. In contrast to what Richards (2006) calls "opinion-sharing" activities (p. 19), consensus activities require that learners do more than simply share their opinions; they must arrive at an agreement that may often entail negotiating a compromise or resolving a conflict of interest.

Discussion activities can be conducted in a number of ways using computers. They differ from information-gap and consensus activities in that the goals of the discussions may vary significantly. The purpose of some discussion activities may simply be to convey information (and may thereby have fewer directions and be less structured) or to solve a problem (e.g., put the following pictures in order). Brainstorming activities, for example, can easily be done in class by asking students to make a list of the advantages and disadvantages of a specific topic (e.g., renewable energy, industrial farming). Discussions about oral or written texts (e.g., Is Madame Bovary evil? Why or why not?) may be better suited for discussions outside of class because it would provide more time for students to consider their responses. In-class discussions would use synchronous CMC such as chat, IM (instant messaging), or IRC (internet relay chat); see Chapter 7), whereas out-of-class discussions would use asynchronous CMC such as bulletin boards, email, and microblogs (see Chapter 8). Discussion activities done asynchronously outside of class can provide advance organizers for activities in class. They can help develop a threshold understanding for readings or culture and allow for more time to be spent on oral communication in class. Asynchronous CMC lends itself easily to out-of-class discussion because learners can participate at their leisure, whereas synchronous CMC must be coordinated for out-of-class discussions so that all participants are present. Asynchronous CMC appears to be counterproductive during class when speech and ink are more efficient media. Moreover, synchronous CMC has a number of advantages in paired discussions for discourse, quality of interlanguage, embedded routines, meaning negotiations, corrective feedback, and self-repair (Pellettieri, 2000). For many of these chat-based tasks, it is important to divide the class into small chat groups, because full-class discussions even with eight to ten learners may be challenging for those unable to follow multiple threads in a given discourse. Thus, it would seem that synchronous CMC is useful for small-group and paired work, whereas entire group discussions are best handled face-to-face.

Ellis (2003) argues for two-way (or multidirectional) information-gap and consensus activities in which information exchange is required from all participants. In most cases, students tend to orient to these tasks as communicative tasks rather than language-practice tasks. Moreover, information-gap and consensus activities tend to be hierarchal and goal oriented, and they encourage development by requiring shared attention among participants. Finally, instructors must always remember to view in-class activities for the purpose they serve, which should always be motivated by the activity rather than politics (to please the administration) or time (to fill time in class).

In short, CALL makes a significant contribution to encouraging the use of the language outside of class through tutorials, simulations, quizzes, drills, and asynchronous CMC. Lomicka, Lord, and Manzer (2003) offer an important A–E checklist for those who want to develop CALL tasks materials: (A) Analyze the task in order to choose the appropriate technology that facilitates the task. (B) Back up your lesson plan with an alternative because you never know what technological glitches may occur during the class. (C) Community is important to any activity and central to linguistic development. Community is also essential for the world language instructor who plans standards-based lesson plans because it is one of the 5 Cs (communication, cultures, connections, comparisons, and communities; Phillips & Draper, 1999—see Chapter 6 for a discussion of the National Standards and CALL). (D) Diversity of activities is essential to promoting motivation in the classroom. WebQuests are good introductory activities in the computerized classroom, but if they are the only type of activity implemented, student motivation may quickly wane. (E) Evaluation of the activity is critical to improve it and to not repeat mistakes made in earlier trials. Activities should be evaluated not only on what works, but also on what provides appropriate scaffolding, cultural authenticity, and classroom preference.

DuBravac (2004) mentions several items to consider when deciding which technologies are most beneficial:

- **Goals.** In any computerized classroom, instructors must constantly reconsider the goals of the lesson, particularly in terms of input required and outcomes desired. This should be a dialogic balance created through interaction with students, technologies, and instructor.
- **Pedagogical advantages of newer technologies over the blackboard.** Newer technologies offer advantages over traditional media, such as the blackboard or the overhead transparency. However, instructors must decide if the returns on language acquisition merit the time and energy required to implement a new technology for a classroom task.
- **Matching appropriate technology with the task.** As Terry (1998) argues, technology should be chosen for its ability to facilitate the task in the classroom and not for its bells and whistles. For example, certain tasks with technology, such as a WebQuest, may facilitate vocabulary recognition but not necessarily vocabulary use. Instructors who want to focus on specific linguistic aspects must first determine how a given activity encourages development of L2 skills.
- **Use of target language.** From an interactionist perspective, most methodologists posit maximum exposure to the L2 as a means of providing the necessary input for efficient language acquisition in a context where all speakers share a common L1 (Brandl, 2008; Curtain & Dahlberg, 2010; Ellis, 2012; Shrum & Glisan, 2010). Practicing teachers have the belief that they should speak the L2 at all times but they often revert to the L1 in a variety of circumstances (e.g., procedural instructions or classroom

management: Edstrom, 2006; Macaro, 2001). Furthermore, because of unfamiliarity with the technology, students and instructors may feel that the computer classroom is the one time that English is an appropriate tool for instruction. Teachers can strive to maximize input by providing appropriate vocabulary during the first day in the computerized classroom (e.g., mouse, screen, click, highlight, save, post, send). From the perspective of sociocultural theory, the tool of mediation (language in this case) is also the activity, so the decision to permit first language (L1) use is essentially a decision to perform a task (mediated by the L1) but forego the overall activity of the class (i.e., getting input in the L2). Hence, instructor use of the L1 is rarely justified. Nonetheless, researchers have also investigated the students' use of the native language to mediate tasks and have shown that student L1 use to regulate the task increases performance and engagement (Brooks & Donato, 1994; Darhower, 2002; Swain & Lapkin, 2000; Thoms, Liao, & Szustak, 2005).

- ***Students' familiarity with technologies.*** Instructors should have an idea of their students' capabilities. Virtually all college students can send and receive email, use the web to find information, use word-processing applications with the fonts appropriate to the target language, and save files to portable or online drives. With minimal instruction, most students will easily learn to keep an online portfolio, use a chat program, or read and post to a bulletin board.

- ***Instructor's familiarity with each technology.*** Instructors should use technologies that are familiar to both the students and themselves. Instructors are ultimately responsible for activity flow and should be able to troubleshoot most problems that occur during classroom activity. Numerous tutorials are available online for the standard applications found in the computer classroom.

- ***Motivation for using technology.*** Administrators (e.g., deans, department chairs, section heads) often feel and pass along the pressure to use technology to establish uniformity across the college or department. Sometimes such pressure comes from the need to justify the monies spent on maintenance and development of technological resources. Sometimes instructors may be required to teach one day a week in a computerized classroom for a variety of reasons (e.g., to be observed, to mitigate space limitations). Students may lack motivation to use computers if they do not have access outside the university or school, or if their connection is slow. Motivation for using technology impacts directly on motivation for doing language-related tasks in class and context dictates when and why technology should be used in the L2 curriculum.

Participation Structures

Participation structures describe the ways that students interact to perform the tasks assigned to them. Hall (2001) lists five: individual, whole group, peer tutoring, team learning, and learning center. These structures are summarized in Table 5.2 and are discussed in greater detail later in this section.

TABLE 5.2 Participation structures

Participation Structure	Number of participants	Example
Individual	1–2: Individual and instructor/computer	Students work on electronic workbooks or online tutorials.
Whole group	Many: Class and instructor/leader	Students use VoiceThread.com to describe an image or video.
Peer tutoring	2: Students work in pairs	Students chat or IM to complete an information-gap task.
Team learning	3–5: Students work in small groups	Students work together to complete a project such as a video or Wikipedia entry.
Learning center	Variable	Teachers designate a portion of the room for an activity such as online Jeopardy! or status updates via Twitter or Facebook for partner institutions.

Much of the activity that has traditionally taken place using the computer is oriented toward the individual as he or she interacts directly with the computer at his or her own pace. Students studying the most commonly taught languages (e.g., Spanish, French, German) now use electronic workbooks that are accessed online, in order to complete their assignments using web sites or stand-alone applications that tend to be tutorials, drills, quizzes, or single-player educational games (e.g., Quia.com or MySpanishLab.com).

Whole-group activities tend to be led by the teacher (although they do not need to be). In a technology-centered environment, this can be a slide presentation (online or off-line) or a whiteboard presentation. These types of activities become interactive by using an audience response system (ARS) or student response system (SRS), often referred to as clickers. Online services allow instructors to create quick online polls using the web (e.g., Flisti.com, TwtPoll.com, Quibblo.com, Survs.com) or mobile phones, Twitter, or email (IVoted.com, PollEverywhere.com). Whole-class discussions can also take place on discussion boards, blogs, or VoiceThreads (see Chapter 8).

Peer tutoring describes interactions between pairs of students. The interchanges are one-to-one rather than brainstorming or collaborative tasks. Tasks that encourage pair work are information-gap or consensus tasks with which students must convey some information to their partners. Applications that facilitate this type of interchange are synchronous CMC such as chat, IM, or short messaging service (SMS); virtual communities; and some asynchronous forms such as email or blogs.

In a team learning structure, people work together to complete project-based products or presentations. Team members have roles and must combine their shared knowledge and agree on the form their presentation to the class will take (e.g., web page, slide presentation, podcast). A number of applications enable collaboration on various project types, such as online document creation (e.g., Google.docs, Zoho.com, CrocoDoc.com, PBWiki.com), brainstorming and mind mapping (Bubbl.us), project management (AdobeConnect.com, Wiggio.com), video creation and editing (Animoto.com, Stroome.com), image art production (Kerpoof.com, Picasa.com, PhotoBucket.com), and broadcasting (iTunes.com, UBroadcast.com, YouTube.com). Team learning structures may be difficult for some students not only because of the language required but also because they are unfamiliar or uncomfortable with the team aspect of learning. Some students may feel that their strengths are not readily identifiable in team structures; others may feel that they spend more time resolving differences than focusing on the task. Classes that use team learning structures tend to include tasks that focus on both language skills and team skills and that foster accountability at both the group and individual levels.

Learning centers are theme-oriented areas that may be popular in schools with a limited number of resources. Students work in groups, pairs, or alone on specific tasks. This is often the participation structure for middle or high school classrooms that have a bank of four to eight computers somewhere in the classroom, with students rotating from nontechnical centers to the computer center. Almost any application supports learning centers because they provide opportunities to work on personal projects (e.g., linguafolio, personal blogs, online newspapers) or group and team projects.

These participation structures can help foster a positive learning atmosphere by enabling different types of tasks within a classroom routine, including tasks encouraging a range of participation structures while allowing a focus on both the cognitive and the social aspects of tasks. Hall (2001) argues that one of the main objectives of education is to "foster the development of communities of learners" (p. 45) that are collaborative and include development in both the social and the cognitive arenas.

Twenty years ago, instructors could improve motivation and impress students with technology, but today's students are so embedded in technology that the task itself must motivate them. This chapter has focused on the notion of task by analyzing the concepts of exercise, task, and activity through the lens of sociocultural theory (specifically activity theory) in relation to CALL. Tasks should encourage interaction within the ZPD by capitalizing on the five principles of activity theory—hierarchical structure, object-orientedness, internalization/externalization, development, and mediation. In other words, tasks that promote scaffolded, goal-driven participation tend to be most beneficial to language learners. Traditional tasks in a CALL environment have ranged from computer-focused tasks such as tutorials and exercises to more learner-focused tasks such as information-gap and consensus tasks. When designing activities, instructors need to match the appropriate technology with the linguistic goals, seek to create a community, and use a routine with a diversity of activity types and participation structures. The technology should support the task and create a better overall experience.

Practical Work

1. Observe a language class taught in a computer classroom. Document when and why the instructor speaks in English rather than the L2. Is there a recognizable pattern? What functions does English serve (e.g., to give directions, to specify the task, to manage classroom behavior, to troubleshoot technical issues, to overcome comprehension and lexical issues, to fix language production problems, to move the class along more quickly)? How is the activity in class modified by the use of English?

2. It is not uncommon for students (and instructors) to speak significantly less in the target language in the computerized classroom or the language center/lab. To help your students (and you) stay in the target language in the computerized classroom, create a short guide for students that includes vocabulary and useful expressions. Some of the vocabulary may include words such as *mouse, keyboard*, and *highlight* or commands such as *click here*, and *Wait! My machine froze up!*

3. Design an information-gap or consensus activity with specific steps concerning how students can accomplish the task (i.e., make sure it is hierarchal). Explain how your task is goal directed.

4. Rate yourselves and your students on familiarity and comfort level with each of the following technologies:

Technology	My comfort level					My students' comfort level				
	Uncomfortable			Comfortable		Uncomfortable			Comfortable	
• Search engines	1	2	3	4	5	1	2	3	4	5
• Online worksheets	1	2	3	4	5	1	2	3	4	5
• WebQuest	1	2	3	4	5	1	2	3	4	5
• Email	1	2	3	4	5	1	2	3	4	5
• Instant messenger	1	2	3	4	5	1	2	3	4	5
• IRC/chat	1	2	3	4	5	1	2	3	4	5
• Social networking sites (e.g., Facebook)	1	2	3	4	5	1	2	3	4	5
• Web authoring software	1	2	3	4	5	1	2	3	4	5
• Blogs	1	2	3	4	5	1	2	3	4	5
• Online discussion boards	1	2	3	4	5	1	2	3	4	5
• Image editing software/sites	1	2	3	4	5	1	2	3	4	5

• Digital audio programs/sites	1	2	3	4	5	1	2	3	4	5
• Digital video programs/sites	1	2	3	4	5	1	2	3	4	5
• Interactive white boards/ SmartBoards	1	2	3	4	5	1	2	3	4	5
• Learning management systems (Blackboard, Nicenet.org, Moodle)	1	2	3	4	5	1	2	3	4	5
• Online gaming	1	2	3	4	5	1	2	3	4	5
• Peer-to-peer networks	1	2	3	4	5	1	2	3	4	5

Which technologies are most interesting to you? Which would you want to use in your class on a regular basis? Plan an activity using one of the technologies listed. Make sure to describe the goals, advantages, and the students' and instructor's familiarity with the technology. Explain what students will do at each step and why the technology you chose is particularly good for this type of activity.

Suggestions for Further Reading

Chapelle, C. (1999). Theory and research: Investigation of "authentic" language learning tasks. In J. Egbert & E. Hanson-Smith (Eds.), *CALL environments: Research, practice and critical issues* (pp. 101–115). Alexandria, VA: Teachers of English to Speakers of Other Languages.

Donato, R. (1994). Collective scaffolding in second language learning. In J. P. Lantolf & G. Appel (Eds.), *Vygotskian approaches to second language research* (pp. 33–56). Norwood, NJ: Ablex.

Ellis, R. (2012). *Language teaching research and language pedagogy.* West Sussex, UK: Wiley-Blackwell.

Hall, J. K., & Verplaetse, L. S. (Eds.). (2000). *Second and foreign language learning through classroom interaction.* Mahwah, NJ: Lawrence Erlbaum.

Warschauer, M. (2005). Sociocultral perspectives on CALL. In J. Egbert & G. Mikel (Eds.), *CALL research perspectives* (pp. 41–52). Mahwah, NJ: Lawrence Erlbaum.

CHAPTER 6

National and International Standards in Teaching with Electronic Media

OVERVIEW

This chapter examines two sets of standards; the first involves the use of technology, and the second targets language learning and teaching. The International Society for Technology in Education (ISTE) published the National Educational Technology Standards for Students (NETS-S) in 2007 and the National Educational Technology Standards for Teachers (NETS-T) in 2008. ISTE is the premier organization that aims to improve learning and teaching by advancing the effective use of technology in P–12 schools and teacher education, but the ISTE standards can easily be applied to postsecondary contexts. The American Council on the Teaching of Foreign Languages (ACTFL) set forth its most recent standards document for students in 1999, and the standards for teacher education (*Program Standards for the Preparation of Foreign Language Teachers*) came out in 2002.

There is significant overlap among the standards for learners and the standards for teachers in both language learning and technology and both sets of standards encourage self-assessment for the group that they target (i.e., students assess themselves using the NETS-S, instructors use the NETS-T). The standards for teachers highlight the importance of maintaining a high level of proficiency in language and cultural knowledge, instructional methods, and technology. Moreover, they underscore the need for teachers to develop personal learning networks (PLNs) using both actual and virtual resources. PLNs can help encourage adherence to national standards and improve teaching skills.

NATIONAL STANDARDS FOR FOREIGN LANGUAGE LEARNING

The National Standards in Foreign Language Education Project (1996, 1999) provides a framework for instructors and administrators around the country to articulate the functions and content students should learn in a world language curriculum. The National Standards present 11 content standards in 5 areas, often called the 5 Cs of foreign language education: communication, cultures, connections, comparisons, and communities (Figure 6.1). They define what students should know and be able to do in a foreign language and facilitate the articulation of performance standards and a justification of world language study. It is important to note that the *Standards for Foreign Language Learning in the*

COMMUNICATION

Communicate in Languages Other Than English

Standard 1.1: Students engage in conversations, provide and obtain information, express feelings and emotions, and exchange opinions.

Standard 1.2: Students understand and interpret written and spoken language on a variety of topics.

Standard 1.3: Students present information, concepts, and ideas to an audience of listeners or readers on a variety of topics.

CULTURES

Gain Knowledge and Understanding of Other Cultures

Standard 2.1: Students demonstrate an understanding of the relationship between the practices and perspectives of the culture studied.

Standard 2.2: Students demonstrate an understanding of the relationship between the products and perspectives of the culture studied.

CONNECTIONS

Connect with Other Disciplines and Acquire Information

Standard 3.1: Students reinforce and further their knowledge of other disciplines through the foreign language.

Standard 3.2: Students acquire information and recognize the distinctive viewpoints that are only available through the foreign language and its cultures.

COMPARISONS

Develop Insight into the Nature of Language and Culture

Standard 4.1: Students demonstrate understanding of the nature of language through comparisons of the language studied and their own.

Standard 4.2: Students demonstrate under-standing of the concept of culture through comparisons of the cultures studied and their own.

COMMUNITIES

Participate in Multilingual Communities at Home and Around the World

Standard 5.1: Students use the language both within and beyond the school setting.

Standard 5.2: Students show evidence of becoming life-long learners by using the language for personal enjoyment and enrichment.

FIGURE 6.1 Standards for Foreign Language Learning

Source: National Standards in Foreign Language Education Project (1999), p. 9. Also available at www.actfl.org/files/public/execsumm.pdf

21st Century (National Standards in Foreign Language Education Project, 2006) is not a curriculum guide, nor does it provide performance benchmarks for all language levels. Furthermore, it does not suggest a scope or sequence of course content, teaching approach, or methodology, and instructors must look to their particular state's standards to identify expectations for the amount of instruction time in class and best approaches to instruction.

Communication

Communication is divided into three standards: interpersonal, interpretive, and presentational. This description of communication diverges from the traditional notion of the four language skills (reading, writing, speaking, and listening) because each of the modes can be written or spoken as well as synchronous (short messaging service [SMS], chat, videoconferencing) or asynchronous (online forums or discussion boards or VoiceThread.com messages). Moreover, these channels can be mixed, for example, in continuing face-to-face a discussion that started online (either as a chat or on a discussion board) or vice-versa (e.g., finishing a class discussion using email). Standard 1.1 focuses on the *interpersonal* mode that enables learners to share information, feelings, and opinions. This mode readily allows for negotiation of meaning and immediate interplay between interlocutors. In other words, students can give and receive help more readily than in the other modes. It has as its primary concerns to establish and maintain relationships by sharing emotions—expressive purposes—and exchanging information—transactional purposes. When students communicate for transactional purposes, their goal is to inform, share knowledge, seek new information, or solve problems. These functions are often expressed with indicators such as *describe, narrate, recount, explain, persuade, ask/answer, argue, invite, tell,* or *exchange* (information). Students who engage in expressive communicative functions endeavor to express emotions, share feelings, or make personal connections with others. Verbal indicators for expressive functions are more difficult to pinpoint than transactional functions because learners can "exchange opinions" as a transactional exercise when their goal is only to provide the needed information but it is difficult to measure the sharing of emotions when students aim to make a personal connection. Common practices that lean toward expressive functioning include update statuses (and comments) on a social network, personal web pages/blogs, recommendations (e.g., GoodReads.com). Both transactional and expressive functions are important as learners seek to understand one another, maintain some control over how they are understood, and make links to the target culture and the classroom culture.

A broad range of activities can emphasize the interpersonal mode in the classroom, including, giving, asking for, and receiving directions; inviting a friend to dinner; expressing opinions; or making complaints. These activities can be completed in a number of media: face-to-face, chat, discussion boards, or email (Blake, 2000; Chun, 1994; Kern, 1995; Ortega, 1997; Pellettieri, 2000; Smith, 2003; Sotillo, 2000; Toyoda & Harrison, 2002; Tudini, 2003; Warschauer, 1996a). Face-to-face activities and online chats (are most obviously useful for developing interpersonal communication skills because students can use short messages to actively navigate turns, negotiate meaning, ask for clarification, and correct misunderstandings to establish and maintain relationships. Asynchronous computer-mediated communication (CMC) such as discussion boards, email, and wikis are less prototypical for the interpersonal mode, but they do provide a medium whereby learners post informational messages but also negotiate meaning, ask for clarification, restate texts, correct misunderstandings, and request elaboration. Asynchronous CMC represents, in many ways, the middle ground between speech and text because it combines characteristics of both (Crystal, 2001).

These exchanges between participants now extend beyond written text alone and include audio, video, or multimedia using such technologies as Wimba® with email, Skype™ for voice and video, avatar chatrooms, or video conferencing whereby participants use voice and gestures. Synchronous and asynchronous communication technologies are discussed in detail in Chapters 7 and 8.

The second mode of communication, identified by Standard 1.2, is the *interpretive* mode, which generally refers to activities that entail reading, listening, or viewing without the opportunity to negotiate meaning with the author. Technology offers advantages for this mode by including interaction with the text, embedded scaffolding, and access. Interaction with the text refers to the learners' ability to use technology to slow down audio and video, isolate and replay various segments, and move among segments more easily and quickly than was possible with analog technology. Digital technology also allows instructors or designers to embed aids that can scaffold students' understanding of text. This assistance can include glosses, subtitles, images, sounds, cross-references, or translations. Technology offers advantages in that it provides extensive authentic texts (including audio and video) that can encourage reading, listening, and watching for pleasure. Both the availability of reading materials and the pleasure associated with reading have proven to be essential factors in learning to read (Wigfield & Asher, 2002; see also Krashen, 2004).

Reading activities can take place in a number of contexts. As discussed in Chapter 3, the large number of authentic texts available on the internet makes the World Wide Web (WWW) a tremendous source for reading material. Activities may include reading a menu, train schedule, or maps for a specific purpose; reading cartoons for enjoyment; or searching the WWW for information as a preparatory activity for a presentation task. The quantity of reading material on the internet allows students a greater choice and may thereby encourage them to read for aesthetic purposes. A number of studies have shown strong correlations between the development of reading skills and the availability of reading material (Ogunrombi & Adio, 1995; Ramanathan, 2003; Tella & Akande, 2007; Wigfield & Asher, 2002).

Reading is the predominant skill that teachers connect to the interpretive mode, but it is not alone in the spectrum of necessary skills for interpretation, since audio and visual literacy are also important. Rubin (1993) offers the term *listenability* to describe the degree to which an audio text is comprehensible. He lists three characteristics that help a text to be more listenable: fewer complex syntactic constructions, less lexical density and diversity, and an information structure that coincides with the listeners' background knowledge and expectations (i.e., presented in the order that a listener anticipates). These characteristics seem to fit well for audio texts that encourage learners to take an efferent stance (i.e., to take away information, or learn from), but they may not be relevant to those texts to which listeners take an aesthetic stance (i.e., to take pleasure in, or enjoy) such as songs, poems, or radio programs. Efferent listeners strive to categorize and connect their listening/reading experience to background knowledge to situate the information. Aesthetic listeners merely seek to enjoy—a construct that is not well understood or defined—the listening/reading experience so syntax, lexical density, and background knowledge may not pay a part in that enjoyment.

Visual literacy is also important to the interpretive mode and includes activities such as watching news reports and movies, and navigating the WWW .Gonglewski and DuBravac (2006) demonstrate how technology plays an important role in developing what they call *multiliteracy*, which includes the previously mentioned forms of literacy as well as functional literacy, critical literacy, and electronic literacy, for example. They conclude that the use of technology in the classroom encourages development in a number of domains that are unavailable without technology. Those who use technology tend not only to prefer multimedia (such as images, audio, and video) to express themselves, but they also develop a different set of expectations for how the computer-mediated multimedia text is expressed and interpreted (see Crystal, 2001, for a discussion of the linguistic conventions of various internet-based communications).

The *presentational* mode, described in Standard 1.3, includes activities involving the creation of text in which the target audience is not normally involved. In the interpersonal mode, both interlocutors are included in the production of a text, whether it be oral as in face-to-face conversation or textual as on a discussion board or email exchange—although some may argue that most textual communications are presentational because the negotiation does not happen immediately. In the interpretive mode, the text is normally created without the participation of the speaker/writer, even though the meaning of the text is co-constructed with the text or appropriated by the learner. Some types of activities related to this mode are written research reports, oral presentations, student web pages and online class newspapers, PowerPoint presentations, audio and video recordings, journal writing, business writing tasks on email, and online team sites. Technology has made and will probably continue to make the biggest impact on the production of presentations (see, in particular, the section on *NETS-S* later in this chapter). Word processing has become an indispensable tool for academic and business writing and the WWW has added new dimensions to artistic writing (e.g., online writing increasingly includes multimedia such as sound, video, twitter feeds, or links to other related information). Technology also offers advantages for instructors who want to present multimedia lessons outside of class time on the web or using a learning management system (LMS) such as Blackboard.com, NiceNet.org, or Moodle.org. Several researchers argue that students willingly spend more time on presentations that are web based than on those that are face-to-face (Gonglweski, 1999; Warschauer, 1999).

TASK 6.1

For each of the following sites and applications, indicate if and how each could be used in a task that focuses on one of the communication standards. The first one has been done for you.

Technology	Interpersonal	Interpretive	Presentational
PowerPoint	No	Yes, for reading or listening comprehension	Yes, for student projects or presentations
Online workbooks, games, tutorials			
Email			
YouTube			
LMS (e.g., Moodle)			
Twitter			
Chat/Instant messaging			
Social networking/ Social bookmarking			
Skype			
Podcasts			

Cultures

Cultures is the second set of standards and concentrates on three main aspects: practices, products, and perspectives. Standard 2.1 states that students should demonstrate an understanding of the relationship between the practices and the perspectives of the culture studied. *Practices* are patterns of behavior of a given society and may include when people eat, how they address one another, what festivals they celebrate, what they do during the day (shopping, work schedules, transportation habits, etc.), and how they spend leisure time.

Standard 2.2 uses identical language to Standard 2.1, with one substitution: Students demonstrate an understanding of the relationship between the products and the perspectives of the culture being studied. *Products* are items created by the target culture, which include both tangible and intangible objects such as games, music, web sites, food items, buildings, laws, and art.

For both standards, the term *perspectives* refers to the belief system of the target culture, including what is valued in the society (money, cleanliness, social responsibility, etc.), or attitudes and meanings that govern the members of that society (Are walls designed to keep things out or keep them in? Why does one member of the society greet another in a given manner?). Perspectives is often the most challenging aspect to teach: Instructors may not normally question the underlying perspectives of the culture or may be insecure about their interpretation of them. A product or practice may not have an easily identifiable perspective associated with it, or the perspective may have lost its historical significance and the contemporary society may no longer subscribe to the beliefs on which a practice was originally based. Cultural perspectives may also be difficult to tap because practices and products may offer seemingly contradictory perspectives. Finally, instructors may feel inadequate to teach culture if they are nonnatives who have limited direct knowledge of and experience with the target culture.

Technology helps alleviate the pressure on the instructor to be the source of all cultural knowledge. First, the web is an excellent source of documents written by native speakers or scholars who study the practices and products of a variety of cultures. Also, email exchanges, web collaboration, and telecollaboration experiences may all help shift the burden of teaching culture from the instructor to native informants (Belz, 2002; Gresso & Lomicka, 1999; Kinginger, Gourves-Hayward, & Simpson, 1999). In essence, these technologies help students gain a greater knowledge of both the target culture and their own culture.

Connections

The third *C—connections*—could be considered the linchpin that holds the other standards together and essentially is an argument for content-based instruction. Standard 3.1 states that students reinforce and further their knowledge of other disciplines through the foreign language.

Standard 3.2 states that students acquire information and recognize the distinctive viewpoints that are available only through the foreign language and its cultures. Basically, students should be learning content that is similar to what they encounter in their other courses. This task appears daunting to many instructors who believe that they must be experts to engage students in an investigation of a specific content area. However, such an assumption is false. Instructors need to feel comfortable as coinvestigators with students in an area in which the student

---

TASK 6.2

Identify a theme or cultural difference that you would like to examine with your class. Choose a product or practice of the target culture (e.g., bread, celebration of Carnival). Use Bubbl (bubbl.us) or Xmind (www.XMind.net)* to create a concept culture map. Set up two separate maps—one for English and one for the target culture with the same product or practice in the center location (e.g., the supermarket/*le marché*). Make associations for each culture to examine how it views the concept differently and has different associations with the concept (e.g., you go to the supermarket once a week, you go to *le marché* almost every day; one is inside, the other is outside). You may choose to do this with invited native speakers.

*Each of these applications is intuitive but also offers tutorials and help support within the site.

TASK 6.3

Identify four content areas in which you would be comfortable incorporating content into your course or courses (e.g., art, math, history/government, science, music, health/wellness, sports). Design a lesson that you could teach in the target language to teach one of the content areas you have indentified above.

can be the content expert and the instructor can be the guide who helps students find and interpret appropriate materials, engage in appropriate tasks, and produce informed presentations. Bragger and Rice (1998) also make the observation that students do not need to know the content in the first language to be able to acquire the content in the second language. With well-structured tasks and guidance with the language, most students should be able to make connections with content that they study outside of the language curriculum.

The idea that learners acquire a language more successfully when they use it for gaining information rather than as an end in itself drives a methodology commonly referred to as content-based instruction (CBI; Richards, 2006). As with the other standards, technology contributes significantly to the realization of this vision by enabling learners to find readily available texts on the web, to contact native speakers for assistance through email or telecollaborative modes, and to establish relationships with multiple target language speakers around the globe. Nevertheless, the instructor retains the responsibility of helping learners identify distinctive viewpoints available only through the foreign language and enabling comparisons on both the cultural and linguistic fronts.

Comparisons

The fourth standard, *comparisons*, focuses on the linguistic and cultural comparisons that students make in studying the foreign language that lead them to an understanding of the abstract concepts of language and culture. Standard 4.1 states that students demonstrate understanding of the nature of language through comparisons of the language studied and their own. Although it is almost inevitable that learners compare their own language to the target language, they may not be able to make comparisons across sociolinguistic boundaries. For example, students may compare aspectual distinctions in romance languages (i.e., perfective and imperfective past forms) with English equivalents to gain an understanding that English relies on lexical aspect (*to know, to think*, and *to be* tend to be understood as imperfective unless marked otherwise in English) or tense (progressive past tense tends to align with imperfect aspects in Spanish—*He was talking = El hablaba*) rather than imperfective markings on the verb. However, learners may be less attentive to dialectal differences in the target language. Technology facilitates this comparison because, for instance, students can easily compare French and French Canadian web sites to examine dialectal distinctions between the two (at a minimum, on a lexical level). This comparison may also lead to an examination of the differences between British English and American English or even among the many varieties of Spanish. Students should also become aware of linguistic practices that occur online, such as abbreviations in chat rooms, standard email conventions, or register, as demonstrated on various discussion boards. These types of exercises lend themselves easily to comparisons among cultures that would be much less available without technology.

Standard 4.2 states that students demonstrate understanding of the concept of culture through comparisons of the cultures studied and their own. As an example of the many activities related to this standard, students could list stereotypes concerning the United States that are common in the target culture, as well as those found in the United States about the target culture. This enables a quick link to products and practices by asking Why do we think that about them? and Why do they think those things about us? The advantage of the internet in this case is that it facilitates multiple perspectives that students can compare using criteria identified by the instructor.

TASK 6.4

Identify two activities that may encourage students to gain a greater understanding of the nature of language or of the concept of culture by comparing the L1 with the L2.

Communities

The final standard involves learning communities both within and beyond the classroom space and time. Standard 5.1 states that students use the language both within and beyond the school setting; 5.2 states that students show evidence of becoming lifelong learners by using the language for personal enjoyment and enrichment. Both standards argue for the agency of the student to perform meaningful projects for the class, the local community, and possibly the target language community in the United States as well as the target communities abroad. This type of learning is often called service learning and has been increasingly used in public education in the 2000s. An example of service learning is students of Italian offering tours of a local museum in Italian. Each student could be responsible for one piece of art. The students then visit the museum and give a tour to the rest of the class as well as any other Italian speakers who are interested. These tours could be made for mobile devices and used by the museum when members of the class are unavailable. In this way, service learning connects the students to the target culture (the art) and the target community (the participants). Another example is a French radio show. Students identify a song in French to research (e.g., the singer, the meaning, the background to the song). Using the information, they create a recording where they introduce and play the song. A local radio station uses the student recordings to present a French radio show that includes French songs with French-language DJs (i.e., students in the class). Radio shows could also be done in podcast or YouTube (for music videos) format. This type of activity enables students to identify a classroom community among all those studying French at the university as well as their own class, in addition to the local French-speaking community. Another activity could be to have students create maps of the campus for students from the target communities, which would be made available online, for mobile devices, or in print at information booths. These project-based community learning modules may also encourage students to become lifelong learners of the language because they encourage students to view the language as a functional tool used by a community that welcomes the learner.

Finally, students may become involved in an online community with chats, blogs, discussion boards, and web sites that they create or in which they participate. These communities can form rapidly and easily because they are available to anyone with an internet connection. Many of today's students are also adept at identifying with members of an online community, as many of them have grown up using social networking sites such as Facebook and massively multiplayer online role-playing games (MMORPGs) including World of Warcraft that inspire communities in which individuals connect with others in common activities.

As can be seen, the five goals and 11 standards of foreign language learning are extensive and require constant attention to balancing the demands of each goal. Instructors should plan all lessons using these standards to govern the direction and to anticipate the outcomes for their students. Because students are engaged in knowledge creation for their own purposes, it can be easier for instructors to guide them to be lifelong learners of the language, which can, in turn, promote continual development along the lines of the rest of the standards.

TASK 6.5

Name several target-language communities in your area and others that are available online. How does one access these communities? What would motivate a language learner to join these communities?

ISTE NETS–S

Although most standards in education target a specific content area or specific age groups, *NETS-S* aims to be content independent and to target all student levels. Many of the content standards for foreign language learning are included in the *NETS-S* standards. *NETS-S* suggests six standards that help students live and learn effectively in a digital world (ISTE, 2007a):

1. **Creativity and Innovation.** Students demonstrate creative thinking, construct knowledge, and develop innovate products and processes using technology.
2. **Communication and Collaboration.** Students use digital media and environments to communicate and work collaboratively, including at a distance, to support individual learning and contribute to the learning of others.
3. **Research and Information Fluency.** Students apply digital tools to gather, evaluate, and use information.

4. **Critical Thinking, Problem Solving, and Decision Making.** Students use critical thinking skills to plan and conduct research, manage projects, solve problems, and make informed decisions using appropriate digital tools and resources.
5. **Digital Citizenship.** Students understand human, cultural, and societal issues related to technology and practice legal and ethical behavior.
6. **Technology Operations and Concepts.** Students demonstrate a sound understanding of technology concepts, systems, and operations.

These standards can be used by content specialist for curriculum development and by school administrators for technology. The ISTE also offers indicators for specific grade levels in conjunction with these standards (ISTE, 2007b). As with the national standards from ACTFL, instructors must contextualize their students' learning and identify appropriate goals, expectations, and activities according to each particular student population and its access to technology. These standards tend to be more easily attainable in a project-based curriculum, as will be evident from the following discussion.

Creativity and Innovation

The standard of creativity and innovation implies that students apply existing knowledge to generate new ideas, products, or processes and to create original works as a means of personal or group expression. These concepts relate to the task-based orientation presented in previous chapters and apply to project-based learning—the idea that students use the language to complete projects. Moreover, the presentational mode (from ACTFL Standard 1.3) lends itself to creativity and innovation. Students can use technology as a support to present information using a variety of applications such as PowerPoint, Flash, or Prezi.com, all of which have a completely online version. Students can also demonstrate creativity by using targeted applications and designing their dream home (using Paint, Photoshop, Aviary.com), presenting their family tree (MyTrees.com, Myheritage.com), or describing a city (Google maps).

Communication and Collaboration

Communication and collaboration can take place when students use digital media to interact, collaborate, and publish with peers, experts, native speakers, or others. Instructors can facilitate these types of activities in the class by promoting online communication using CMC (e.g., email, discussion boards, chat, Skype) and by designing projects that require collaboration. In addition, students should learn to communicate information effectively to multiple audiences using a variety of formats such as blogs, web pages, webinars, and podcasts. Instructors can also promote community by facilitating communication between L1 and L2 speakers of the language through keypal activities, telecollaboration, or guest speakers. Increasingly, this type of collaboration is facilitated with shared wiki spaces, a variety of methods for CMC, and sites with the sole purpose of connecting native speakers with learners (EPals.com, TandemCity.com, Italki.com, LiveMocha.com).

Instructors can begin collaborative projects by identifying a project, finding a collaborating instructor or class, and negotiating the exact parameters of the exchange (e.g., frequency of the exchanges, nature of the final project, date of the final telecollaboration). In his book *Intercultural Language Activities*, Corbett (2010) offers activities and practical suggestions for setting up and managing intercultural exchange projects.

Research and Information Fluency

This standard focuses on students' ability to plan, locate, organize, analyze, evaluate, synthesize, and ethically use information from a variety of sources. Some faculty members may complain that students begin their research with Wikipedia and end with a Google search. However, one of the advantages of Wikipedia is that many of its pages exist in other languages and often have information that conflicts with that on the English pages. Instructors can capitalize on these discrepancies to show the importance of evaluating sources and developing critical literacy concerning online materials.

The internet increasingly contains shared information rather than information from one monolithic authoritative source (De Freitas & Conole, 2010). Collaborative notetaking is rendered simple via social bookmarking (e.g., Delicious.com, Digg.com, Reddit.com), one of the many collaborative note-taking sites (e.g., Evernote.com, Springnote.com, NotePub.com), and outliners (e.g., Thinklinkr.com, TheOutlinerOfGiants.com). Unfortunately, the field lacks research that shows whether these collaborative tools actually help students produce more cohesive or sophisticated reports; however, they may help make the process more transparent for the rest of the team because all members can see who shares what information and how it gets organized during the writing process.

Critical Thinking, Problem Solving, and Decision Making

The fourth standard makes another appeal for project-based learning in that students must be able to plan and conduct research, manage projects, solve problems, and make informed decisions about which digital tools and resources to use. Students could investigate a problem or issue in the target country or their own environment and make presentations about strategies or approaches to address the problem (e.g., poverty, racism, deforestation, waste disposal).

Digital storytelling projects typify this kind of involvement. Students must first identify the elements of a good story and the types of stories that contain significant information. Next, they must plan and manage activities that help them record their audio story with its visual accompaniment (e.g., collage, video). As they share their projects in class, students identify weak and strong aspects, identify difficult parts of the process, and brainstorm possible alternatives for the task. Students can use any number of applications to produce a digital story, from the very simple Photo Story from Microsoft to a more complex edited video using Adobe® Premiere®. The price of digital video recorders has fallen considerably whereas their ease of use has increased. Mobile recorders such as the Q3 Zoom (Zoom.co.jp) and Flip camera (TheFlip.com) are good options for institutions because they are durable and require no cords or extra storage media. Video cameras are also part of most handheld devices (e.g., iPhone, iPad, Android). Students can shoot the footage, download the video and upload it to other sites, and edit it (online or offline) with little training. Digital storytelling is an option for all levels of instruction (see relato-digital.blogspot.com).

Digital Citizenship

Unfortunately, the ISTE documents do not offer a solid definition of digital citizenship, but it is commonly understood to mean a student's ability to understand the legal and ethical issues that surround the use of technology. Ribble (2010) defines the term using nine elements:

1. **Digital etiquette.** Digital etiquette means that students know and practice the proper online behavior. Too often we may be tempted to ban certain technologies rather than discuss their appropriate use. Some schools have banned social networking sites or Twitter in an effort to curb undesirable behavior, but ISTE takes the position that it is more beneficial to teach the appropriate use of technology.

2. **Digital communication.** Everyone can now communicate with anyone at anytime (e.g., instant messaging, SMS text). The result is that individuals are faced with so many digital communication options that they may find it difficult to make appropriate decisions. Rules help students determine which technologies to use and when to use them.

3. **Digital literacy.** Just as learners need to be taught the appropriate time and form of communication, they need guidance on how to use the technologies to learn. These skills are included in the previous two standards on research and critical thinking, but they also contribute to overall digital literacy and digital citizenship.

4. **Digital access.** Good digital citizens support access to technology for all, and learners should demonstrate awareness of and advocate for digital equality. This is of particular importance to instructors in choosing the technology for the course. For example, if an instructor uses Twitter for daily journaling and expects regular updates, students who have and use mobile devices will have a significant advantage over those who do not, because it is much easier to post while one waits for the bus (for example) than it is to log in to a public computer at the library. The same can be said for the use of pay sites versus free sites or video projects that require students to use their own cameras.

5. **Digital commerce.** Learners should be aware that although a large share of the market economy happens online, dangers are associated with it. Additionally, illegal or immoral goods are available, and students should learn to be safe, effective consumers.

6. **Digital law.** Just as students are taught to be law-abiding citizens in the physical world (e.g., don't shoplift, don't vandalize), they are responsible

for knowing and obeying digital laws including illegal music sharing, plagiarizing, virus proliferation, hacking, spamming, and identity theft.

7. **Digital rights and responsibilities.** The rights and responsibilities of digital citizens should be discussed in class and clarified for students. Concepts such as *free speech* and *privacy* clearly constitute rights that also entail responsibilities.

8. **Digital health and wellness.** Students should be aware of what constitutes healthful and safe behavior such as distance from and time on screen, sitting position, and repetitive movements. Good health also concerns psychological issues such as internet addictions.

9. **Digital security.** Although we strive to maintain a safe society with reliable contacts and trusted members of the community, not all members of the community abide by the same standards. Students should know how to protect the technologies they use (e.g., against viruses and surges, and with passwords and backup protection).

In short, digital citizens exhibit a positive attitude toward technology for collaboration, learning, and productivity. As instructors use technology in the classroom, they should take opportunities to reinforce current knowledge while clarifying the boundaries and pitfalls of technology to promote a culture of digital citizenship.

Technology Operations and Concepts

The standard of technology operations and concepts refers to the ability to use software and hardware to complete tasks in class. As students use applications to complete an assigned project, they become increasingly familiar with the hardware, software, and online applications they use. Instructors can help by making tutorials and lists of frequently asked questions (FAQs), and by structuring activities in a carefully sequenced manner. It may also be advantageous to establish roles in the class such that each person becomes responsible for a specific technology; if others in the class have a question or need to troubleshoot that technology, they can seek out the student responsible for it.

The *NETS-S* provides six basic goals for using technology in class. Although these goals will not guide instructors as they plan their language curriculum, they do provide a useful checklist for inclusion or improvement of activities that use technology. These activities should promote creativity, innovation, communication, collaboration, critical thinking, and digital citizenship. In addition, they should help students refine their research and presentation skills, their online social skills, and their technological prowess to use, troubleshoot, and share a variety of technologies. The *NETS-S* and the *National Standards for Foreign Language Learning* provide standards for students and aim to help instructors design efficient curricula. ACTFL and ISTE also publish standards for teachers. These standards support the training of teachers but also sustain professionalism as teachers strive to improve their language and teaching skills.

ACTFL TEACHER STANDARDS

The *ACTFL Program Standards for the Preparation of Foreign Language Teachers* (2002) lists six content standards for language teachers. These standards were designed as accreditation and evaluation measures for foreign language teacher education programs. They are discussed here because the knowledge, skills, and dispositions mentioned in the teacher standards are too often attained outside of a teacher education program. Some foreign language teachers may get certified to teach through alternative means in which much of their training comes in the form of in-service, workshop, or conference participation. Post secondary instructors may not ever be exposed to teacher standards. The *ACTFL Program Standards* were created specifically for K–12 teacher certification programs, yet they are applicable beyond K–12 to both postsecondary and postgraduate contexts. With the use of technology, in-service teachers at all levels can and should participate in online social networks and maintain a personal and professional learning network (PLN) to improve their linguistic, cultural, instructional, and management proficiency. A PLN is a network of individuals who share information that contributes to their professional development. At the postsecondary level, the PLN for language teaching tends to be composed of the teaching assistants for that language. Nonetheless, individuals do not need to meet members of their PLN in person; instead, they simply rely on the connection (e.g., via Twitter, social networking sites, or email) to regulate their personal and professional development. Technology can help teachers find the information they need, develop the skills they require, and be inducted into a society of language teachers.

The six content standards are

1. Language, Linguistics, Comparisons
2. Cultures, Literatures, Cross-Disciplinary Concepts
3. Language Acquisition Theories and Instructional Practices
4. Integration of Standards into Curriculum Instruction
5. Assessment of Languages and Cultures
6. Professionalism

In large part, these standards emphasize the need for teachers to be good models of language, culture, learning, and teaching practices.

Language, Linguistics, Comparisons

The first standard is divided into three aspects: language proficiency, linguistic understanding, and ability to identify language comparisons. This standard calls for teachers to be at least advanced-level speakers of their language of instruction (French, German, Hebrew, Italian, Portuguese, Russian, or Spanish) and at least intermediate-high speakers if their langauge of instruction is Arabic, Chinese, Japanese, or Korean. Technology can help instructors maintain and improve their language skills.

Krashen (2004) makes a strong case for free voluntary reading as a means to maintain an instructor's language ability. He argues that free voluntary reading in the target language provides the necessary input at sufficient levels to maintain and even improve language skills. Technology facilitates free reading as a means to improving instructors' language skills because it grants access to substantially more reading material. Libraries, booksellers, and news kiosks were the source of written texts until the advent of the computer. When print newspapers, magazines, and journals began publishing material online, many instructors used bookmarks or link lists to collect their favorite news sources in their language of instruction. They could access the information by simply clicking on the appropriate addresses to read the daily news. More recently, instead of bookmarks to manage their information flow, they use RSS feeds that update whenever the content at the requested site is updated (see Chapter 8 for further discussion). RSS aggregators such as Google reader, Bloglines.com, Mozilla's live bookmarks, or Internet Explorer (IE) feeds let users know when content has been updated so that they can read only the new information. Several social networking sites (Orkut.com, Facebook.com) portals (Yahoo.com, iGoogle .com), and mobile devices (e.g., iPad, Android) allow users to switch the interface to the language they prefer, and they will retrieve news in the language they select as their interface.

Instructors have access to millions of documents written by native speakers that can be tapped to find out exactly how the language is spoken or written according to the most frequent uses on the internet. Numerous sites provide conversation partners, including Italki.com, MyLanguageExchange .com, ConversationExchange.com, or Language-Exchanges.com. These sites enable instructors to form relationships with native speakers based on both language and culture. These relationships become part of a PLN that supports and develops the instructor's skills.

Cultures, Literatures, Cross-Disciplinary Concepts

The second standard emphasizes cultural understanding, literary and cultural text comprehension, and the integration of other disciplines into foreign language instruction. Teachers should be able to demonstrate that they understand the connections between the perspectives of the target culture and the practices (e.g., greetings, eating out, using the post office) and products (e.g., food, clothes, phones) which demonstrate those perspectives. They should also recognize the value and role of literary and cultural texts for illustrating the perspectives of the target cultures. This standard echoes the third C of previously mentioned *National Standards for Foreign Language Learning* (i.e., Connections) by encouraging teachers to integrate knowledge from other disciplines and identify distinctive view points that are accessible only through the target language.

Godwin-Jones (2006) indicates that one of the more difficult challenges that we face in the effective use of the web for learning and teaching is finding the appropriate resources. Although there is no shortage of videos that depict cultural activities, it may be difficult for instructors to know what they should be seeking. Franklin (2007) argues that a site such as MERLOT (www.merlot.org) can play a key role in identifying appropriate activities, content, and materials.

MERLOT is a peer-reviewed repository for activities that have been vetted for quality of content, potential for teaching and learning, and ease of use.

Moreover, participation in online book discussion groups (e.g., GoodReads .com, BookTalk.org, and others via Facebook.com) can help instructors identify others who are interested in reading and discussing foreign language books. Enthusiastic participation in literature- and culture-oriented PLN activities such as these enables teachers to maintain and improve their knowledge of the target culture and literature. These types of activities can also encourage deeper understanding of how products and practices of the target culture relate to the perspectives of the target speakers.

Language Acquisition Theories and Instructional Practices

Instructors can develop a greater understanding of language acquisition to support classroom activity by participating regularly in conferences and reading journals that advance knowledge in the field of second language acquisition (SLA). Likewise, participation in online communities can help instructors develop or adapt instructional practices for their contexts.

Several professional organization offer regular newsletters and journals online (e.g., ACTFL.org, NECTFL.org), and subscriptions to listservs also enable teachers to receive regular updates on SLA and teaching methods (e.g., FLTEACH). In addition, video collections and online workshops are available from the Annenberg Foundation (Learner.org) and STARTALK (STARTALK .umd.edu). Federally funded language resource centers offer webinars on a regular basis (e.g., NCLRC.org, LARC.sdsu.edu) to help language teachers increase their knowledge of SLA and instructional practices.

Instructors can also seek evaluations from other instructors, mentoring professors, or content specialists. Classroom observations can be facilitated when instructors use web cameras in their classrooms that others can view in real time in various locations. This can be particularly useful to instructors who would like to observe classes at different institutions but do not have the means or time to travel between them. Video Skype and ooVoo (ooVoo.com) make two-way video chat easy to set up. Long-distance observations are necessary when members of an instructor's PLN are not local.

Integration of Standards into Curriculum and Instruction

Integration of the standards into the curriculum, Standard 4, depends on a clear understanding of learner standards, planning, and instructional sequencing and execution. Providing a sweeping generalization about how to integrate the standards at all levels is difficult for at least two reasons. First, the *National Standards for Foreign Language Learning* have different implications according to course level, student population, and state or institutional requirements. Second, instructional materials (e.g., videos, web sites) may not contain any clear reference to the standards, and instructors (particularly novice instructors) may find it overwhelming to design instructional sequences that integrate the standards unless they have significant support or examples.

Technology can help teachers integrate standards into the curriculum by providing access to information through a PLN. Models and examples of standards-based lessons and activities are widely available through professional organizations (see the section on professionalism later in the chapter) and language resource centers (see clear.msu.edu/clear/otherlrcs/). MERLOT and blogs (e.g., Technorati.com, EduBlogs.org) provide a wide variety of resources for instructional methods for those striving to integrate the standards at all levels. Twitter, social bookmarking, and social networking strengthen an instructor's PLN and allow participants to share tools for evaluating, selecting, designing, and adapting resources. Franklin (2007) states that "seasoned practitioners use less of a prescribed road map than a very deep toolkit" (p. 203). The toolkit for language instructors can consist of technical tools (e.g., web sites, presentation templates, CMC options), task ideas (e.g., jigsaw, consensus, problem-solving activities), social connections (intercultural exchange opportunities, guest speakers, peer teachers), or even management tools (classroom rules and routines, feedback considerations, discipline ideas). Instructors should begin with the standards to establish benchmarks and then use their toolkit to reach those benchmarks. These toolkits include members of a PLN who can provide innovative methods of integrating the standards regularly into instruction.

Those who are active in PLNs receive constant reminders of the importance of the standards, standards-based planning, and instructional materials that promote the standards for language learning. Using a PLN can bolster both integration of standards and integration of technology. As teachers participate in these online networks, the use of the applications that support them (e.g., social networking sites, Twitter) becomes second nature, and it becomes easier to integrate the technological tools into their standards-based curriculum.

Assessment of Languages and Cultures

Standard 5 focuses on assessing learners through multiple measures, reflecting on these assessments, and reporting the performance to those involved (students, parents, administrators). One benefit of using technology in the class is that it often pushes instructors to use multiple assessment types, particularly projects that can serve as both formative and summative and integrated performance assessments. Chapters 9 and 10 discuss these aspects more fully and how computer-assisted language learning (CALL) has helped transform practices in language assessment.

Several excellent professional development sites are devoted to assessment. The Educational Communications Board offers an exceptional online development guide (www.ecb.org/WorldLanguageAssessment/index.htm). The Center for Advanced Language Proficiency and Research (calper.la.psu.edu), the Center for Applied Linguistics (www.cal.org), and the Center for Advanced Research in Language Acquisition (carla.umn.edu) offer resources for understanding assessment and building tests and rubrics. The tutorial on testing produced by the Center for Applied Linguistics is particularly useful for teachers. Other online resources that may help instructors implement purposeful assessment measures include rubric makers (e.g., rubistar.4teachers.org), which facilitate the creation of informative rubrics to help assess students and to help students assess their own work. These rubrics offer a variety of options that can be adapted to fit the particular circumstances of a given level, language, or student population.

Standard 5 also emphasizes the need to report the results of student measures. Technology facilitates conveying and storing information. Students have access to notes posted online from anywhere. LMSs (e.g., Blackboard, Moodle) also enable students to check their grades. Linguafolio and other electronic portfolios may offer important advantages over the single number/letter grades because stakeholders can examine the performance itself and not just its evaluation. Most portfolios also allow students to make reflective comments and evaluations, and they allow for discussion of the performance. As these types of measurements of learner outcomes are stored in electronic (searchable) format, they allow for evaluation of the curriculum, better curricular articulation between language levels (from elementary through college), better content articulation among classes at the same level, and impact of programmatic changes (Morris, 2006).

Professionalism

Professionalism has two major aspects. First, teachers should engage in professional development opportunities to strengthen their linguistic and cultural skills and reflect on their practice. Second, instructors should understand the value of foreign language learning and advocate with students, colleagues, and members of the community to promote the field.

Participation in professional organizations is also important; each of the major associations maintains a presence on the web. The most prominent is the ACTFL (ACTFL.org). Instructors can also attend several regional conferences (see Table 6.1). The National Capital Language Resource Center (NCLRC; NCLRC .org) maintains a list of state organizations for language teachers at www.nclrc .org/profdev/organizations_resources.html. There are also language- specific organizations for the commonly taught languages (see Table 6.1) and one that targets the less commonly taught languages (NCOLCTL.org, pronounced *nickle-tickle*). Many other support organizations exist for a variety of interests (e.g., early education, applied linguistics, CALL).

These national and regional organizations serve both an academic purpose and a political one. They provide numerous resources for professional development while being strong advocates for learning foreign languages in the public schools. They disseminate research to both improve the teaching and learning of language and to justify and clarify the value of foreign languages.

As has been emphasized continually throughout this discussion on teacher standards, the most important use of technology for in-service professional development is active participation in PLNs. PLNs help instructors

TABLE 6.1 Resource list for professional development

Regional conferences	The Northeast Conference on the Teaching of Foreign Languages (nectfl.org)
	The Central States Conference on the Teaching of Foreign Languages (csctfl.org)
	The Southern Conference on Language Teaching (scolt .webnode.com)
	The Pacific Northwest Council for Languages (pncfl.org)
	The Southwest Conference on Language Teaching (swcolt.org)
Language specific	American Association of Teachers of French (frenchteachers.org)
	American Association of Teachers of German (aatg.org)
	American Association of Teachers of Spanish and Portuguese (aatsp.org)
	Chinese Language Teachers Association (clta-us.org)
	American Association of Teachers of Slavic and Eastern European Languages (aatseel.org)
	Alliance of Associations of Teachers of Japanese (aatj.org)
	American Classical League (aclclassics.org)
	American Association of Teachers of Italian (aati-online.org)
	American Association of Teachers of Arabic (aataweb.org)
	National Council of Less Commonly Taught Languages (ncolctl.org)
	Teachers of English to Speakers of Other Languages (tesol.org)
Particular interests	National Network on Early Language Learning (nnell.org)
	American Association of Applied Linguistics (aaal.org)
	Language Resource Centers (clear.msu.edu/clear/otherlrcs/)
	Center for Applied Linguistics (www.cal.org)
	Computer-assisted Language Consortium (calico.org)
	International Association for Language Learning Technology (iallt.org)
	World CALL (worldcall.org)

on a regular basis to reflect on their practice and improve their linguistic, cultural, teaching, and technological skills. PLNs can be formed in a number of ways: social networks such as Facebook, Orkut, or Ning (in particular Classroom 2.0); listservs such as FLTEACH; or microblogging sites such as Twitter. Twitter may be confusing to some because its purpose is not clearly evident: You read a webpage, you chat in a chat room, you search using a search engine, but tweeting with Twitter doesn't seem to be self-explanatory. The main purpose of Twitter, however, is to follow individuals with similar interests. In other words, the principal intent is to establish a PLN with people you don't know but who are interested in the same things you are. For example, you begin by following someone who has similar interests; if you're not sure whom to follow, you can start with Twitter4Teachers (twitter4teachers.pbwiki.com/Foreign-Language-Teachers), which lists a variety of language teachers by their Twitter accounts. As you read their Twitter sites, you may find someone they follow who is interesting to you, so you follow them as well. Your site will be updated regularly as they post comments about new practices, activities, and technologies. If you find that some of the people you are following are not interesting to you, you simply stop following them. Twitter also allows users to send personal messages to ask for clarification. You can just read posts for several weeks until you feel comfortable posting yourself. For many instructors, their PLN may simply be the other language teachers at their institution. Twitter and social networking sites expand instructors' PLNs to include state, national, and global trends in language education.

ISTE NETS-T

The *NETS* for teachers includes five standards that echo those for students. As instructors strive to model and apply the *NETS* for students, the *NETS* for teachers emerge as logical standards for designing, implementing, and assessing student learning experiences. The five NETS-Ts follow:

1. Facilitate and inspire student learning and creativity.
2. Design and develop digital-age learning experiences and assessments.
3. Model digital-age work and learning.
4. Promote and model digital citizenship and responsibility.
5. Engage in professional growth and leadership.

Unlike the *NETS-S*, which focus on learning and demonstrating skills and dispositions that learners develop in authentic task realization, the *NETS-T* concentrate on modeling behaviors and attitudes consistent with the digital-age world view.

Facilitate and Inspire Student Learning and Creativity

Two interesting performance indicators are evident in this standard. The first is that instructors must lead by example and modeling. Teachers are responsible for modeling creative thinking and innovation in both face-to-face and virtual environments. Instructors should be concerned with both pedagogy and technology. They should be the experts in pedagogy, but they need not be experts in technology. They should be competent enough to be able to orchestrate pedagogically sound and technologically enhanced language learning tasks. In many ways, the situation with technology is similar to the circumstances of a nonnative (NNS) instructors who teach native speakers (NS). The NNS instructors may know more about the content area (or pedagogy) than their

NS students, but their NS students may know more language. Nonetheless, NNS instructors gain respect by maintaining a high proficiency level in the target language. Likewise, instructors should know more about the pedagogy than their students, and some students might know more about technology, particularly those instructors who did not grow up with the technology. However, instructors can gain the respect of he students by maintaining a high proficiency level in the technology tools they use in class.

The second point is that language learning experiences are both face-to-face and virtual. It may be easy to get carried away by the excitement of technological advances and focus on implementing new and creative technology solutions at the expense of face-to-face interactions. In fact, it is often the case that the non-virtual classroom experiences are an important aspect of bringing about positive virtual encounters (Kassen & Lavine, 2007; Oblinger & Oblinger, 2005; Sharpe, Beetham, & DeFreitas, 2010). Online collaborative tools work in conjunction with, not in lieu of, face-to-face contact that encourages mutual construction of knowledge in the class.

Design and Develop Digital-Age Learning Experiences and Assessments

Digital-age learning experiences are characterized by self-assessment and personalized learning goals. To meet the performance indicators in Standard 2, instructors incorporate digital tools into learning experiences, develop technology-enriched learning environments to help students identify and pursue their own learning trajectory, customize learning activities, and provide multiple and varied assessments (including self-assessment). These types of assessments have been mentioned earlier with the other standards and will be investigated further in Chapters 9 and 10.

Model Digital-Age Work and Learning

Digital-age work and learning are mainly about communication and collaboration. Instructors should demonstrate the ability to work with students, peers, parents, and community members for the success of the students. This cooperation includes relevant and effectively packaged communication using a variety of media and formats. For example, teachers can use web sites, blogs, or Twitter to communicate homework and assignments, online grade books to communicate grades, ePortfolios to communicate progress, or email or SMS to communicate concerns.

In addition to good communication, teachers should demonstrate the ability to find, learn, and use resources to support teaching, learning, and research. This is most easily done by establishing a PLN. Kathy Schrock (twitter .com/kathyschrock) and Steven Anderson (twitter.com/web20classroom), for example, post new ideas, technologies, or applications for learning several times a day. These connections help maintain the flow of communication so that teachers find out about new developments without having to search for them.

Promote and Model Digital Citizenship and Responsibility

This standard's key concept is modeling appropriate behavior. Promoting and modeling digital citizenship entail advocating safe, legal, and ethical uses of digital information, such as respecting copyright and intellectual property regulations and appropriate documentation of sources. It also includes promoting equal access and using learner-centered strategies to meet the needs of all students and modeling appropriate online interchanges (i.e., netiquette).

Standard 4 also requires engaging with colleagues and students of other cultures. The need for direct interaction with native speakers has been reiterated throughout this chapter. Instructors who develop a PLN and are in regular contact with native speakers can easily meet this standard. Because the teacher standards tend to focus on modeling the behaviors, digital citizenship would entail inviting guest speakers (via Skype or other technology) to the classroom as well as instructors' being a guest speaker for others.

Engage in Professional Growth and Leadership

The performance indicators for professional growth and leadership appear to describe active participation (and leadership) in local and global communities for both technology and content (such as PLNs) and promoting leadership among others. The performance indicators also signal regular evaluation of current research and professional practice (available, for example, through webinars, online workshops, or online tutorials) and contributions to the effectiveness, vitality, and self-renewal of the teaching profession on various levels. Overall, few studies look at the high school language learning population. With the advent of Twitter, wikis, and blogs, however, practitioners are increasingly sharing their practices online. Newer technologies have enabled all teachers to contribute to a growing body of literature on the practices of teaching and learning a foreign language.

This chapter has examined the ACTFL and the ISTE standards that target both learner and teacher development. Some important themes have been reiterated throughout the discussion. The first is that student projects, presentations, and learning can be facilitated using technology and that language activities should also be used to reinforce digital skills in meaningful and creative ways. Second, the student standards are inextricably linked to the teacher standards, the latter often echoing the former. Teacher standards emphasize the need for teachers to provide good models of the skills and dispositions required by the student standards. These skills and dispositions include a positive conceptualization of the target language and culture and the use of technology; appropriate background knowledge to design, implement, and assess learning activities; and continual participation in professional activities. PLNs play a key role in educators' ability to meet the demands of continual improvement and maintaining a high level of professionalism in the classroom, the schools, and the community at large.

Practical Work

1. This chapter noted a number of technologies and resources. Complete the following table using some of the technologies mentioned in this chapter and earlier chapters (you can peek ahead to Chapters 7 and 8 if you have difficulty thinking of items).

Technologies I know how to use	Technologies I don't know how to use	Technologies I would like to try in class	Technologies I've never heard about
1.			
2.			
3.			
4.			
5.			

2. Complete the following table.

Tasks I use in class (e.g., Survey—interview those around you)	Tasks from column 1 in which I or the students use a computer	Tasks from column 1 in which I or the students haven't used a computer but could	Tasks that use a computer but that I have never used in class

3. Find and list resources that are available to you at your institution. Be sure to include campus-wide, department, and individual resources. Good places to start are the help desk, the technology specialist, and another instructor or administrator who uses technology for teaching.

4. Using the resources mentioned in the chapter, identify at least six entities you could include in your PLN. These can be listservs, blogs, or newsletters from professional organizations that you can subscribe to; people you can follow on Twitter; or social networks that you can join.

Suggestions for Further Reading

American Council on the Teaching of Foreign Languages (ACTFL). (2002). *Program standards for the preparation of foreign language teachers (Initial Level–Undergraduate and Graduate) (for K–12 and secondary certification programs)*. Alexandria, VA: Author. www.actfl.org/files/public/ACTFLNCATEStandardsRevised713.pdf.

Corbett, J. (2010). *Intercultural language activities with CD*. Cambridge, Eng.: Cambridge University Press.

de Freitas, S., & Conole, G. (2010). The influence of pervasive and integrative tools on learner experiences and expectations of study. In R. Sharpe, H. Beetham, & S. de Freitas (Eds.), *Rethinking learning for a digital age: How learners are shaping their own experiences* (pp. 15–30). New York: Routledge.

Ducate, L., & Arnold N. (Eds.). (2006). *Calling on CALL: From theory and research to new directions in foreign language teaching* (pp. 43–68). San Marcos, TX: CALICO.

ISTE. (2010). *Standards for global learning in the digital age*. www.iste.org/standards .aspx (contains links to both *NETS-S* and *NETS-T*).

National Standards in Foreign Language Education Project. (1999). *Standards for foreign language learning in the 21st century*. Lawrence, KS: Allen Press.

CHAPTER 7

Synchronous Computer-Mediated Communication

OVERVIEW

Chapters 7 and 8 discuss computer-mediated communication (CMC). This chapter focuses on synchronous CMC, which Murray (2000) defines as communication that occurs in real time using computers to enable the communication. The typical example of synchronous CMC is an online chat application. This chapter investigates some of the many CMC technologies, including instant messaging (IM), short messaging service (SMS), audio conferencing, and video conferencing. We examine the uses, advantages, and disadvantages of synchronous CMC. We also compare and contrast face-to-face (F2F) interaction with CMC interaction. Another topic we cover is how to implement, manage, and assess synchronous CMC activities within a curriculum. Key aspects of using synchronous CMC include the task preparation, articulating the task, and the follow-up. Task preparation for synchronous CMC includes orienting the students to the task, providing the linguistic conventions of CMC, and ensuring that students have the technological ability to use the applications. Guidelines for CMC tasks include limiting the number of participants, setting time limits, and identifying clear goals. Follow-up and maintenance include helping latecomers or inattentive students and using the transcripts to analyze the conversation. We also discuss the technical issues of identifying and using CMC applications in the classroom such as choosing the appropriate application, inserting foreign characters, using international fonts, and learning target culture internet chat customs. A well-articulated synchronous CMC activity includes pre- and post-CMC activities that familiarize students with the software and the language while encouraging them to take advantage of the text type that is produced.

SYNCHRONICITY AND TOOLS FOR SYNCHRONOUS CMC

Synchronous CMC differs from asynchronous CMC in two important ways: (1) Participants engaged in synchronous CMC need to be online at the same time, and (2) participants generally have far less time to edit and revise their messages in synchronous CMC than they do in asynchronous CMC (Levy & Stockwell, 2006). The fact that participants must be online at the same time creates difficulties for instructors who would like to connect with a target culture in a different time zone; in some cases, the time difference between countries may be eight or more hours, which may make it impossible to arrange class interactions. The fact that students have less time to edit and revise generally means that their discourse will have more errors and show more attributes of colloquial speech than it might during asynchronous CMC. Despite these drawbacks, there has been significant interest in synchronous CMC in recent years (Blake, 2008; McCourt, 2009; Van Compernolle & Williams, 2010). Initially, examples of synchronous CMC were limited to internet relay chat (IRC), audio and video conferencing, and the MOO group (see the next section); however, newer models of CMC have arisen such as IM, and technological developments have made internet chat available through a variety of methods (web based; PalTalk; and Voice over IP [VoIP] such as Skype™, Ventrilo, or TeamSpeak). This section discusses the various technologies available for synchronous CMC and looks at the advantages of CMC.

MOO

The MOO group of technologies (sometimes referred to as MU*s) includes MUD(D)s (multiuser Dungeons and Dragons), multiuser domain, or multiuser dimension, MOOs (MUD object-oriented), MUSHs (multiuser shared hack, habitat, or hallucination), MUSE (multiuser shared environment), MUVE (multiuser virtual environment), and MUCK (acronym unknown). At its core, a MU* is a database that enables users to communicate with one another and interact with the virtual environment (e.g., take a virtual drink, sit in a virtual chair). Groups of instructors and students are still using MU*s for language instruction, but they are decreasing in popularity; Mundo Hispano claims to be the "first (and the last?) all-Spanish MOO" (www.umsl.edu/~moosproj/mundo.html). Many MU*s and traditional MU* participants have drifted toward Second Life SecondLife.com, MMORPGs (massively multiplayer online role-playing games) or other technologies mentioned later in this chapter. Many instructors may avoid MU*s because of their association with games, free-for-all speech, and disorder than with learning in a structured environment.

In any case, instructors wishing to integrate a MU* into their teaching should be mindful that MU*s are generally open areas created by for specific purposes. Kötter (2006) recommends that instructors visit several MU*s on multiple occasions to make an informed decision concerning their class's participation and the planned activity.

There are still a number of language-specific MOOs such as LeMOOFrançais (www.umsl.edu/~moosproj/moofrancais.html), DreistadtMOO in German

(cmc.uib.no/dreistadt/informationen2.html), and MundoHispano (www
.umsl.edu/~moosproj/mundo.html) that provide opportunities for learners to
communicate synchronously with others in the target language. Although both
text-based and audio- and visually enhanced MU*s are available, some instructors
argue in favor of the text-based environment (Shield, 2003). Others suggest the
use of MU*s for tandem learning (Kötter, 2003), online presentations (Svensson,
2003), and exploratory learning where students explore their surroundings in a
virtual world (Levy & Stockwell, 2006), but there has been no boom or flurry of
interest in MU*s in recent years as there has been for chat or instant messaging
systems.

Internet Chat

The prototypical example of synchronous CMC is internet chat. The term
chat can refer to any kind of synchronous communication over the internet
but generally refers to text-based chat that is either group oriented (many-
to-many) or direct (one-on-one). An IRC works on a client–server paradigm.
An individual has a client application on his or her computer (at least a box
for writing and a box for reading what one's interlocutor has written). When
the user enters text (or speaks if it is voice chat), the message is sent to a
server. The server sends a copy of the input to all individuals logged into
the system.

Instructors can easily set up their own server–client system using
HyperChat Suite (fhsoftware, 2000). This free software enables teachers to use
their desktops as the server and have students log in as the client from their
own computers. Instructors may also choose to use a learning management
system (LMS) such as Blackboard or Moodle that offers chat as a module of
the program. A number of other free chat servers are available for download
with sufficient supporting documentation. An able information technology (IT)
support person will be able to set up an internet chat server for an instructor.
Setting up a private server for class use allows the instructor to maintain direct
control over the language in the chat room. These situations are referred to as
closed chats, and the instructor limits the participants in the class (or classes if
instructors are communicating with a class in the target country, for example).
Instructors may also choose to use public servers.

Public IRC servers are available across the internet on web pages or using
proprietary client software. This use is generally referred to as an *open chat* and
is available to any participants who wish to join. The advantage of using this
type of chat is that students are introduced to native speakers using authentic
online chat conventions and authentic expressions. One major drawback is that
students are exposed to language that may be above their level or inappropriate
for their age or includes nuances of the expressions used that nonnative speakers cannot comprehend. Instructors using a public chat server should familiarize
themselves with it by spending sufficient time in the chat room before exposing
students to that particular room for a classroom activity. If the chat room proves
acceptable, instructors need to prepare their students by providing frequently

used abbreviations and instructing them to read the chat for a while before participating.

One major benefit of the standard chat systems that are freely available for public use is that, in many cases, they permit the transcript of the conversation to be saved in an easily accessible location for both students and instructors (e.g., for corpus studies). This feature not only allows the instructor to monitor how well students communicate in an online discussion, but it also provides an important data source for how well certain prompts, activities, and tasks are designed from an action research point of view. Instructors can easily determine how quickly students begin and complete the task, how well they stay on topic, and what gaps in their interlanguage systems prevent or hinder them from accomplishing a given task in a chat room.

SMS, Text Messaging, or Texting

SMS is a method of sending messages to and from mobile phones. Indeed, in numerous settings, text messaging via mobile phones has replaced passing notes (e.g., during class, business meetings, or religious services). It seems only natural that this means of communication be implemented in academic settings for language learning. However, using SMS in the classroom can pose significant hurdles for instructors, particularly if they desire to design a tandem activity. For example, students may have different phone plans that can make the messages costly, unreliable, or inconvenient. Reception (although improving) is not guaranteed, resulting in the loss of messages that can be a source of frustration for students and instructors. Some plans do not allow the transfer of text messages from the mobile phone directly to email or other easily transferable media, so instructors have little control over when and how they receive the messages and how or where to store them for later analysis. Additionally, instructor, program, or institutional policy may make text messaging impossible. Finally, SMS systems do not lend themselves easily to instruction or research because the messages are often impossible to retrieve, and the communication activities are often difficult to coordinate. For short message interaction, instant messaging is clearly preferable to text messaging for the time being.

Instant Messaging

IM generally refers to a slew of programs that function like AOL's Instant Messenger (AIM; e.g., Yahoo Messenger, Windows Live Messenger, gtalk, iChat). Throughout the early 2000s, IM increasingly became one of the most popular forms of online communication and has well more than 1 billion users, with 1.7 billion users expected by 2014 (Radicati, 2009). Since 2009, however, this growth has slowed because users have moved more toward to community sites (e.g., Facebook, LinkedIn, Twitter) where they can conduct the same activities more efficiently (Online Publishers Association, 2009). IM systems function similarly to chat rooms except that users can log so that only friends or buddies can determine their availability. IM applications tend to be light (i.e., it use very little memory and processing power), nonsecure protocols that send information through a server that relays the information only to those to whom the user directs the messages. Most IM clients, therefore, are good for pair work but not for larger group work because sending messages to multiple participants can be cumbersome, in most IM applications, to send the same message to multiple users. IM, however, is now included in a number of applications (e.g., Skype) and community sites (e.g., Facebook, Twitter) that enable conference IMs (i.e., more than two participants).

VoIP

Voice over IP (VoIP) technology (also called internet telephony) is increasingly popular; it allows individuals to communicate in real time as they would on the phone, and communication to other countries is normally inexpensive, if not free. The quality of the audio and video depends largely on the quality of the network, so it is important that these calls take place over a dependable broadband network to provide the most comprehensible conversation. Dependable high-speed networks abound today, and most institutions offer support for VoIP calls. The majority of the client software used for VoIP is free (i.e., Skype, Gong, Ventrilo, TeamSpeak) and does not use many computational resources (i.e., memory, processing time), because many of applications were originally designed for online gaming, which mainly uses computing resources.

Of all the forms of CMC mentioned previously, text-based chat has been the most popular because it requires little bandwidth, has greater durability and manipulability (students can see, save, and work with the texts created), allows for greater time for thought in the second language (L2), and is one of the more frequently used form of CMC by the current generation of digital natives (i.e., those who grew up with technology; Lenhart, Ling, Campbell, & Purcell, 2010). Nonetheless, according to Lenhart and colleagues (2010), faster forms of communication such as VoIP continue to compete as the preferred method of communication for certain groups.

TASK 7.1

Search the internet to identify three chat systems you could use in your class and evaluate them for activities you would design with them for your students. What tasks would you use (be specific)? Does the chat system use public or private servers? What advantages does it offer? What disadvantages can you identify? Is it free? If not, what is the cost? Is there a limit on the number of participants? How user friendly is it? Does additional software need to be installed or is it web accessible? Can you save and reuse transcripts?

FACE-TO-FACE VS. CMC

Abundant research has reported on the advantages and disadvantages of CMC compared with F2F communication. F2F communication occurs when all students are present and talk directly to one another; CMC occurs when students communicate via the computer. In their review of the literature from 1990 to 2000, Liu, Moore, Graham, and Lee (2003) note that the advantages of CMC for

L2 learners have been "one of the most commonly discussed topics in foreign language literature" (p. 252). Several early studies showed increased motivation (Beauvois, 1994; Chávez, 1997; Meunier, 1997). Others indicate a positive impact on oral production, interactive competence, noticing, and repair (Beauvois, 1997a, 1997b; Blake, 2000; Chun, 1994; Fitze, 2006; Jepson, 2005; Kitade, 2000; Lai & Zhao, 2006; Pellettieri, 2000; Salaberry, 2000; Smith, 2003, 2004; Smith & Gorsuch, 2004; Sotillo, 2000; Toyoda & Harrison, 2002; Tudini, 2003; Volle, 2005; Warschauer, 1996a). Yet other studies point out the benefits of CMC in terms of intercultural understanding, access to native speakers, and construction of a community of learners (Belz, 2002; Belz & Müller-Hartmann, 2003; Kinginger, Gourves-Hayward, & Simpson, 1999; Kramsch & Thorne, 2002; Lomicka, 2006; Meskill & Anthony, 2005; Shin, 2006; Thorne, 2003).

The benefits of anonymity in CMC are extensive and were documented early as reasons for increased participation among students (Marjanovic, 1999; Sullivan, 1998). This anonymity allows students in a native speaker chat room to observe (i.e., read but not contribute to the conversation). Nonetheless, although it may appear easy for participants to not participate, synchronous CMC has consistently proven to have important advantages in balancing student participation (Beauvois, 1992, 1998; Bohlke, 2003; Braine & Yorozu, 1998; Chun, 1994; Davis & Theide, 2000; Gonglewski & DuBravac, 2006; González-Bueno, 1998; Kelm, 1992; Kern, 1995; Kivella, 1996; Mabrito, 1991; Smith, 2003; Warschauer, 1996a). A balanced student participation structure means that all members participate equally in the conversation rather than a participation structure in which a few dominant members guide the discourse.

Some researchers attribute this balancing of participation to the turn-taking mechanisms involved in CMC (Beauvois, 1992, 1998; Kelm, 1992). In F2F discussions, participants must wait until the speaker has finished before they begin to contribute to the conversation (if they choose to be polite), whereas in CMC discussions, all participants can formulate their next contribution at the same time. As such, CMC has been called "conversation in slow motion" (Beauvois, 1992) because students have more time to think about and articulate their contributions to the conversation. This increased time allows for a wider range of lexical items (Warschauer, 1996a). Yet, even though CMC may be slowed down, Fitze (2006) found no significant difference in the amount of language produced by participants in F2F discussions and those involved in CMC. So although students do not necessarily produce more language in CMC, they do have enough time to plan their speech and focus on both form and message.

TEACHING PRINCIPLES FOR SYNCHRONOUS CMC

Although abundant literature describes the benefits of using synchronous CMC in L2 classes, surprisingly little research discusses effective tasks and how to manage student CMC activity. This section offers advice for instructors looking to use synchronous CMC in language classes with suggestions for effectively designing and implementing a synchronous CMC activity, managing it while in progress, and following up on student performance.

Instructors must decide if they will use a public chat or a private chat. As discussed previously, a private chat has a number of advantages over a public chat, and public chats are not without danger. In a public chat room, the conversation generally goes so fast that beginning language learners are usually unable to follow the multiple threads of the conversation. Private chat rooms tend to be better for beginning language learners, younger students, and students who have no experience in chat rooms.

Preparing for Chat

Before performing the task, students should be familiar with the technology. Although many students may already be aware of how to read and post messages in a chat room, the only way to make sure that they are familiar with the particular technology to be used is to ask them to perform a task using it. Students should be able to engage in a preparatory chat (often called an ice-breaker task) that encourages them to use familiar language to introduce themselves or to brainstorm on a given topic. A short brainstorming activity of two to three minutes such as "Decide on the ten healthiest things to eat" (if the discussion is on food) has two important benefits. First, it creates a guided activity that has students using the technology in such a way that instructors can tell who is accustomed to it and who are the fast typists in the class. Second, it guides students to produce simple language (i.e., lists rather than phrases) using familiar vocabulary so that their energy can be spent figuring out how to be most efficient with the technology.

A subsequent activity could be geared toward orienting students to the language of chat rooms. A number of researchers (e.g., Crystal, 2001; Gonglewski & DuBravac, 2006) have made the case that the type of language used in a chat room is not, and should not necessarily be, the same as the language used in F2F interactions. Students should learn a few of the conventions of synchronous CMC language. Instructors can help students be productive by providing a list of expressions that are common in a chat, such as the English IMHO (in my humble opinion), French qq1 (*quelqu'un*) or C (*c'est*), or Spanish xq (*porque*; see Table 7.2) and then asking them to perform a task using as many of the expressions as possible. This type of activity enables students to make connections and comparisons between their own culture and the target culture. It also enables them to see how English has spread to other languages even though the letters of the acronyms don't translate; lol for *laughing out loud* and asap for *as soon as possible* are almost ubiquitous in chat rooms regardless of the language. Instructors may also explain appropriate behavior in online environments (called *netiquette*) at this point so that students are polite and respectful in their interactions (e.g., they don't write in all caps or mock others' responses).

Once students are accustomed to the technology and have access to appropriate language for the chat room, they are ready to begin a chat that has an objective and more direct significance and personal relevance for them.

TABLE 7.1 Text abbreviations in most commonly taught languages*

English phrase	English	French	German	Italian	Spanish
as soon as possible	asap	dqp	asap	asap	asap
Hello	hi	bjr/slt	gT	ciao	hl
Today	2da	auj	Heu	OJ	oy
Who	who	ki	Wo	ki	kien
With	w	avec	mit	kn	cn
Please	plz	stp/svp	plz	xfavo	xfa
Goodbye	cya/bbb	a+	AWS/bbb	adm	a2
Someone/ Anyone	sm1/ne1	qqn	MN	qkl1	algn
Kisses	xxx	xxx	xxx	xxx	xxx
Always	4ever	tjs	4e	smpr	smpr
a lot	alot	bcp	v	molto	mx
Thanks	thx	mr6 b1 (merci bien)	dnk	graz	gcs/ghx
Numbers	b4 i 4get = before I forget	b1 = bien c5pa = c'est sympa 2m1 = demain	8ung = Achtung	dv 6? = dove sei	to2 = todos

*Some common SMS abbreviations can be found online. Some sites are listed here for English (www.webopedia.com/quick_ref/textmessageabbreviations.asp), French (french.about.com/library /writing/bl-texting.htm), German (home.arcor.de/gratis-sms/free_sms_abkuerzungen_sms_kuerzel /free_sms_abkuerzungen_sms_kuerzel.htm), Italian (http://www.wired.com/beyond_the_beyond /2009/07/web-semantics-italian-sms-abbreviations/), and Spanish (www.braser.com/spanish-information /spanish-sms-abbreviations.html).

The Task

As with any task, a chat activity should have a specific objective to be accomplished in a limited amount of time. The guidelines and suggestions listed here and described in more detail in the following sections are designed to help in setting up and executing an effective activity:

- Limit the number of participants.
- Have specific time limits.
- Identify a clear goal that students can complete in the time allotted to them.
- Help latecomers and/or those who weren't paying attention.
- Use the transcripts.

Limit the Number of Participants

As discussed previously, a chat room with too many individuals tends to elicit a discourse that learners find difficult to follow and contribute to. In most cases, instructors can focus the conversation by dividing the class into groups of three to five students. Using a private chat enables instructors to establish areas or rooms (also called channels) for each group. Instructors can assign each student to a specific channel or room, and students in that room form a working group. Those in a specific room do not see posts from outside their room, so they tend not to be distracted. A limited number of participants in the same room also reduces the speed of the incoming messages so that even when a thread is loose, other participants can quickly regain the momentum of the conversation.

Have Specific Time Limits

It is important to set clear starting and ending times. Time limits help keep students focused on a task. In most cases, individuals and groups tend to manage their time better when they know how long they have to complete the task. The amount of time allotted to a task also helps students determine how thoroughly they need to complete the task.

Identify a Clear Goal that Students can Complete in the Time Allotted to Them

Conversations that have no goal or objective tend to stray in undesirable directions and not have a definable endpoint. For example, "Introduce yourself to your partners" is a little vague, and students may be unable to assess when they have completed the task. On the other hand, a task such as "Introduce yourself to your partners and make a list of six things you have in common" helps students begin the task (by introducing themselves) and complete the task (when they have a list of six items). When instructors delineate an obtainable objective, learners use the language as a tool, and the conversation tends to maintain a better focus, with more appropriate interchanges and negotiation of meaning (Ellis, 2003). Mynard (2002) suggests several additional techniques for making the chat activities meaningful for students: using worksheets that enable the students to clearly understand the purpose of the chat, allowing them time to prepare, and offering them practice in the language area. Among these activities, Mynard (2002) also suggests interviewing native speakers using a chat room.

Stevens (2004) describes several task-based activities that include synchronous CMC and web page development. For example, a group of students collaborated to create a virtual cooking school in which they held an online chat and posted images of the dishes they created. Other task-based CMC options include consensus, information-gap, and problem-solving activities.

Consensus activities encourage students to come to an agreement about a given topic and make concessions to others in the group to arrive at a mutually beneficial conclusion. All of the information about all of the options is available to all of the participants. Some good examples of consensus activities are (1) a travel itinerary, for which students decide where they should travel in the target country; (2) a dating wish list, for which students agree on the most important characteristics of a date or spouse; and (3) a list of the ten worst or best jobs, for which students agree on jobs and identify the criteria for why they are either desirable or undesirable.

Information-gap activities allow each partner to have a portion of the information necessary to complete the task. Groups must work together to share information to accomplish the task. Examples of information-gap activities include a treasure hunt race for which students have a series of questions that they must answer using online resources and share with the rest of the group (for questions such as "How many of the countries in South America are French speaking?" see the example at the end of this chapter).

Problem-solving activities encourage students to identify a problem and suggest various solutions for it. An example of a problem-solving activity is students being given a topic (e.g., food) and asked to use the internet to identify at least five problems or current events in the target country related to the topic (e.g., diminishing lunch times, expense, lack of fresh vegetables, cholera, genetically modified grains) and suggest at least one viable solution for one of the identified problems. To accomplish the task, groups must work together to glean the important information about the problem they have selected and the viability of the solutions they offer.

Each of the activity types mentioned previously happens in tandem with other activities, and CMC is merely the modality for communication. As with other activities, CMC activities may be done quickly in class or spread out over a number of meeting times. Nonetheless, even though the activity can be divided over several class periods, it is important to have achievable goals throughout the project that can be accomplished in the time allotted for each class period.

Help Latecomers and/or Those Who Weren't Paying Attention

Just as in F2F communication, it is important to keep an eye on students who lose their way or have difficulty getting started, although the medium of communication may make it difficult to monitor students. Often with newer technologies, students are already more familiar than the teacher with the applications, or they may be so eager to begin the activity that they do not pay attention during the model and explanation. In many cases, some technological hand-holding may be necessary once the activity has begun.

Use the Transcripts

Every online activity has (or can have) a log of all text and commands that were entered by the participants. Some logs of CMC activity are easily generated and some are more difficult to locate, or the instructor must copy and paste from the conversation window. Some transcripts are nearly impossible to get into a workable format (e.g., SMS cell phone texts are difficult to share if the participants are not included in the original message). The transcripts in the logs from CMC activities have numerous advantages for the instructor and for the students. The instructor can use the transcripts as data for action research by analyzing learners' language and gauging improvement over time. Many CMC applications also allow instructors to quickly determine the number of words generated by participants as well as the lexical density (i.e., the variety of words used). These statistics may indicate the difficulty of a task or the level of engagement from the students.

Students can profit in a number of ways from analyzing the transcripts. Learners can reexamine their production and analyze their errors as performance errors (e.g., "I knew that . . . I just missed it!") or competence errors (e.g., "Oh really, you can't say that?"). Having students recognize their errors and label them as items they knew but missed or items they didn't know can give them confidence in the language despite their errors, while helping them notice gaps in their interlanguage. Recognition of errors can also be helpful when students make many errors of the same type (e.g., agreement). The instructor can write an error on the board and have students scan their own discourse for instances of the same error type. Students can also use the transcripts as a guided follow-up to develop self-assessment skills. For example, students can be asked to identify three well-formed questions, three poorly formed questions, two vocabulary words that they did not know, one fact that they learned in the activity, or any combination of these items.

One disadvantage of synchronous CMC is that, unlike asynchronous CMC, it does not tend to lead students to expand on topics or use more syntactically complex language (Hirotani, 2005). Indeed, it is a common challenge to get students to expand on topics and develop their discourse competence in asking follow-up questions (Mynard, 2002). Learners can use the transcripts to identify a number (set by the instructor) of instances in the activity when it would be appropriate to ask follow-up questions to expand on a topic. For example, a transcript may read "What do you like to eat?—I like chocolate. What sports do you like?—I like basketball," particularly for students at the lower levels. Using the transcripts, students can develop self-assessment skills and discourse competence by asking follow-up questions that expand on topics discussed in the online environment, such as What type of chocolate white or dark? What is your favorite basketball team?

The major advantages of synchronous CMC that can be exploited in class are synchronicity, anonymity, and persistence. The synchronous aspect of CMC enables students to speak (albeit via the keyboard) as they would in a F2F environment except at a slower pace. Learners have more time between interchanges and less responsibility to wait until the other interlocutors have completed their contributions before beginning their own. Synchronous CMC enables students to participate equally and at a slower rate, which allows for greater lexical variety without reducing the amount of *in lingua* production. Synchronous CMC also allows students to connect in real time with native speakers without the expense of bringing native guest speakers to class or taking the class to the target language country.

Anonymity is also an advantage afforded by synchronous CMC. Student can enter chat rooms without feeling that they must post before they are ready. Likewise, anonymity allows for more authentic task types; in a classroom, it is somewhat odd to ask information about someone when you can see the person (e.g., What color is your hair? How old are you?), but if students log in anonymously and are given the task to associate online names with class names, they can authentically ask "What color is your hair?" Introductions, greetings, and closers are also more authentic as students enter and leave the chat area. Synchronous CMC also allows for persistent data. Persistence means that CMC conversations are recordable; students can examine the texts they produce at any time to evaluate their strengths, weaknesses, or changes over time.

Instructors can evaluate the tasks they wish students to complete using synchronous CMC and determine if students are benefiting fully from the anonymity, synchronicity, and persistence of the technology. Although instructors need not exploit the advantages in every activity, it is wise to analyze CMC activities to make sure that the tasks are designed to facilitate authentic communication among students and that the technology improves and supports the task rather than being an additional task in and of itself.

TASK 7.2

Skype™ has a number of advantages including voice and videoconference as well as free add-ons that allow you to share your desktop. Design a collaborative task that uses Skype to unite participants (e.g., telecollaboration, guest speaker.). What are the limitations on the activity that you design? How long does your activity take (class periods? weeks? months?)? How do students know when they have completed the task?

TECHNICAL CONSIDERATIONS

The major hurdles for those just beginning to use CMC in the classroom are (1) inability to determine a suitable chat room for the class, (2) using accented characters and special fonts, and (3) chat customs. This section deals with each of these topics with advice on facilitating the use of the technology for students.

Many instructors may be reticent to use synchronous CMC because they are not familiar enough with the technology to find suitable applications for use in class. In recent years, asynchronous CMC applications have become increasingly easy to find and to use. Many teachers are comfortable using chat applications that come with LMSs, such as Blackboard or Moodle; other instructors may prefer to use free sites such as Bravenet.com or the Palace (www.thepalace .com) or a MOO; yet other instructors may prefer to have more control and use self-contained applications such as HyperChat (software.emule.com/hyperchat -suite/), IM and conferencing through Skype, Gong (gong.ust.hk), or Google. To select the most appropriate software, instructors should first identify their comfort level with not having control over what students post. Each of the forms of CMC mentioned has advantages and disadvantages in this regard that will affect the decision on the most effective platform for CMC.

LMSs such as Blackboard and Moodle have easy-to-use software and automatically saved transcripts of the chat, and they allow only students registered for the course to join the chat room (private chats). When the LMS is on a reliable server, this option appears ideal for class chats, but it is difficult (although not impossible) to invite guest speakers; instructors would need to add the guest speaker to their class and give the guest speaker the appropriate privileges and uniform resource locator (URL) for the site. This format does make it cumbersome for international or even extramural CMC. CMCs also tend to be slow and can be unreliable depending on the time of day and resources available to the institution.

Online chat sites or MOOs are useful and engaging for students involved in international exchanges. Both groups simply join the same site and the same channel, chat room, or location in the MOO. Most of these sites are reliable because they serve thousands of individuals per day. The major drawback for some instructors is their lack of control over what their students encounter. Anyone in the world can wander into their activity or join their conversation without being invited unless there is an option for a private chat that uses a password (which many do have). These sites may also have a large number of advertisements on the sidelines that could annoy instructors (but there is no convincing evidence that these advertisements are distracting to the students). A number of sites also offer audio and video chats for instructors who wish to experiment with different media. Finally, instructors must visit these sites several times to ensure that the instructions they give to students are clear and that students are able to find the space in which they are to meet.

Instructors who prefer a high degree of control are most likely to prefer establishing their own arena using a chat server that they install on their own server. HyperChat studio is probably the easiest to use because it can act as a server from any networked computer (even behind a firewall) and can be run from a removable disk drive such as an online drive or flash drive. Setting up your own server can have a number of advantages, such as allowing students to see web pages that you deem important for the chat or the ability remove (kick) people from a chat room if they do not speak the target language. All of the transcripts are saved in one location on the server (which can be the instructor's computer), and instructors can print them out immediately following the activity for follow-up discussions. The instructor can enable or disable features of the software, such as commenting, making commands, or transferring files. Instructors can also block certain words from being used. If instructors do not want students to use inappropriate terms and acronyms, these words can be added to a list of items that will not be sent through the server; other members of the chat room will simply see that something was said but they won't know what. Each service has different options, and instructors should be familiar with the application they choose in order to troubleshoot potential issues or log in from multiple machines or accounts to help students who are having difficulties.

Finally, for instructors who prefer a high level of control and have little desire to explore the technology from the server side, online IM allows instructors to form specific private groups of students and present activities without worrying about the reliability of the server (Skype, Yahoo!, MSMessenger, and Google have reliable servers), and they are still able to use audio and video chat. One of the major advantages of IM is that most students are already familiar with the technology and will generally need little guidance; the disadvantage is that they are often more proficient than the instructor, so instructors must be comfortable receiving technical assistance from their students. Other major disadvantages to using IM clients include that they are insecure (the data can be intercepted by nonparticipants), they are not uniform in appearance or function (although this has been changing), and many are unable to support non-roman characters. Some applications (specifically AIM) will not support foreign characters without downloading the appropriate language-specific client.

Fonts

Fonts for synchronous CMC are generally not an issue if instructors use web-based software. In most cases, if students can see Russian or Greek characters in a web browser and can produce them on their computers, there should be no problem in a browser-based application (such as Yahoo!, Google, Skype, or MSN—the exception being AIM). Additionally, a number of chat rooms allow learners of Japanese to chat in either hiragana or romanji (e.g., apricotweb .com). The easiest way to facilitate fonts in synchronous CMC environments is to set the language environment to the target language (e.g., Japanese, Arabic, Russian); on Macs the fonts are already installed, and on PCs they need to be installed. Finally, install an appropriate keyboard to accompany that font. The most significant problem with foreign fonts is lack of standardization among fonts (e.g., a ж on one machine should look like a ж on another machine). This standardization has become important, and many systems now use UNICODE fonts, which produce the same characters across systems. Nonetheless, adherence to the standard is far from complete, and many messages may still suffer from font changes across systems.

The more commonly taught languages (French, Spanish, German) do not have a font problem because many of the American English characters are the same or can be easily substituted (e.g., German *ß* for *ss* or *ö* for *oe*). Instructors should be aware of any diacritical marks or special characters that would be needed in the particular target language. In most cases, even native speakers make substitutions. For example, in Spanish and French, many participants in chat rooms simply use capitalization instead of the accent mark (e.g., *durmiO, espaNol,* or *parlE*). For language learners, the practice of substituting capital letters may help increase the speed of the interchange while still enabling students to be aware of accented characters. In most chat rooms, many accents are simply left off in words that do not have meaning differences (e.g., French *bete* is almost never written *bête* in the chat rooms), so it may not be as important that students included accents in their text; nonetheless, some instructors may require the inclusion of an accent in all cases (particularly when the accent make a semantic difference such as *Tengo 19 años*). Substitutions for accented characters clearly provide the most efficient and authentic method for enabling students to function in synchronous CMC without installing additional fonts and keyboard configurations.

Chat Customs

Another important technical consideration is the need to help students realize the customs of a given chat arena. Instructors should make clear the rules and expectations for censoring, flaming, and sidelining and using text conventions, acronyms, and emoticons.

Instructors may want to consider chat rooms in which they have the option to censor students who do not act correctly (e.g., are rude or consistently use the L1). In some applications, the instructor can eject students from the chat room who then miss out on the conversation and must log back into the chat room. This causes such students to lose participation points according to language produced (determined by the transcripts). In lieu of gaining server access (needed to censor students), instructors may wish to make it clear that the transcripts are available to the instructor and everyone else and that the evaluation criteria for the activity include appropriate chat room conventions.

Flaming refers to the act of provoking other students through insults or name calling or of attacking others because of their point of view rather than discussing any differences. Flamers or cyberbullies can easily eliminate any motivational advantages created by using the synchronous CMC tools. Instructors can make it clear from the beginning that this is unacceptable behavior in a private classroom chat.

Sidelining, also called lurking, is the act of reading without contributing to an active chat session. Although many instructors may consider this acceptable behavior in a public chat room with native speakers for a particular activity, most would agree that sidelining is unacceptable in a private classroom chat. Sideliners can be guided into the conversation early by simple reminders on a private channel (many chat systems allow individuals to send private messages or *whisper* their message to another party). The issue of sidelining should also be addressed in the chat rules.

Text conventions generally refer to how participants convey meaning other than by the words they use. For example, although capital letters can substitute for accented characters, entire phrases in uppercase characters often signify shouting, yelling, and possibly belligerence. When students wish to accent words or correct mistakes, it is better to use asterisks(*) before the targeted material (e.g. I was going to fall you.. –*call). Acronyms also allow students to communicate substantial content rapidly. As mentioned earlier, students profit from having a list of acronyms in the target language that they can use during the conversation. Along with the list of acronyms, students may want to qualify their utterances using emoticons for happy :-) or sad :-(. Most students will have a repertoire of emoticons at their disposal, but instructors might consider soliciting a selection of emoticons for use in the class such as :) for smiling, XD for joking, or :S for worried, which allow students to express themselves in an acceptable manner.

Conclusion

In this chapter, we have examined a variety of synchronous CMC tools and methods and explored the advantages of using synchronous CMC in the classroom. Synchronous CMC provides a significant complement to traditional F2F communication in that learners tend to show increased motivation, a wider range of lexical items, development in oral production, interactive competence, noticing, meaning repair, access to native speakers, and more balanced involvement among synchronous CMC participants. The benefits of synchronous CMC are far reaching, and instructors who wish to profit from synchronous CMC should properly prepare participants for the activity by allowing them to explore the technology with a familiar task before using it to perform new tasks. Participants also benefit from a limited number of individuals in their group, specific time limits, clear goals and a well-defined task, support for latecomers and those who fall behind, and appropriate and judicious use of the transcripts from the online conversation. As instructors take advantage of the synchronicity, anonymity, and persistence afforded by synchronous CMC, students can also profit more fully from the activities.

Practical Work

1. In the following table, list four chat systems that are available to you and complete the table to decide which application is best for your circumstances. These systems can be available at your institution or online.

Name of the chat application (e.g., Blackboard)	Private? Public?	Instructor permissions (blocking participants or words)	Server reliability and speed	Interesting features
1.				
2.				
3.				
4.				

   Which of the chat systems that you examined is the optimal choice for your teaching situation?

2. Set up a chat on pros and cons of synchronous CMC.
   Begin an online chat with those in your class or colleagues at another institution. Brainstorm advantages and disadvantages of synchronous CMC. Discuss task type, ease of use, and feasibility at your institution of learning.
   Make a list of five obstacles to overcome at your institution for using synchronous CMC.

3. After using a chat room, download and examine the transcripts. Figure out if it would be easier in your teaching position to print the transcripts yourself or to have the students print their own transcripts. Print out the transcripts and analyze them for content and accuracy.

4. Set up a guest speaker chat (e.g., with a native speaker).
   a. Identify a topic and a meeting time for a native speaker virtual visit.
   b. Create a worksheet to help students prepare for the activity. The worksheet should make the purpose of the chat explicit. If you are inviting someone to discuss recycling in Germany, for example, it should be clear to the students

that they should focus on concepts related to recycling and not, for instance, German music. Other topics that work well and increase cultural insight are interviewing recently married couples about their wedding, interviewing new business owners about the difficulties and successes of starting up their business, interviewing students who have just passed major exams, or discussing current events in the country (e.g., elections, major sporting events). The worksheet should also have a space where students can prepare questions that they wish to ask the guest speaker. In some instances, it may be necessary to require students to prepare a certain number of questions.

   C. Identify a colleague or native speaker whom you would like to ask to participate in a conversation with your students.

   d. Tell the guest speaker that he or she will be answering questions on a specific topic for the class and delineate the meeting times. For example, if the class meets from 2 pm to 5 pm, the guest speaker would need to come from only 2:30 pm to 3:00 pm to allow time for other activities besides the guest speaker chat.

5. Chose a chat platform and perform activities A and B in class. Then discuss the activity using the questions in activity C.

Activity A: As an entire class, go online (to any chat room or MOO) and introduce yourself to others in the chat room. Talk about your interests and hobbies and try to find three other people who have similar hobbies. Report on your activity to the class.

Activity B: In groups of four, meet in a private room or channel of a chat room. Establish one person to be the leader, one person to be the recorder, one to be the timekeeper, and another to be the fact checker. Racing against the other teams, use the internet to find the answers to the following trivia questions and communicate them to your group. Leaders should divide the work evenly, everyone should report to the recorder, the fact checker is responsible for verifying questionable answers, and the timekeeper is responsible for balancing the fact getting and the fact checking. You should have eight to ten minutes to complete this activity.

   i. What was the name of the manifesto written by André Breton in 1924?

   ii. What is the name of René Magritte's painting of a pipe?

   iii. Name four paintings by Salvador Dalí.

   iv. Where is the Salvador Dalí museum?

   v. Who painted *La tour rouge* in 1913 and where was he born?

   vi. What type of music is generally associated with the surrealist movement?

   vii. What political parties are generally associated with the surrealist movement?

   viii. Name three television shows that can be considered surrealist.

   ix. Name three films that can be considered surrealist.

   x. How would you describe surrealism?

Activity C: Compare the discourse from both Activity A and Activity B using the following questions as a guide:

How does the discourse elicited in the first discussion (A) differ from that in the second discussion (B)?

Did you find the discussion easier to follow in A or B?

Did you stay on task better for A or B?

Did you feel more productive in A or B?

Discuss the advantages of one task type over the other.

Suggestions for Further Reading

Belz, J. A., & Thorne, S. L. (Eds.). (2005). *Internet-mediated intercultural foreign language education*. Boston: Thomson Heinle.

Blake, R. J. (2008). *Brave new digital classroom: Technology and foreign language learning*. Washington, DC: Georgetown University Press.

Charbonneau-Goudy, P. (2009). Awakening to the power of video-based web-conferencing technology to promote change. In R. Oxford & J. Oxford (Eds.), *Second language teaching and learning in the net generation* (pp. 199–216). Honolulu: University of Hawai'i Press.

Crystal, D. (2001). *Language and the internet*. Cambridge, Eng.: Cambridge University Press.

Shin, D.-S. (2006). ESL students' computer-mediated communication practices: Context configuration. *Language Learning and Technology, 10*(3), 65–84.

Wang, Y. (2004). Supporting synchronous distance language learning with desktop videoconferencing. *Language Learning and Technology, 8*(3), 90–121.

CHAPTER 8

Asynchronous Computer-Mediated Communication

OVERVIEW

Asynchronous computer-mediated communication (CMC) has become one of the more standardized and reliable forms of communication in education. Most teachers are competent in email and have little difficulty thinking of appropriate uses for online discussion boards, blogs (short for weblog), podcasts, and wikis. Asynchronous forms of CMC have a few advantages over synchronous CMC because of their simpler logistics (not everyone needs to be present at the same time), the ubiquity of synchronous CMC (there are about 3.9 billion email accounts worldwide; Radicati, 2010), and the standardized conventions of asynchronous CMC. Indeed, although the use of synchronous CMC is supported thoroughly by the language learning theories discussed in Chapter 4, asynchronous CMC can also facilitate classroom management and can be easily added to the formal classroom setting. It provides opportunities for comprehensible input and gives ample time for students to articulate their responses. This chapter discusses the advantages offered by asynchronous CMC, specifically email and related activities (e.g., listservs), discussion boards, blogs, podcasts, wikis, and social networking sites. Each of these technologies has particular advantages depending on the activity, the level of the students, and the overall design of the tasks. Along with providing an overview of technologies for asynchronous CMC and related appropriate tasks for students, this chapter identifies guidelines for choosing between modes of CMC (asynchronous or synchronous).

ASYNCHRONOUS TOOLS

A number of asynchronous CMC tools are available to language instructors today. In general, these tools provide a collaborative platform for communities of language learners. Both synchronous and asynchronous CMC have been shown to improve participation, particularly among students belonging to minority groups, shy students, and physically challenged students (Beauvois, 1992, 1997b; Braine & Yorozu, 1998; Bruce, Peyton, & Batson, 1993; Chun, 1994; Curtis & Roskham, 1999; Davis & Thiede, 2000; González-Bueno, 1998; Hartman et al., 1991; Kelm, 1992; Kern, 1995, 1997; Kiesler, Siegel, & McGuire, 1984; Kivella, 1996; Mabrito, 1991; Meunier, 1997; Smith, 2003; Spiliotopolis & Carey, 2005; Warschauer, 1996c), even though they may sometimes hinder more verbally expressive students (Palloff & Pratt, 2007).

Although both asynchronous and synchronous CMC have been shown to provide helpful support to students, there are important distinctions between them. Asynchronous CMC, for example, is more permanent because most users do not review chat scripts or save instant messages (IM), but they do expect to refer to wikis or re-listen to podcasts. Unlike synchronous CMC, asynchronous CMC does not permit the rapid exchange of short utterances and therefore generally requires a longer period of time for communication to take place and enables more detailed responses. With a shorter response time, synchronous CMC may place additional demands on speakers simply because of the speed of the conversation and students' typing ability and familiarity with the technology (Beauvois, 1992, 1997a; Cech & Condon, 1998; Hata, 2003). Synchronous CMC includes all the same discourse functions as face-to-face (F2F) communication, whereas asynchronous CMC displays only a limited number of discourse functions (Sotillo, 2000) and fewer interactional features (Warschauer, 1996a). In contrast, asynchronous CMC provides more opportunities for learners to produce syntactically complex language (Hirotani, 2005; Sotillo, 2000). Asynchronous CMC has also been shown to be effective in creating learner communities (Spiliotopolis & Carey, 2005), an important characteristic for effective second language (L2) learning (Hall, 2001). A clear advantage of asynchronous CMC over synchronous CMC is its flexibility in accommodating students with varying schedules. With synchronous CMC, all learners must be online at the same time, which can make cross-institutional communication difficult for institutions in different time zones (e.g., those in Japan and the United States). Asynchronous CMC allows learners to take time to formulate opinions, seek appropriate vocabulary, and catch up on missed work. This extra time may help increase confidence and reduce discomfort in the class by lowering the affective filter (Hata, 2003). Table 8.1 summarizes some notable differences between synchronous and asynchronous CMC.

We cannot discuss all the many forms of asynchronous CMC; moreover, most of the literature groups the various applications under the label *Web 2.0*, rather than dealing with each one separately (Lomicka & Lord, 2009). This chapter examines the following forms: email, listservs, discussion boards, blogs, podcasts, RSS feeds, and wikis. Many readers are already familiar with email;

TABLE 8.1 Major differences between synchronous and asynchronous CMC

Synchronous CMC	Asynchronous CMC
Accommodates the here and now	Maintains an expectation of permanence
Allows rapid exchange of short utterances	Encourages lengthy, detailed utterances
Shows all of the discourse functions included in F2F interaction	Shows a limited number of interactional features
Focuses on frequent (and often simpler) syntactic structures	Provides opportunities to produce syntactically complex language
Emphasizes peer interaction and one-to-one relationships	Helps create communities of learners
Requires all participants to be present for the task	Accommodates students with different time schedules
Necessitates on-the-spot language creation, and correction and monitoring occur in real time	Permits learners to take time to formulate responses, seek appropriate vocabulary, and catch up on missed work

a short definition of the other terms may provide a clearer picture of how these tools can be used for language learning. A listserv is an electronic mailing list; subscribers receive copies of email messages sent to the server from all participants. A discussion board is also called an online bulletin board, a forum, or message board. Participants use an internet browser to post and respond to comments. Blogs (previously called weblogs) are online journals on which writers post information and readers respond using comments. Podcasts are episodic online audio recordings; subscribers are notified when new episodes are posted and can listen via the computer or other electronic device. RSS feeds are similar to podcasts—subscribers are notified of new online content (i.e., text, audio, video, status updates) and retrieve the new media via a feed reader on the computer. Wikis are editable online documents—Wikipedia is the prototypical example of a functioning wiki, for which all participants are readers, writers, and editors. These tools can be used separately or in conjunction with one another to facilitate communication among learners. One issue with CMC is that it does not necessarily make the role of the instructor less prominent in the classroom. In fact, some practices may cause the instructor to engage in extensive communication with the class. Instead of technology helping automate the instructor's job, asynchronous CMC can increase the instructor's workload because the instructor must respond to more email, and students expect rapid responses.

EMAIL

Email exchanges, keypals, and email tandems have been used for a number of years for four purposes: (1) to develop interlanguage and communicative skills, (2) to promote intercultural education, (3) to train teachers, and (4) to develop a sense of community among target language users (cf. Lantolf, 2000; Lantolf & Appel,

1994). Although none of these purposes excludes the others, most research has concentrated on the first. Agreement is widespread that email improves communication skills, whether it is with native or nonnative speakers (González-Bueno, 1998; González-Bueno & Pérez, 2000; Kasper, 2000).

Other studies provide a variety of pedagogical benefits of using email in addition to traditional F2F activities. Discourse analyses have revealed similar characteristics among speech and email exchanges (Beauvois, 1992, 1997b; Crystal, 2001; Pelletieri, 2000), and classes that use email exchanges have demonstrated significant language improvement over those that do not (González-Bueno, 1998; González-Bueno & Pérez, 2000; Kasper, 2000). Gonglewski, Meloni, and Brant (2001) list several pedagogical benefits of email, including extending language learning time and place, providing a context for authentic communication, expanding topics beyond classroom-based ones, promoting student-centered language learning, encouraging equal opportunities for participation, and enabling quick connections to native speakers. Using email in the classroom has been found to reduce anxiety and promote language awareness (LeLoup & Ponterio, 2003). Additionally, email communication uses standard conventions (Crystal, 2001), so it promotes an alternate form of literacy that student need to experience if they are to function in the target language (Gonglewski & DuBravac, 2006).

Although the advantages for using email are numerous, the design of the task can determine the success or failure of the activity for the students. The design of an email exchange activity hinges on a number of variables that include the purpose of exchange, the class size, and the coordinating instructor. Activities tend to be accomplished successfully when the targeted text type and discourse functions guide the design of each exercise. An email exchange with another class requires agreement between instructors concerning the structure and purpose of the exchange. Instructors may want to focus on cultural knowledge, language development, or a combination of the two and it is clear in the minds of the instructors and the students what they are doing and why.

During the growth of the internet in the 1990s, email was the most readily available form of CMC for students and instructors. Hence, email exchanges were quickly embraced as one of the most efficient and effective ways to communicate with those with little technological experience. Even more than 20 years later, the most frequent use of the internet on any given day is to send or receive email, with the average corporate user sending about 110 email messages per day (Radicati, 2010). Although, people have been claiming since as early as 2007 that young people do not use email anymore preferring texting or IM instead (Lorenz, 2007), a Nielsen study (Gibs, 2009) found that high social media users (18–34 year olds) actually used email more than those who do not use social media (e.g., Facebook, Twitter, LinkedIn). Even with the increase in mobile devices, the majority of time spent on the internet continues to be for email (Nielsen, 2011).

Some of the simplest email exchanges occur between instructor and student. One method of using email to enhance productivity is requiring that completed assignments be emailed to the instructor. Teachers can easily provide feedback using the reviewing features in Word, which allow instructors to add comments, make changes, and highlight content or linguistic problems. In many cases, however, the submission of assignments is more easily done through a digital drop box in a learning management system (LMS) such as Blackboard, Moodle, Nicenet, or Sakai. Students can drop assignments in a folder located in the LMS and instructors can collect all of the completed assignments at once.

Despite the advancements in email technology and the facility that students and instructors have using it, the realization that email exchanges could be time consuming and "messy" (Robb, 1996) made it clear that many of the tasks that took place via email could more easily be done using other forms of CMC, such as discussion boards, digital dropboxes, wikis or microblogs. In addition exchanges, electronic journaling became popular for a time. Email journaling with the instructor may still be a useful activity for classes, but email exchanges with individual students can be prohibitive when instructors have four classes of 24 students and feel like they must respond to all messages—with only one email per student per week, instructors would need to file over a hundred messages.

Even so, it is unlikely (and possibly not the best use of time) for instructors to respond thoughtfully to each posting. Many instructors have turned instead to blogs and microblogs to facilitate online journals (see the section on blogs later in the chapter) for which students give feedback in addition to potential instructor comments.

Voicemail and other technologies such as Wimba allow students to send audio recordings as email attachments. These attachments may encourage students to work on both the written and oral aspects of email communication. However, like most applications in email, these functions have moved to audio drop boxes that are easier to manage than multiple emails or to podcasts that are also aggregated into a central location (see later in the chapter).

Intranet Email Exchanges

Intranet email exchanges occur within a single class. Students are paired (called tandem groups) and are given tasks to complete with their partners. Gonglewski et al. (2001) offer advice for establishing email exchanges, and much of the following discussion builds on their comments. They list several email activities that an instructor can use to prepare students for class:

1. Using email, students in pairs or as a group can brainstorm a potential list of subjects for a writing assignment.
2. Students can share background knowledge on a topic to prepare for a listening activity.
3. Students can prepare for a discussion by emailing short summaries of a reading assignment.
4. Students can prepare for a debate by discussing it via email and using the transcripts as a basis for their position.

In all of the preceding activities, a different medium could work better for the instructor. Brainstorming and information sharing may be more efficient using a discussion board or a wiki (see later in the chapter) so that the information is stored in a central place and is available to everyone simultaneously. Preparing for the discussion is also more easily done on a discussion board because students can produce and respond to all messages in a common thread. Instructors may prefer a discussion board or wiki because the related messages will be channeled to a common spot, and the instructor's inbox will not be overwhelmed by redundant messages (each message would include the previous communications).

At a minimum, these activities may be more effective using a listserv instead of individual pairings. A listserv sends all postings to all participants at once, thus all members of the class rather than to limited subgroups receive them. For activities 1 through 3 of the previous list, it seems advantageous for all students to get all of the information. See later in the chapter for further discussion of listservs.

The fourth activity, preparing for a debate, requires additional preparation and planning. If an instructor divides the class into two sides before the debate, it may be advantageous to use email as the medium of communication for planning with each group separately so that each side is effectively excluded from knowing the other's arguments. If, however, the instructor prefers that all students see what the other side is planning, the discussion may be more easily done using a discussion board or a listserv on which each side of the debate would join a common listserv or wiki site to further its discussion of the topic.

Bauman (2000) provides an excellent example of using email to further class discussion in an ESL course. During the first session, he gave students criminal case studies in the target language and asked them to discuss the cases and determine appropriate punishments for the offenders. Next, students were given the assignment to write an original criminal case and email it to the instructor. The instructor then emailed two cases to each student and asked them to decide the punishment before coming to class. During the following class session, students who received the same criminal cases were put in groups to work on coming to an agreement on an appropriate punishment for the crime. Gonglewski et al. (2001) note that the use of email as a preparation for class reserves valuable class time for F2F interaction.

Manteghi (1995) also describes an interesting activity in which each student writes part of a fairy tale. After reading a fairy tale in class, the instructor began a fairy tale email, "Once upon a time there was a little girl who . . . " and emailed it to the first person on an alphabetical list of members in the class. That person was to add at least one sentence and then forward the message to the next person on the list as well as to the instructor.

Bauman's (2000) and Manteghi's (1995) ideas appear more conducive to the email medium for at least two reasons. First, only individual students received and responded to any given email. With some exceptions, email works better with individual and tandem responses, whereas a discussion board lends itself to whole-class and small-group activities. Too many authors on a single email can make a conversation hard to follow because email tends to encourage shorter, more immediate responses than discussion boards or other asynchronous CMC tools (Crystal, 2001). Second, both of these activities require students to respond to the entire email. In Gonglewski et al.'s (2001) four activities (brainstorm, share information, prepare for discussion, or prepare for a debate), the students are merely required to participate in the communication and not respond to the entire message. With Bauman's (2000) and Manteghi's (1995) projects, students are required to read the entire email, evaluate its content, and build on the information to prepare for class.

Three major advantages of using email are based on its ubiquity. First, very little (if any) training is needed for students because virtually all of them have used email extensively (even if it is not their preferred mode of communication). Second, most of today's email is web-based or runs through standardized servers, which largely avoids the problem of foreign fonts discussed in previous chapters. Third, the major LMSs (Blackboard, Nicenet, Moodle, Sakai) as well as social networking sites (e.g., Facebook, Ning, Orkut) offer an email list for students in the class so that instructors need not spend time retrieving and assembling email addresses. Instructors can also organize email exchanges between individuals who are not in the same institution; these exchanges are called internet email exchanges because they extend beyond the local network.

Internet Email Exchanges

Internet email exchanges can take several forms: exchanges between classes in different institutions (class exchanges), exchanges between individuals in different institutions (tandem activities), and exchanges between individuals who may or may not be students. The advantages and challenges associated with these types of exchanges are discussed later in this section.

The most common goal of exchanges between classes in different institutions is to collaborate on a joint project that involves reading and writing in the target language, and a strong cultural component. Van Handle and Corl (1998) describe an exchange between students enrolled in intermediate German at Ohio State University and Mount Holyoke College in Massachusetts. Greenfield (2003) describes another interchange between a 10th grade ESL class in Hong Kong, and an 11th grade English class in Iowa. In both cases, groups of students worked collaboratively to discuss assigned topics and create presentations on the target culture. Their findings echo Beauvois's (1994, 1998) results that participation increased in the class discussions that followed the online exchanges. Numerous versions of the "cities project" (Meloni 1995, 1997) ask students to describe via email an aspect of their city to students who live in another city. Students research the information and produce a multicity guide depending on the number of cities involved. Van der Meij and Boersma (2002) note, however, that some tasks may facilitate an "I'll tell you my story, you tell me yours" approach to communication (i.e., the presentational mode) rather than encouraging questions and feedback (i.e., the interpersonal mode). It is therefore important to define the task in such a way that students are required to negotiate meanings, elicit elaboration, and take cultural stances, as well as solicit and provide information via email.

Other American universities have paired with foreign universities for email exchanges. Lomicka (2006) describes a collaborative project with the Lycée Paul Heroult in which a class of American students learning French was paired with a class of French students learning English. Students collaborated to produce an online magazine that focused on cultural similarities and differences. They emailed regularly to collaborate on the project. Several email tandem projects have been described in the literature on computer-assisted language learning (CALL; Greenfield, 2003; Hertel, 2003; Kern, 1996; O'Dowd, 2003; Ware & O'Dowd, 2008). More recent exchanges are not limited to email but include VoIP (Voice over IP) technology or telecollaboration whereby students collaborate orally in real time (Mullen, Appel, & Shanklin, 2009; O'Dowd & Ritter, 2006).

In general, most efficient class-to-class exchanges have several common characteristics. First, they involve considerable planning and coordination on the part of the instructors. Instructors must meet before the semester begins to determine if they have similar goals and expectations for their students. It would be unwise for instructors to collaborate if they have vastly differing opinions on how languages are learned or how frequently students should correspond, or if the parameters of participation are not explicitly presented to the students.

Second, efficient collaboration focuses on the final result of the task and not solely on the collaboration. Although many of the projects mentioned here have requirements for the number of times that students must post messages (e.g., at least one per week), the overall purpose for the exchanges is clear (e.g., to produce a city guide, an online magazine, or research paper). Students may exchange emails more frequently than the minimum to complete the task. With parameters such as these, students tend to focus on accomplishing a goal together rather than merely on completing the requirements of the assignment.

Third, email is supported by other means of communication, such as web page production, wiki management, videoconferencing, audio chat, or text chat. In some cases, the project concludes with a short visit to the partner institution. Although a simple email exchange may be beneficial on many levels, it may be insufficient with young students (i.e., digital natives) to maintain their interest for an entire semester. Additionally, online collaborative projects with cooperating institutions are not easy to establish and with the amount of effort necessary to begin the process, it is worth the extra effort to establish multiple points of contact (e.g., chat, web page production) to strengthen the intercultural relationships that form during the collaboration.

Keypals are pairs of learners (also called tandem groups) who correspond with each other via email. Keypals can be organized by an instructor who pairs his or her class with another (either in the same institution or in a cooperating institution in the target language) or by individual learners using resources available on the internet (see discussion on social networking sites later in the chapter). It can be advantageous for an instructor to organize an individual email exchange (in the L2) between classes whose students speak the same L1 because authentic communication that contains characteristics of oral speech but with the speed and reviewability of written text provides innumerable advantages concerning grammar (Kendall, 1995), proficiency (Stockwell & Harrington, 2003), social responsibility (Wong & Cohen, 1995), and cultural awareness (Liaw & Johnson, 2001).

Here are five important considerations for organizing tandem exchanges:

1. A threshold level of interaction is necessary for the exchange to be beneficial to the students (Stockwell & Harrington, 2003). Instructors should establish a clear set of guidelines and parameters from the beginning of the project. Instructors should address frequency, length, and quality of emails exchanged, and how and when the instructor should be included (cc:ed) on the email exchanges.
2. As with all technology, it is beneficial for students to begin with an icebreaker task. An icebreaker introduces them to the technology by performing a task that is below their current level of proficiency. For example, students at any level should be able to introduce themselves with little effort concerning the language. Icebreaker tasks ensure that the instructor knows that students can perform the task with the technology.
3. It is important that students realize that having a keypal is much like having friend; each has responsibilities to maintain the relationship through active participation (Wong & Cohen, 1995).
4. Relationships between tandem partners can easily be enhanced by special sessions of synchronous communication such as videoconferencing, audio chat, or text chat.
5. Instructors should remember that success in one semester does not necessarily mean that the second connection will be easier or more successful. Every email exchange offers new challenges: different student personalities, different group dynamics, different majors, and new applications of current technology (Baron, 2008; Wong & Cohen, 1995).

An intercultural exchange requires much forethought but can offer enormous advantages to the students, such as authentic interaction, student-centered learning, a written record of class participation, a social and cognitive link to other language learners, and possibly a friend in the target culture.

TASK 8.1

Create a worksheet that you could give to students who are beginning an email exchange. You should describe the following items: Which groups are included (e.g., from the same university, a partner in the target country, beginning, intermediate)? What is the theme of the exchange (e.g., festivals, stereotypes, literature)? How frequently and how much should students write? Will there be synchronous support? What will they produce from their interaction (e.g., web page, video, PowerPoint)? Make sure to provide a rubric for contributions to ensure that students meet the requirements for frequency, length, quality, and appropriateness.

Listservs

Listservs are declining in popularity. A listserv is an electronic mailing list that distributes messages to the email addresses of all those who subscribe to it. Some examples of prominent listservs include FLTeach, which is popular among high school language teachers (see web.cortland.edu/flteach/ for additional information) and LCTL, which targets less commonly taught languages (see www. carla.umn.edu/lctl/resources/listservs.html for additional information). The most prominent listservs target the professional development of teachers. Although certain listservs could be used for language learning (e.g., Causerie, listserv@uquebec.ca for French), RSS feeds or social networking sites are replacing many language learning listservs (see later in the chapter for further discussion of this topic).

   Listservs may be more suitable as an addition to a personal learning network (PLN) or specific target language courses (Business French, Greek for New Testament Scholars, etc.). Many of their functions have been taken over by discussion boards, blogs, and RSS feeds. Discussion boards are technically distinct but functionally similar to listservs and are easier to manage on a class-by-class basis. Additionally, blogs and RSS feeds have replaced many of the functions of listservs because they eliminate spam and allow moderators to stream new updates to all who are subscribed to the RSS feed. Today many of the activities of listservs are done more efficiently using other forms of technology.

TASK 8.2

Join a listserv for one week and determine if the discussion is beneficial to you. Make note of how many messages you receive and how many apply to your situation. Report to the class at least one thing you learned.
Optional resources:

ESPAN-L—for teachers of Spanish literature and language: listserv@taunivm.tau.ac.il

SLART-L—for discussion on second language acquisition: listserv@cunyvm.cuny.edu

TESL-L—for teachers of English as a second language: listserv@cunyvm.bitnet

TESLK-12—for teachers of English as a second language in K–12: listserv@cunyvm.cuny.edu

CHINA-T—for teachers of Chinese languages: listserv@vm1.spcs.umn.edu

MULTI-L—for discussion on language and multilingual education: listserv@barilvm.bitnet

FLAC-L—for discussions on foreign language across the curriculum: listserv@brown-vm.brown.edu

FLASC-L—for coordinators of foreign language programs: listserv@uci.edu

FLTEACH-L—for FL teachers in general, particularly useful for K–12: listserv@listserv.buffalo.edu

DISCUSSION BOARDS

Discussion boards are also called internet forums, bulletin boards, threaded discussions, and message boards. A number of sites offer forums or discussion boards that are free to users; however, for most instructors, the easiest and most efficient discussion boards are part of a LMS such as Moodle or Blackboard.[1] A discussion board is hierarchical and includes the following levels forum, subforum, topic, thread, and reply. A person begins a discussion (thread) by making an initial post. Students respond to the post (called a reply), thereby creating a list of responses in chronological order. Instructors can begin new discussions at any point by simply creating a new thread.

The discussion board moderator (usually the instructor or teaching assistant [TA]) can set options on the discussion board to limit access, restrict usage, or allow anonymity. For example, access to posts on a certain topic can be limited to the beginning and ending dates of the week, thus focusing the discussion and providing a conclusion. The use of the board to post and to read can be restricted to students in a given course; this type of restriction helps prevent students from displaying private work in the public sphere. Anonymity (a benefit of online communication noted by Vonderwell [2003]) can be permitted, or instructors can require that the author attach his or her name to any posting on the discussion board. The options available are as varied as the number of discussion board applications available. Many discussion boards available as part of a LMS offer the ability to count the number and frequency of postings in order to facilitate grading based on quantity of postings.

Like many of the technologies described in this chapter, no expensive software is necessary because discussion boards are accessible through any internet browser. Bikowski and Kessler (2002) claim that a discussion board allows learners "to take control of their own learning in a supportive and collaborative environment, and encourages them to reflect on how they accomplish tasks. Together, these experiences lead to increased motivation and greater achievement" (p. 28). When used consistently as an anchor in the course and not as an add-on, discussion boards can encourage group cohesion and collaboration.

Another major advantage of most discussion board systems today is that they allow for attachments such as audio, video, images, or multimedia such as PowerPoint slide shows and Flash animations. A few discussion boards are mainly voice rather than text (e.g., VoiceThread.com, VoxoPop.com). In undergraduate classes, discussion boards enable learners to complete cooperative tasks. On the graduate level, students can post their final papers as an optional activity. They may see the advantages of knowing what others are

---

[1]There are several discussion board services beyond the typical LMS such as Blackboard (Blackboard. com), Nicenet (NiceNet.org), and Moodle (Moodle.com). It is best to look at several services before adopting one for class. ExcoBoard.com and HostBoard.com are possible alternatives to an entire LMS. Nonetheless, unless there is a specific reason for choosing a discussion board outside of a LMS, most instructors would be content with the discussion board resource available in a LMS, even if only the discussion board feature is used.

doing or receiving peer feedback on their work. The use of a discussion board can also provide models of writing to students in a class.

Specific considerations and preparations for using discussion boards can make a difference for student participation. When students are clear on the parameters of the task, they can focus on doing the task content rather than trying to figure out how to do the task. Instructors should clearly delineate the responsibilities of the students, monitor their performance closely for the first few weeks, and provide a frequently asked questions (FAQs) area online where students can find and post answers to their questions.

Clarifying the Task

Clear guidelines are needed as to frequency, length, and quality of each posting. It may be ineffective to simply request that students participate and write something every week. Students may be more willing to participate when they know exactly when they need to post (e.g., by 5:00 pm on Friday). The length of the posting is also important and minimums can be set at the word level (e.g., 150 words) or phrase level (e.g., at least 10 phrases). The quality of the posting is generally improved if instructors design recursive tasks. A recursive task requires students to read and respond to the postings of others. Instructors may find that unless the task requires the students to respond to others' comments, students will just post their own messages and not necessarily read what others have posted. The following is an example of a recursive task: The instructor asks students to write five sentences describing themselves (e.g., I am tall, I am from Virginia, I like chocolate, etc.). As a follow-up, students are required to read the postings and find the two people in the class who are most like them and say why. The second posting requires all students to read all of the postings, understand them, evaluate them, and reply to them. As a follow-up to the second posting (who is most like you), students could be asked to find two students who are most unlike them. By making the task clear and recursive, students have the opportunity to focus on the language and content and not on the technology or number of words.

Monitoring

Instructors need to monitor students in the initial stages of the task to ensure that they are all participating equally and appropriately. The instructor's activity in the discussion board may also help set the tone and keep students on task, as well as model appropriate comments and accurate structures. Once the instructor has verified that student participation is appropriate, adequate, and meaningful, students can often continue on task without the instructor's constant encouragement. Nevertheless, it is important that instructors check the discussion weekly even if they decide not to make comments.

As with all technology, it is important that the students be given the opportunity to begin with an icebreaker task that does not require significant language skill and simply allows the instructor to gauge which students are capable of dealing with the technology. The most common icebreaker task with discussion boards is to have students introduce themselves in a few short sentences. Most students can accomplish this task with minimal effort. (e.g., "My name is Sam. I like to eat pizza.")

TASK 8.3

Design a series of three prompts that you could use with your classes. Begin by creating an icebreaker task that ensures that everyone is familiar with the parameters of the activity (both the technical aspects and the social aspects). Next, design an activity that requires all students to post and read others' posts. Finally, design an activity that ensures that all students have read others' posts and are able to respond in a synthetic or antithetic manner (e.g., "I agree or disagree with X . . ." "I'm like or unlike X . . . "). This type of activity is particularly useful if you teach a literature course.

FAQs

Instructors may find it useful to maintain a separate forum for FAQs. Students often have questions that crop up repeatedly, and it can save the instructor some time if students can find answers on the discussion board. These questions can be technical (How do you put a smiley face in your text?), academic (How long is the final paper?), or social (When is the instructor's birthday?). The FAQs can also be a resource for external links where students can find more information about a given topic.

An important characteristic of discussion boards is that they advance or prolong the conversation that occurs in class. For the most part, however, students are theoretically still writing for their peers. The writing is authentic but the audience is limited to the classroom. For students to begin addressing a larger audience, a blog may provide adequate exposure to the internet as a whole.

MICROPUBLISHING

Micropublishing involves students creating a text for consumption on the web. We talked about some forms of micropublishing in Chapters 1–3. Uploaded written documents, photos, PowerPoint presentations, web page production, and blogging are forms of micropublishing. This section will not revisit PowerPoint and web page production, but rather it will explore blogs, microblogs, RSS feeds, and podcasts.

Blogs

A blog (short for "weblog") is an online journal. Most reports indicate that blogs are personal in nature (Winn, 2009). A blogging services allows individuals to create reverse chronologically structured web pages with little effort or technical knowledge. The writer, or blogger, enters information in an online form and submits it. The server formats the text using templates and adds the new text to the home page. Blogs differ from discussion boards in that only authors may post on the site. They offer the opportunity for an individual to keep a journal online and contribute to it daily (i.e., blogging). Originally, a single author maintained a blog, but there is now a trend toward collaboration, with multiple authors posting to a blog. This format resembles a discussion forum by a limited number of authors. Blogs began in the early 1990s but did not gain popularity until after the turn of the century. Blogging has become an important source of information, revenue, political opinions, and social networking.

Blogging offers many advantages to foreign language instruction, such as allowing students to write journals without having to submit them on a weekly basis. One problem with paper journals is that students have to turn them in and instructors have to respond and then return them to the students. If instructors collect journals weekly (e.g., on Friday), students are without their journals for the weekend, which for most of them is the most interesting part of the week. With blogs, instructors can visit students' blogs and make comments at their convenience. Students can also respond to instructor comments, make changes to previous posts, or make new posts without ever relinquishing their journal.

Blogging may have legal ramifications because it requires students to work in the public sphere. Although many students already maintain blogs to record their daily activities and communicate with friends, publishing their schoolwork may create censorship and privacy concerns with parents, administrators, lawmakers, and others. Instructors should be aware of the issues associated with their particular context.

Teachers, however, can use a blog for their entire course with relatively little time investment. They can specify due dates and parameters for homework with links to resources and reminders of upcoming events. Instructors can also use a blog to provide notes on what happened in class on a specific date. For some classes, instructors may decide to add students or teaching assistants to the blogging list to make additional comments about what happened in class. An instructor's blog generates easily accessible course information. It also provides a written record so that students can review materials or make up for missed days. Likewise, prospective students can refer to the blog to determine course content or as a measure of what is expected. Substitute teachers

TASK 8.4

Join a blog and keep a daily journal for the next week. Try to "blog your course" as described previously. Included details such as how long some activities took and reactions to some of the activities.

The most prominent sites are listed here, but you can find many other sites by searching the internet for *free blogs*:

www.blogspot.com

www.livejournal.com

www.typepad.com

classblogmeister.com

can also refer to the blog for an accurate summary of what has been covered. Administrators may also find this application useful because it gives them a quick view of the activity of any given course.

Microblogs

Blog content is generally posted from a computer, but more services are allowing content to be posted from email accounts and mobile devices. Because many mobile devices do not lend themselves to extended discourse, users who post from them tend to prefer microblogging to blogging. Microblogging is the posting of short texts (fewer than 200 characters), video, audio, or pictures and is in many cases the same as Twitter (twitter.com), although microblogging takes other forms besides Twitter (e.g., tumblr.com—note that sites designed for mobile devices generally do not have "www" in the URL). Microblogging frequently takes the form of status updates in social networking sites such as Facebook, LinkedIn, or Orkut, on which members post updates of what they are doing so that friends are aware of their activities (see the discussion of social networking sites later in the chapter). The usefulness of these sites to foreign language education is that students can focus on novice-level discourse without seeming artificial. Updates are expected to be short, often bulleted (list form), and frequently in the present tense. As such, even novice learners are able to post without feeling overwhelmed.

Microblogging, specifically Twitter, can be useful for teachers not only for professional development purposes as mentioned in Chapter 6, but also for instruction. Twitter is an excellent way to keep in touch, share ideas, and create a learning environment that encourages students to think about the course more frequently than they would otherwise. Twitter.com and Tumblr.com are excellent tools: They are free; they require minimal setup; and unlike other forms of CMC, learners feel no obligation to write more than 144 characters. Additionally, Moodle has a Twitter add-in that allows direct access to Twitter, with other LMSs sure to follow.

General preparation for microblogging activities includes prewriting, deciding on a theme, and providing assessment rubrics for student participation and presentation. Prewriting activities include reading microblogs (or subscribing to them) to familiarize students with the genre. Prewriting also includes subscribing to the feeds from everyone else in the class (called *following* on Twitter). Once students are ready to begin writing, they need to identify an overarching theme for their posts for the class: Will they be simple status updates or comments about the theme of the chapters (so they change regularly), food, sports, public transportation, and so on? Will they focus on specific assignments such as commenting on films, plays, or conferences? Having a concrete theme enables students to focus their attention and language skills on more coherent conversation than is characteristic of microblogs.

Upon presentation of the theme, instructors should take time in class to provide appropriate models of what is expected. Microblogs began as stream-of-consciousness publications but have since evolved to a more focused form albeit with regular tangents. Therefore, finding the most authentic tasks can be difficult if appropriate models of acceptable posts are not provided. Microblogs are often used for public relations, marketing, or social purposes. People post what they are doing, experiencing, or thinking, so effective microblogging tasks aim to emulate these purposes. For example, a literature course may use micro-blogging to encourage students to explore their attitudes concerning characters in the text. The prompt might include instructions such as "Give your opinion of Madame Bovary and describe three actions to justify what you think of her." Students make multiple posts with short messages to complete the task. The length of microblog posts helps alleviate the feeling of the need to formulating a long, supported essay that students might have using a discussion board. For a culture course, instructions might include something such as "Identify prod-ucts or practices from various Hispanic countries that demonstrate the value given to healthy eating." Students can make several posts of products or prod-ucts that lead to the same perspective of the culture. Language classes focusing on persuasive writing could simply reply to a teacher's post such as "Which movie should I go see this weekend?" Finally, posts are often expected on a daily basis (as opposed to a weekly basis as with blogs) and occur throughout the semester. Microblogging is an activity for the course (i.e., theme based) and not an exercise for a week (i.e., not time based or grammar based).

As with any assignment, final evaluation rubrics encourage focus and en-able student self-assessment (see Chapter 10 for a discussion of rubrics). A ru-bric that gives 50% of the assessment to the instructor and 50% to the student/microblogger may encourage effective self-assessment. With a well-articulated rubric, students tend to rate themselves appropriately, and the instructor's com-ments serve to validate what the student already believes. Assessment criteria for microblogging activities can include frequency (e.g., I posted every day or more frequently), focus (e.g., I usually posted on topic), content (e.g., my comments were interesting, thoughtful, entertaining, and related to others' com-ments), and accuracy (e.g., my grammar was good and I used culturally cor-rect abbreviations). Regular self-assessment has numerous benefits; it promotes learner autonomy (Kjisik, Voller, Aoki, & Nakata, 2009), student achievement, (Andrade & Valtcheva, 2009) and self-confidence (Butler & Lee, 2010).

Microblogs and blogs generally emphasize texts and links, but they can include any number of media including audio, video, and multimedia presen-tations. Blogs that focus solely on video or audio are known as vlogs and vodcasts or audioblogs and podcasts, respectively.

TASK 8.5

Open an account with a microblogging service (e.g., Twitter.com, Tumblr.com). Spend a week microblogging at least twice a day on any ideas for activities you would like to do in your class (including technology, classroom management, parties, etc.). After a week, decide on an activity that you would like to do with your students using a microblog. Identify the frequency and the theme, and write a rubric for assessment that you could give to them.

TASK 8.6

Identify three target language news sites that may be useful to you as an instructor (e.g., Zeit.de, ElPais.com, France24.com) and subscribe to the RSS feeds. After a week determine their usefulness to you as an instructor and unsubscribe from those that are not helpful.

RSS Feeds

RSS[2] feeds are a way of subscribing to various blogs, podcasts, vodcasts, wikis, or any other regularly updated information on the web regardless of whether it is text, audio, video, or multimedia. The advantage of subscribing to an RSS feed is that the user no longer needs to visit the site to keep abreast of discussion happening on the internet. The user generally subscribes to a site using an

RSS feed that is shown by an orange button XML or 🔳. When new documents are uploaded from the parent site (e.g., CNN.com, NPR.com, Blogger.com, Digg.com, News.Yahoo.com), they appear in the subscriber's feed aggregator. A feed aggregator can be an online service such as bloglines (www.bloglines. com), Google reader (www.google.com), or Yahoo! (my.yahoo.com). Feed aggregators are often wrapped into other programs that access the internet, such as a mail client (Microsoft's Outlook, Mozilla's Thunderbird), a digital entertainment library (Apple's iTunes, GPL's Juice), or—most conveniently—placed right in your internet browser (Flock). Subscribing to a feed depends on which feed

aggregator you use; it is often sufficient to click on the button (🔳) in your web browser to subscribe to a feed. Simply go to your favorite news magazine (e.g., Lemonde.fr, Zeit.de, ElPais.com), look for the RSS button, and click on it to add the link to the content you want to read. Once you have subscribed to an RSS feed, new headlines will appear in your reader each time they are posted by the parent site. Subscription to news or culture sites may be of use to instructors who are constantly seeking updated cultural information for their students.

Vodcasts and Podcasts

Podcasting has become a prominent activity among language classes. The term *podcasting* comes from a blend of "broadcasting" and "iPod." The popularity of podcasting in higher education is due, in part, to the ubiquity of the iPod, as well as to the simplicity of production and distribution of the medium. Users download audio feeds (called podcasts) using a feed aggregator such as iTunes (iTunes.com), Doppler (DopplerRadio.net), or Juice (JuiceReceiver. sourceforge.net) to play them on their iPod or other MP3 player (although the majority of users listen to podcasts from a computer). The term *vodcasting* is a

---

[2]RSS stands for really simple syndication and is a summary of the content of a text, audio, or video file on the internet.

combination of "video" and "podcasting" and refers to video feeds rather than audio feeds. For the purpose of this section, podcasting will be used to refer to both video and audio files stored on the web. Students can use podcasting two ways in the classroom: as subscribers or as producers. As subscribers, language learners can select their favorite audio feeds to practice listening and gain cultural knowledge. Instructors can also assign specific feeds as homework. As producers, students can practice speaking, hone pronunciation skills, focus on content, and show off their creativity (DuBravac, Gonglewski, & Angell, 2008).

PODCAST SUBSCRIBERS   The audio that users download can come from an audio blog or an RSS feed from a well-known radio station such as the BBC, NPR, Deutche-welle, or RFI. Students can also use a podcast directory to find foreign language podcasts. It is best to use a foreign language podcast directory, or many of the results will be "how to learn the language" or "phrase of the day" podcasts. Although these may be useful, they are not generally authentic communication because they do not target native speakers of the language.

These types of feeds may be particularly useful if students are in need of listening comprehension activities. Although it is possible for instructors to listen to the podcast ahead of time and create an accompanying worksheet activity, instructors may decide to use an approach that enables students to follow their own interests in the target language. Students can find their own podcasts and instructors can ask simple questions or give tasks that would apply to almost any podcast: What is the main idea? What is the source? List 15 cognates that you hear. Write a short summary. Find a written news story at one of the online newspapers, and so on.[3]

Most podcasts are stored on the server for a minimum of seven days but are often removed to preserve server space. This removal can be frustrating to instructors who spend time creating specific activities to accompany a certain podcast that is no longer available when assigned to students. Instructors would benefit therefore from formulating more general questions that can be discussed at greater length and in more depth on a discussion board, blog, or via email. This method allows learners to choose podcasts and control the topic, listen for information (rather than just practice), listen for entertainment, and determine when to begin and end the listening activity. These opportunities for learner-driven activity may not be available if instructors determine the content, but learner control may improve motivation among learners.

As with any text, audio, or video, it is recommended that students have pre-reading, reading, and post-reading tasks. These pre-reading or pre-listening tasks should activate appropriate background knowledge and vocabulary which can be done using quizzes, short answer questions, watching without the sound

---

[3]Target language podcasts that are comprehensible to beginning and intermediate learners may be difficult to identify. Podspider.net offers lists of podcasts in French, German, and English. There are also lists of Spanish podcasts (Podcastellano.com) as well as the less commonly taught languages (Podomatic.com).

(for vodcasts), images, or brainstorming, for example. The main purpose of the pre-listening task is to enable students to predict content and anticipate what they might hear, thus allowing them to verify their predictions rather than de-cipher the message in real time. Many podcast feeds are accompanied by titles, taglines, and synopses. The accompanying data may facilitate the pre-listening activity (What is the source? Who are the target listeners?).

The listening activities should focus on the actual listening task such as scanning for information (e.g., List the cognates you hear. Name three interest-ing points that you hear.), skimming for main ideas and cultural concepts (e.g., What would be another title for this podcast?), and checking for comprehension (e.g., What two things did you learn from this podcast? Write two questions you still have about this podcast).

Finally, the post-listening activities build on what students learned from the listening activity and are facilitated through technology because students can be asked to perform a number of different tasks using technology. For ex-ample, students can post comments on the discussion board of the podcast (if one exists), email the author for additional comments, or respond by creating their own podcast.

PODCAST PRODUCERS   Most students are able to produce a podcast without significant effort. Producing their own podcast is an excellent activity to pro-mote student self-assessment because students tend to record themselves sev-eral times before being satisfied with their podcast. To structure a podcasting project, instructors need only three items: a concept, equipment, and a method of assessment.

The concept behind a podcasting project is central to its success because it will provide structure, promote creativity, and establish an audience for the podcast. It is important to remember that a podcast project is not a single audio file on the internet. As seen in the previous section, podcasts are theme-based, episodic audio recordings to which individuals subscribe. Although many in-structors have chosen to use podcast equipment to record their students, these single audio files are neither episodic nor interesting to other listeners. Not many of us would subscribe to a podcast of individuals describing their fami-lies, for example. Thus, the concept ought to be episodic, theme based, avail-able to all, and interesting.

Instructors who wish to use audio for a single, nonepisodic activity should consider an audio dropbox (clear.msu.edu/teaching/online/ria/audioDropbox) rather than a podcast format. An audio dropbox allows students to record their sample online and post it in a location where instructors can access the audio files for their course. This approach allows for more privacy and easier grading of all of the assignments. For video tasks that are not vodcasts, instructors can use a video repository such as YouTube.com or TeacherTube.com.

The equipment necessary to record a podcast is minimal, and the type of platform used for podcasting will determine the materials needed. Generally, a connection to the internet, a microphone, and a home site where the pod-casts will be posted are sufficient. Most podcasting home sites are free, and many blogging sites also offer free audioblogging. Vodcasts can happen easily through YouTube.com. Instructors should visit several sites and examine the ease of posting, reading, and reacting to podcasts, as many options are available.[4]

The assessment for a podcasting project should include a rubric so that students understand how each episode will be evaluated. Students often profit more from a podcasting project if they know they will receive feedback from several sources: peers, the instructor, and possibly the general online public.

When assigning a podcast project, instructors may want to consider the following tips and hints:

1. ***Articulate the entire activity.*** Both students and instructors can benefit by identifying parameters and the end goal for the project. Some initial questions to ask include the following: How many episodes of the podcast will there be? How will each subsequent podcast relate to the previous one (i.e., How will they be episodic?)? How will each podcast be assessed? When is each podcast due? What do students do as they listen to podcasts (Rate them? Ask follow-up questions? Draw a picture? Suggest a title?)? It is important to establish early that everyone in class is responsible for evaluating all of the podcasts. As usual, student evaluation is facilitated by providing a rubric or creating one with the students.

2. ***Do the initial recording in class.*** Even though many students may already be familiar with digital recording technology and most could figure it out without difficulty, it is important to conduct the first recording in an environment where immediate help is available and where the instructor can be reassured that all individuals are capable of completing the task.

3. ***Create the motivation for others in the class to listen to each podcast.*** The goal to have all students listen to each podcast is more easily achieved if the episodes are interesting to others. It is unlikely that students would be as motivated to listen to podcasts entitled "Introduce yourself" as they would to one entitled "The school gossip line," for example. In addition, the podcasts generally include talk and music shows, interviews, storytelling, tutorials, commentaries, and sportscasts, but instructors should guide students toward types of podcasts that will promote creativity, recruit subscribers, and solicit feedback.

4. ***Begin by producing podcasts and then to listening to foreign language podcasts.*** Contrary to what may be intuitive—listen first, then produce—it may be easier to have students produce podcasts first and then listen to others for comprehension purposes. There are two

---

[4]Many popular sites include music, whereas others target voice podcasting and others target videos. Some sites allow you to make a podcast using a telephone or mobile device (Cinch.fm, Yodio.com, Ipadio.com), some provide their own proprietary recording software (AudioBoo.fm), and others allow you to upload only content that you have produced on your own (YouTube.com). Nearly every site that provides hosting for podcast content also provides a tutorial on how to use the site. The tutorial is a great place to start for instructors who are planning on having students produce their own content.

significant reasons to attempt a production project before a comprehension project. First, although students may have a schema for how a podcast is done, the structure and variability do not become apparent until students are asked to produce podcasts of their own. Second, much of the vocabulary they would need to comprehend a podcast would be available to them at a slower rate in student-made podcasts, thus facilitating the eventual reception of native speaker podcasts.

Podcasting has been one of the fastest growing technologies for language instruction in recent years and will likely continue to be used in language classes with an accompanying support such as a discussion board, blog, or wiki.

TASK 8.7

Look at the ideas for podcasts listed here and identify which would be the most interesting for students. Choose one of the listed activities or create your own and design the accompanying episodes of the series. Be sure to identify the goal for the project, the role of peer evaluation, and the rubric for assessing each podcast in the series.

1. **Music show.** Individuals or groups research and present music from their language around the world in a class radio show. In each podcast, a new performer, music type, country, or band is featured.
2. **Mini-biographies.** Students interview and create biographies for local heroes or favorite teachers.
3. **Advice line.** The class solicits questions in the foreign language from other students, and each week one question is answered in a creative way.
4. **Game show.** Students design a game show with unique rules (or a twist on the old rules), and each week bring new contestants on board (use NPR game shows as a model).
5. **Community roots projects.** Students reach out to local ethnic and language heritage resources in the community or school and produce a weekly broadcast featuring a person or one aspect of that community's culture (e.g., music, sports).

WIKIS AND SOCIAL NETWORKING SITES

Wiki technology has boomed in the past several years. Like a blog, a wiki is a web site that one can edit with no knowledge of HTML. Unlike a blog, anyone can edit a wiki. One of the most prominent wiki-based sites is Wikipedia (www.wikipedia.com), which offers encyclopedia entries that are written by individuals around the world. The term *wiki* comes from the Hawaiian word *Wikiwiki* ("quick"). There are numerous other wiki sites but none that compares in size to Wikipedia. For classroom purposes, Blackboard and Moodle offer wiki pages. Other sites that are free to educators include WikiSpaces.com and PBWorks.com.

Wiki technology has provided the easiest method for collaborative writing of all of the technologies mentioned in this chapter. The fact that anyone can add, delete, or modify any part of the wiki means that the writing is driven by peer contributions and corrections. Students can participate in the creation of knowledge as a web site rather than as a final paper or presentation. Literacy for a wiki extends beyond the linear structure posited in traditional academia.

Although students may be familiar with the concept of a wiki through their experiences with Wikipedia, many of them may not be willing to jump right into the activity of web site creation without significant guidance and support. The following are suggestion for enabling students to perform better in class wiki activities:

1. Provide an icebreaker task with multiple steps, such as (a) edit an assigned page, (b) add to or edit a page that someone else created, and (c) add a link.
2. Establish a clear set of guidelines concerning participation on a wiki. A wiki is a collaborative space and should be treated more like a participation activity than an assignment. It is also important to have a clear goal for students to accomplish on the wiki that goes well beyond frequency of postings. This is not to say that frequent and regular posting is not important; for courses that meet only once a week, it may be feasible and important to have students post more frequently than once a week.
3. The instructor must model most of the activity that occurs in the classroom. For example, the wiki should start with several pages already established but not complete. A links page should contain at least one link. A page for frequently asked questions should be started with some key questions answered. Students tend to be slow to work on a blank wiki with no direction. It should be clear from the onset that there are important pieces of the wiki that are missing.
4. Instructors should check the wiki often and encourage students to post early and frequently. During the first weeks of the course, the instructor should remind students to post and/or modify the posts of others according to the needs of the courses. As with email exchanges, if students do not have enough contact with the wiki, they will see it as busy work rather than a productive part of the course.
5. Participation works best when students have a precise task to accomplish. The best types of tasks are cooperative and require significant editing. For example, brainstorming can be productive because students can simply add to a list. Instructors can also assign a debate topic that students can write about online before the class. This permits students to have an adequate understanding of the issues before the class begins, therefore saving important class time. With all of these tasks, it is important to specify the quantity of writing required.

It is now relatively easy to use a wiki for educational purposes because several sites offer excellent support and free hosting (e.g., PBWiki.com, WikiSpaces.com). These services make a convenient portal for wiki production because instructors can choose their own domain (e.g., *MyClass*.PBWiki.com), and instructors can decide who has access to read, edit, or create new pages. This level of security and flexibility has quelled many concerns related to exhibiting students' work in the public sphere. Whereas those who embrace Web 2.0 concepts have difficulty understanding why anyone's work should not be shared (particularly because no public assessment is available for each student), others have voiced concerns related to forcing children or students to place their work in the public sphere. Publicly hosted wikis also control for wiki spam or floods (malicious overwriting of wiki pages with links or other unrelated and undesirable content) by filtering out IP addresses that have been reported as spammers. Instructors need not worry about replacing data, maintaining order, and controlling unwanted contributors; they can instead focus on using the technology to further the needs of the class.

Social networking sites include Facebook.com, LinkedIn.com, Flickr.com, Vimeo.com, and Ning.com. These sites are created and maintained by individuals in a social group. A number of activities enable the strengthening of social bonds, for example, updates, photos, messages, virtual gifts, and activities. At the university level, a LMS tends to take care of many of the functions that would be available in a social networking site. Nonetheless, for ease of use, teachers who are active on their Facebook accounts may decide to open a fan site for their course. A number of researchers (Harrison & Thomas, 2009; Redecker, Ala-Mutka, & Punie, 2010; Thomas, 2009) argue that the use of social networking sites can promote lifelong learning of the target language as stated in Standard 5.2 of the National Standards for Foreign Language learning mentioned in Chapter 6, because the aim of these sites is to promote community around a specific cause. The tasks for a social networking site are similar to those mentioned earlier for discussion boards, microblogging, and wikis. It is not recommended that teachers use their personal accounts to participate in the activity. Instructors who create an alternate account for class purposes tend to avoid issues with their students by maintaining distance and thereby promoting professionalism. Additionally, social networking sites work better over a longer period of time (e.g., for majors in the university, for high school classes).

In short, the tools available for asynchronous CMC are so numerous that it is not possible or advisable to attempt to include all of them, particularly in a given semester. Instructors should evaluate the activities they would like to attempt and then identify the appropriate form of asynchronous CMC to accomplish that task. The general rules for using asynchronous CMC that have been repeated throughout this chapter follow:

- Envision the entire project and articulate the beginning, middle, and end by providing an assessment rubric to the students.
- Provide a model or icebreaker task.
- Monitor closely at the beginning of the activity to ensure comprehension.
- Make sure that the task or activity fits the technology chosen.

As instructors follow these basic guidelines, asynchronous activities become much more manageable and rewarding for the entire class.

TECHNICAL CONSIDERATIONS

One final point that instructors may consider teaching is netiquette. As mentioned briefly in previous chapters, the term *netiquette* is a blend of "internet" and "etiquette"; it refers to how individuals should behave online. The need for training in netiquette may arise because newbies (those new to the internet) or n00bs (those who disrespect the rules) send email or post items that are inappropriate for a certain forum. They may be inappropriate because of content, manner of writing (e.g., all caps is considered yelling), or simple inconsistency with the established discourse structure of the forum. Several sites have established guidelines to help newbies become responsible netizens (those experienced with the internet), such as www.NetManners.com. Users can find any number of sites by entering the word in a search engine. Some important hints for netiquette include thinking before you post or send, rereading for offensive language, using emoticons, and so forth.

Digital natives, those who grew up with social networking sites, tend to have a good sense of what is acceptable and what is not. However, it may still be worthwhile to review a couple of the general rules of conduct. This review may be done most efficiently as a class, and the rules are easily assembled on one of the technologies mentioned earlier such as a discussion board or wiki.

Practical Work

1. Blogging
   Create a blog or microblog. Here are some suggested sites:
   - www.blogger.com
   - www.typepad.com
   - www.bravenet.com
   - www.wordsmith.com
   - www.twitter.com
   - www.tumblr.com

   Keep a blog regularly for the rest of the semester by writing in it once a day. You should exploit the power of your blog by (a) creating links from your team members' blogs to your own; (b) making comments on your students' blogs; and (c) posting in various media such as text, hypertext, audio, and video.

2. Using a wiki
   Set up an account with PBWiki.com or WikiSpaces.com. Identify a presentation activity that you could do with your class. Themes could include important historical sites throughout Germany, Chinese festivals, French cheeses, or Spanish lexical variants. Design at least four pages to get your class started and provide a model. The pages should include at a minimum the welcome page, an FAQ page, a model page, and a partially completed link page.

3. Podcasting
   Make a podcast targeting other instructors learning about technology. This can be an individual project or you can team up with others in the class. Begin in the first podcast to introduce yourself (or group) and identify the subjects to be treated in the subsequent podcasts (e.g., wikis, blogs, chat, blogs). Make a minimum of four podcasts

(these can and should be relatively short to begin with, less than 10 minutes). Here are some suggested sites for recording yourself:
- www.podbean.com
- www.mypodcast.com
- www.ipadio.com
- www.podomatic.com
- www.yodio.com

4. Social networking sites
   Set up an account on ITalki.com and note the purpose, flexibility, and navigability of the site. Join a group and participate for at least two weeks. Other social networking sites include LinkedIn.com (search groups for education or language), Ning.com, and Facebook.

Suggestions for Further Reading

Blake, R. (2008). *Brave new digital classroom: Technology and foreign language learning*. Washington, DC: Georgetown University Press.

Clarke, A. (2008*). E-learning skills,* 2nd ed. New York: Palgrave Macmillan.

Ducate, L., & Arnold, N. (Eds.). (2006). *Calling on CALL: From theory and research to new directions in foreign language teaching*. San Marcos, TX: CALICO.

Oxford R., & Oxford, J. (2009). *Second language teaching and learning in the net generation*. Honolulu, HI: National Foreign Language Resource Center.

Pallof, R. M., & Pratt, K. (2007). *Building online learning communities: Effective strategies for the virtual classroom*. San Francisco: Jossey-Bass.

Richardson, W. (2009). *Blogs, wikis, podcasts, and other powerful web tools for classrooms*. Thousand Oaks, CA: Corwin Press.

CHAPTER 9

Computer-Based Language Testing

OVERVIEW

Computers have been used for many years for testing purposes, such as managing item banks, scoring responses, and analyzing and storing responses (Baker, 1989). Computer-assisted language testing (CALT), also known as computer-based testing (CBT), received a boost in the late 1990s when the Educational Testing Service (ETS) began offering the TOEFL, a test of language proficiency, in a computer-based format. A number of books have been published on computers and testing (e.g., Chapelle, 2001; Chapelle & Douglas, 2006), but it is usually researchers who pass information on assessment to practitioners. Social, cultural, or administrative conventions require all teachers to test, but not all teachers consider themselves assessment specialists. In fact, a look at several methodology books for language teachers reveals three or more chapters dedicated to teaching and one, if any, dedicated to assessing language skills (see Brandl, 2008; Curtain & Dahlberg, 2010; Hall, 2001; Horwitz, 2008; Omaggio-Hadley, 2001; Shrum & Glisan, 2010). This chapter begins with a discussion of the purpose of testing, which then leads to a comparison of CALT and paper-and-pencil tests.

This chapter examines several CBT tools for instructor-created exercises, quizzes, and tests, notwithstanding their limitations, as well as several commercially available alternatives. Because CALT is a rapidly developing field, we also discuss its future and some considerations for instructors aiming to integrate it into the language curriculum.

PURPOSE OF TESTING

Assessment is generally defined as information gathering, but unless the purpose to which the information will be put is understood, it does not prove to be a useful endeavor. Klapper (2005) indicates six purposes for language testing: aptitude, placement, diagnosis, progress, achievement, and proficiency. Identifying a test's purpose is essential to determine whether or not the test is valid. Validity refers to whether or not a test actually measures what it says it measures, is a central concern for psychometrics, and will be discussed later. First, however, the question is why should students take a language test: To see if they are good at language? To see what language skills they lack? To show their learning? Without identifying the purpose of a test, it is impossible to determine if it is a good test. This section discusses the six purposes outlined by Klapper (2005).

Aptitude tests are designed to identify a student's ability to learn a language. Language aptitude is considerably complex and controversial because of the need for a model of both the language that is learned and the process of acquiring a language. As seen in Chapter 4, researchers have yet to agree on a well-articulated model of transition and state theories. The modeling of the learning process often indicates that aptitude tests are generally valid only for the program into which students will be sent. For example, the Defense Language Aptitude Battery (DLAB) tests language aptitude for those in the military to determine if they qualify for the Defense Language Institute (DLI). The DLAB measures phonetic awareness and syntactic and morphologic skills and attempts to predict the likelihood of success for those who enter the DLI to learn the language assigned to them. Theoretically, then, the DLAB would be valid for the teaching methodologies used at the DLI (because its goal is to predict future success at that institution); if the teaching methodologies used at the DLI change, then the characteristics of the DLAB should change also, because of the relationship among teaching methodology, language learning success, and items on the test.

According to Carroll and Sapon (2002), the Modern Language Aptitude Test (MLAT) or the Computer-Based MLAT (CB-MLAT) can be used to predict how well a candidate will perform relative to other individuals in a particular time frame (generally intensive) under specific conditions (generally formal instruction). The DLAB and the MLAT are designed for adults. A number of other tests have been created for children, such as the Pimsleur Language Aptitude Battery for students in grades 7 to 12 and the MLAT-Elementary for children in grades 3 to 6.[1] It is important to remember that tests of academic language aptitude are of limited usefulness; they are inherently bound to the context of the learning. For example, aptitude tests rarely measure attitude or motivation, which are key elements in teaching and learning second languages (Dörnyei, & Ushioda, 2011), but instead focus on a limited set of skills (e.g., verbal memory, grammatical sensitivity) to help predict the learning that can occur under specific environments with particular teaching approaches.

---

[1]See Second Language Testing, Inc., for more information at http://www.2lti.com.

Placement tests are designed to determine where in a particular curriculum students should begin so that they enroll in the appropriate course or level. Klapper (2005) states that "one would expect the test material to be related to the curriculum or syllabus of the various levels" (p. 91). Many institutions create their own placement tests—for example, the final exam for French II may also serve as a placement test to determine whether incoming students belong in French II or French III. Others may rely on instructors or program directors to interview incoming students to place them into the appropriate level. However, the amount of time required for these interviews is significant, and some program directors (particularly in Spanish, because of typical high enrollments) can spend many hours each semester interviewing new students (or even a sampling of those students). The time requirements for placing students appropriately have prompted many language program directors to seek more efficient methods. One widely used computer-based placement test in the United States is the Computer-Assisted Placement Exam (CAPE) from Brigham Young University (BYU). The CAPE series helps place students in the first three semesters of college-level study and is offered in Chinese, English as a Second Language (ESL), French, German, Russian, and Spanish. After completing the exam, students receive a score that is compared to a placement chart listing the cutoff scores for each semester of study. A computerized placement test such as the CAPE has numerous advantages for program directors (e.g., time, reliability). The significant drawback with the CAPE is that it does not consider the various syllabi of the subscribing institutions. Students receive a performance level score and although BYU does offer its own institutional cutoff scores, program directors from other institutions must still determine what that score means for their particular context. In short, the program directors are still responsible for student placement, but a computerized version of the test provides standardized, easily collectable data that students can access on their own.

Diagnostic tests pinpoint strengths and weaknesses of a learner's developing linguistic system so that instructors and tutors can plan appropriate activities for advancement or remedial purposes. The most widely available test that best resembles a computer-based diagnostic test is the DIALANG system (DIALANG, 2002). DIALANG uses both self-assessment and computer-adaptive assessment (see the discussion below on reliability) to test their reading, writing, listening, grammar, and vocabulary skills in 14 languages. DIALANG enables test takers to identify their language ability relative to the European Common Framework of Reference (CEFR), a document used to set standards for successive stages of language learning (Gouiller, 2007). Placement tests and diagnostic tests differ in their goals. Placement tests help student select the appropriate course level; diagnostic tests identify linguistic gaps and can be used by instructors (to know what to teach) or by learners (to know what to study). Diagnostic tests should help identify current weakness or areas in which students might concentrate to improve their language skills or cultural awareness. They can allow test takers to decide whether to enroll in additional courses to meet their language proficiency goals.

Progress examinations are important for instructors who wish to measure how students are continuing to improve their language skills. Online courses generally have progress examinations after each module, often called comprehension checks or posttests. Most language courses have an assessment at the end of each chapter or unit. These tests are usually designed to assess learners' assimilation of the material in the chapter or unit rather than their global linguistic development (in fact, linguistic development can be inferred by users only through the difference of test–retest scores). Progress examinations are linked directly to a curriculum and measure student advancement toward the end goal of the curriculum. They generally occur at regular intervals throughout the semester or year.

Achievement tests may also take the form of final examinations or culminating tests for a semester or year of study. Achievement tests do not necessarily assess learners' overall language abilities, but rather how well they have absorbed course material such as culture, grammatical rules, and vocabulary from the topics addressed in class. Achievement tests tend to be summative assessments of a learners' progress over an entire semester, year, or even a curriculum.

Proficiency tests differ from achievement tests in that they aim to evaluate global linguistic ability regardless of the course of study context in which the language is learned. The American Council on the Teaching of Foreign Languages (ACTFL) Oral Proficiency Interview (OPI) is the prototypical example of a proficiency test for speaking ability (see Liskin-Gasparro, 1984). Language proficiency levels are well-defined stages, and progression through them takes time, making proficiency tests inappropriate for measuring change over short periods. However, a proficiency test may provide useful information when administered at the conclusion of an undergraduate major in the language or when there is reason to expect significant advances in language skills (e.g., study abroad or an intensive summer program).

Instructors can use tests for all of the purposes mentioned here. Historically, these tests have been oral or pen-and-paper tests, but computer-based tests for a variety of these purposes are rapidly becoming the norm. In fact, instructors can anticipate seeing more computer-based tests and particularly more web-based tests (WBTs). Limits on technology have tended to restrict the level of sophistication that instructors can use on the tests that they produce themselves (e.g., web-based voice recognition is not readily available to everyone); nonetheless, instructors can still profit from many of the tools available to educators online and the following section discusses some of these tools and their limits.

TASK 9.1

Give examples from Klapper's categories (aptitude, placement, diagnosis, progress, achievement, and proficiency) of tests that you have taken or given. Are there types of tests that you have never taken? Which types of tests have you taken most frequently and why? If you have created or administered tests, which types were they? Compare your list to those of others in the class.

CHARACTERISTICS OF ONLINE ASSESSMENT

CALT has a number of important advantages, but many are not available to some instructors because of the technical and statistical knowledge needed to exploit their potential. Nonetheless, online testing options are increasing, and continuing developments in technology have eliminated some obstacles and facilitated implementation. This section begins by examining some fundamental concepts in testing, such as reliability and validity, in relation to several technological applications described in the chapter. We then discuss the benefits and limitations of CALT in terms of delivery, presentation, scoring, and washback effects.

Reliability

Reliability refers to the consistency of the test, for example, if a student receives similar scores on multiple administrations of the same test. Similarly, if different raters were to give varying scores to the same essay test, we would say that the ratings are unreliable or that they have low inter-rater reliability. Reynolds, Livingston, and Willson (2009) list several threats to reliability. Among these threats, they list time sampling errors which relate to changes over time of the learner (e.g., fatigue, illness, anxiety of the test taker), the scoring (e.g., fatigue, attention, consistency of the rater), and the test administration conditions (e.g., the proctor and instructions, temperature, noise, distractions). CBTs manage to mitigate many of these threats. Test administration, for example, tends to be more consistent on a computer; for each iteration of the test, the instructions do not vary, the interface does not vary, the reporting of time does not vary. Likewise, fluctuations in scoring are minimal because many computer-based tests consist of machine-scored items that do not rely on subjective judgments and are not susceptible to human error (e.g., the computer grades responses the same way every time, whereas human raters may differ depending on fatigue or distractions). Finally, fluctuations in the learner are generally attributable to influences such as learner maturation (e.g., ability to pay attention longer, increase of interest in an area), fatigue, sickness, or stress. These sources of variability would theoretically be the same whether the test were a CBT or a paper-and-pencil test because they are all attributable to the learner and not to the test.

Reliability can be calculated using a variety of methods (e.g., test–retest, parallel forms, split-half[2]), most of which depend on correlations (between tests, forms, item responses, or graders). It is important to be aware that the length of a test does not necessarily improve its reliability. The relationship of items to reliability is asymptotic, which means that the addition of items increases the reliability significantly for the initial items. However, lengthening a test

---

[2]Test–retest reliability is the correlation between two administrations of the same test to the same person. The parallel forms (also called random parallel forms) method calculates the correlation between two tests that are supposed to be similar. Split-half reliability measures internal consistency by dividing the test into two nearly equal parts and correlating the scores between the two parts.

beyond a certain point provides diminishing returns; the test may simply become longer rather than more reliable. For example, the fifth item on a 5-item test may increase the reliability significantly; the two hundredth item on a 200-item test will increase the reliability very little, if at all. This relationship is important to remember because the computer can monitor the reliability of a test and allow shorter and more reliable tests because it can determine, in real time (called *adaptability*), items that contribute to the reliability of the score.

Validity

Validity is not a characteristic of the test itself; rather, it refers to the use of the test for a particular purpose. Messick (1989) defines validity as "an integrated evaluative judgment of the degree to which empirical evidence and theoretical rationales support the adequacy and appropriateness of inferences and actions based on test scores or other modes of assessment" (p. 13). Henning's (1987) statement may be even clearer: "A test is said to be valid to the extent that it measures what it is supposed to measure" (p. 89). Statistical tests are not used to determine validity. Instead, researchers must consider a body of evidence to justify the appropriate uses and interpretation of test scores. Messick (1996) argues that a theory of validity should focus solely on construct validity and posits validation through argument rather than a single empirical study. Kane (2006) explains that validation involves two arguments. The first is that the interpretations and uses of the test should include content, students' abilities, scoring, generalizability, external factors (who pays for, or requires the test), and decisions based on performances (e.g., admission, placement, certification). The second is a validity argument that provides an evaluation of the interpretive argument. The validity argument claims that "the interpretive argument is coherent, that its inferences are reasonable, and that its assumptions are plausible" (p. 23). In short, instructors cannot determine if a test is valid; instead instructors make a case that the uses for the test are valid based on the content and context of the test.

Instructors make an invalid application of a test when they use the results for purposes that the test does not intend. For example, an instructor who uses a placement test as a final exam for a course is misusing the test. Instructors may inherently create an invalid test by including test items that do not match the content or objectives of a course. A good example of this problem would be an exam that required students to talk about their vacation when they had never been exposed to vocabulary concerning leisure-time activities. Another threat to validity is lack of cooperation on the part of the learner. For example, a test taker may attempt get a low score on a placement test in order to be placed in a lower (seemingly easier) class. Lack of cooperation from the test taker threatens validity because the decisions for placement should be based on true language ability and the uncooperative learner's score does not represent true language ability.

An inappropriate norming population is also a threat to test validity. Inappropriate norming occurs when the designers of the exam administer it to a population other than the target population to determine its discriminative value. The most common form of this occurs when instructors use a generic version of a test (e.g., the tests that come from publishers along with the textbook) without accounting for its particular context. Two main threats to validity identified by Messick (1989) are underrepresentation and construct-irrelevant variance. Underrepresentation means that the test fails to measure the important aspects of the construct (e.g., key vocabulary from the chapter, essential grammar in the chapter). Construct-irrelevant variance means that the test attempts to measure too many variables, some of which are irrelevant to the construct. Two types of construct-irrelevant variance can be identified. Construct-irrelevant difficulty stems from questions that stray from the construct being measured to make the test more difficult for some groups (e.g., a test on numbers in the target language that includes math problems). Construct-irrelevant easiness occurs when extraneous clues in the test or test format permit some individuals to score higher on the test (e.g., a unit test where many of the grammatical constructions are contained in the reading portion of the test—learners can simply use the reading portion to check their work in the previous or subsequent sections). When possible, instructors might mitigate invalidity of off-the-shelf tests by examining the test for underrepresentation or irrelevance. This is difficult to do without having identified the parameters of the construct ahead of time. As instructors and language program directors (LPDs) identify the end results/goals of a chapter or unit before looking at the test, they ensure that the goals of the curriculum are identified by the context rather than the test or textbook (Angell, DuBravac, & Gonglewski, 2008). For example, a Spanish program in a large university in South Florida in which diversity and exposure to Spanish culture may (and most likely should) have different curricular goals for its students than a small Appalachian college in which many students have had little exposure to foreign cultures. Instructors and LPDs can then use the identified curricular goals to identify where each test shows underrepresentation of the targeted goals or irrelevant items. The convenience of using an off-the-shelf test and striving to administer a valid measurement of students need not conflict. In fact, Kane (2006) argues that evaluating test validity is not a static, one-time event but rather a continuous process. Hence, instructors will need to evaluate any test both before and after it has been administered.

TASK 9.2

Rudman and Schafer (2002) argue for a variety of instructional roles for testing. Identify a test that fits each of the testing roles listed here:

- Tests can aid in grouping students in class.
- Testing can diagnose what students know.
- Testing can help determine the pace of classroom instruction.
- Tests can be used to help make promotion and retention decisions.
- Test results can show instructional effectiveness and learning.

In most cases, it is enough to use common sense to evaluate the validity of a given test. If instructors are judicious and moderate their use of test scores for specific purposes, the question of validity can be controlled. It is not enough to say that a test is valid or invalid; it must be valid for a specific construct, for a specific group, and for a specific purpose. Both validity and reliability apply to all tests, and efforts should be made to ensure validity and reliability whether it is a CBT or a paper-and-pencil test.

Delivery

The most notable and frequently mentioned advantage of CALT over paper-and-pencil tests is the physical and temporal flexibility of its delivery. The ability to deliver a test at the convenience of the test-taker has long been promoted as an important advantage of computerized testing (Carr, 2006). Teachers can easily instruct students to take a test online at home, at the library, or wherever there is a computer with an internet connection. Moreover, instructors are less involved in the test-taking interaction because much of the feedback, help, and scoring is automated.

The three basic variations of CBT delivery are computerized fixed tests (CFT), automated test assembly (ATA), and computer-adaptive tests (CAT). CFTs are basically pencil-and-paper tests delivered on the computer, so transferring a pencil-and-paper test to a CFT usually takes a short amount of time with few changes to the original document. CFTs are fixed-length and fixed-sequence tests that resemble a take-home exam via the computer. ATA is used to produce multiple equivalent versions of the same test by using a bank of questions that are coded for content. Instructors set the number of questions for each concept that should appear on each test, and the computer creates a version of the test by selecting the corresponding items from the question bank and presenting them in a semi-random fashion. The main concern for instructors using ATA is to ensure that the tests are, in fact, equivalent. ATAs offer more security where item sharing (i.e., when students ask other students what was on a test) or copying are of concern. Finally, CATs use enormous item banks to adjust the sequence and difficulty level of the items according to an individual's responses. If a response is correct, the following item will have a higher level of difficulty; following an incorrect response, the computer selects items of lower difficulty. CATs generally vary in length and difficulty for each test taker because the computer does not select items that are too easy or too difficult for the individual; test takers see only the items whose difficulty is near their level. Most instructors are not capable of producing a CAT without some significant institutional support. All of these tests may be delivered via the web or on a stand-alone computer.

Physical and temporal circumstances can also be a drawback for test designers. When tests are delivered via the web, it is difficult to provide technical expertise and maintain test security, which has been and always will be a concern for WBT. The stakes of a particular test largely determine the importance of test security. For example, the Test of English for International Communication (TOEIC) exam can determine if individuals are eligible for a particular job; the stakes are high, so the security should also be high. On the other hand, a test on which scores are inconsequential (e.g., surveys) gives students no motivation to cheat, so test security can be low. Moreover, test administrators have techniques to make a WBT tamper resistant, but arguably none to ensure that a test is tamperproof.

For individual instructors, online tests may be the best option for student self-assessment, review, or comprehension check purposes. Final examinations, certification tests, or other high-stakes tests would probably not be the best candidates for anytime–anywhere tests because there would be no proof of who actually took the test and what support they used (e.g., dictionaries, grammars, native speakers). Additionally, if instructors decide to monitor the test in a classroom, there may not be enough computers for the students.

Presentation

Multimedia capabilities are most commonly noted as an interesting feature of CBTs in comparison with paper-and-pencil tests, because they allow for a more stimulating test environment. Multimedia and interactivity can enhance the test items, the responses, and the feedback mechanisms. Test items can be enhanced with video and audio in the prompt as well as in the responses to improve contextualization and authenticity (Chapelle & Douglas, 2006). The questions can be presented in audiovisual format with or without textual support to adapt the test for the specific needs of learners (e.g., those with visual or audio impairments). Eventually, online tests could include authentic and current texts taken directly from online journals or live interviews. Responses could be scored in real time with raters via text, audio, or video chat.

Students' interaction with the test is also enhanced in online formats. Recent online tests generally include animation, pull-down menus, drag-and-drop matching, and other features that enhance the appearance of the items and the activity of the test taker. Students can record their voices, select a number or letter on the keyboard, select an item on the screen using the mouse, move items into groups using the mouse, or even make a short video of themselves that can be automatically sent to raters.

The interactive nature of the computer has enabled test takers to receive automatic feedback immediately or as a delayed response in an audio, video, or text format. Test takers can receive feedback by redirection to a web site or a page containing more information (grammatical, cultural or other) on the topic. The feedback may also take the form of additional items similar to one a student answered incorrectly. For example, if students enter an incorrect response to an item, a computer-based test can direct them to other items on the same topic and of the same difficulty level. This interaction of feedback allows CBTs to be formative as well as summative.

Consistency of presentation, which contributes to reliability, is another advantage of CALT. Every learner receives identical instructions, time allocation, and guidance in how to respond. Paper-and-pencil tests may vary according to the number of students (e.g., because of noise in the room, distance from the proctor during instruction, distractions from acquaintances), the frame of mind of the test administrator, and the guidance given to students. With most CALT formats, students can read the instructions as slowly or as quickly as they wish, practice on several model sentences before beginning the test, and even change the interface language (see www.lancs.ac.uk/researchenterprise/dialang/about for example).

Drawbacks of the rubrics or instructions of online tests are that students may get lost in the guidance sections or the help sections may be too extensive for students to get the information they actually need. The complexity of the delivery system may often require significant tutorials and practice materials. It is not difficult to create the support mechanisms, but instructors using online tests, quizzes, and interactive worksheets should be aware of the need for a online support, such as FAQs and practice questions.

Scoring

Computer-scored tests can save time, but not without concessions on other fronts. Computers can score a range of item types: true/false; multiple choice; matching (also with drag-and-drop); ordering jumbled letters, words, sentences, or paragraphs; crosswords; and cloze (fill-in-the-blank). The computer does not score short-answer responses, open dialogues, and essay questions for content or accuracy. Most instructors need to evaluate constructed responses (e.g., essays) individually, and they do not use the computer to help them in most instances.

The question types that facilitate computer scoring generally have only one correct setting for each response (either correct or incorrect). Instructors can code responses easily for these items because of the limited number of acceptable responses. In contrast, cloze (fill-in-the-blank) activities create problems for computer scoring because they are string based. A string in computer science is a finite sequence of characters. In the case of language testing, the computer compares the string provided by the students (the response) with the string or strings provided by the test writer in the list of acceptable responses. The issue arises when students forget to provide an accent, misspell a word, put a space before or after the word, capitalize or fail to capitalize letters correctly, or input the string in a form other than what was identified by the test writer. Instructors and online systems have generally circumvented this problem by creating a list of correct responses rather than one acceptable string. However, the response bank still creates significantly more work for the instructor, who must anticipate all possible acceptable or nearly acceptable responses. This task is augmented even more if instructors want to provide corrective feedback for specific errors (e.g., "Don't forget the accent"; "Did you check for agreement?" "Make sure it is past tense"). The use of strings for the responses simplifies the construction of the test, the answers, and the feedback, but there is a consistent shift toward using a mathematically intensive method of automatically extracting meaning from natural language (and often error ridden) input called natural language processing (NLP). The use of NLP and other sophisticated measures in CALL is generally called iCALL, or intelligent CALL, and testing has seen the greatest advances in iCALL. You can get a taste of what is possible simply by typing in the letters "langauge" into Google's search engine; the first response should be "Showing results for *language*." The algorithm for analyzing the question can ignore capital letters and extra spaces and it can account for missing accents, synonyms, and misspellings.

The scoring of constructed-response tests (i.e., essays and short answers) takes advantage of NLP and is discussed later in greater detail in the section on creating and grading. For now, it is a limitation for most instructors, because the majority of instructors lack the technological skills and the data required to create automated scoring tools for constructed-response exams.

Washback

Washback is an area of concern for all tests and teachers. It is also referred to as test impact. Washback is defined as the effect of testing on teaching and learning. A test is normally a measure of what students have learned or the language they have acquired over a period of study. In some cases, the test dictates the learning—this is washback from the test. Washback is not necessarily negative; it can be beneficial if the test is valid and reliable and measures the multidimensional competences inherent in language development. One of the problems with testing foreign language ability is that language use is multidimensional by nature and testing strives to measure skills unidimensionally (i.e., measure one skill at a time). Negative washback occurs when there is a mismatch between the construct definition or the content and the test. The task types mentioned earlier (e.g., matching, true/false) do not coincide with any performance that language students will use in an authentic situation. For example, being able to identify an utterance as true or false will rarely enable a language learner to order a croissant at a café or get directions to the train station. If washback is to be positive, then the test should measure the skills or functions that are to be encouraged (e.g., asking questions, introducing one's self). For these purposes, many instructors have turned to alternative assessments such as portfolios, self-assessments, and projects (see Chapter 10).

Nonetheless, as this section shows, CBT provides numerous advantages in terms of delivery, presentation, scoring, and washback effects for particular types of tests. These tests tend to be large-scale, programmatic tests that can take advantage of a delivery system that is independent of time and place, are able to accommodate copious amounts of data associated with various forms of presentation, provide sophisticated (and often complex) scoring procedures, and have significant washback effect (either positive or negative). The future of CBT will arguably include advancements in computer technology and sharing of information (i.e., corpora from a variety of sources) that will enable individual instructors to score constructed-response tests automatically. For the immediate future, however, these procedures are available only for the large populations that can provide the threshold data and profit from the significant time investment required to validate the results from the test. The next section explores language tests that instructors can create for their own purposes and commercially available language tests.

TASK 9.3

Numerous tests have been created for assessing language skills, each with a different purpose. Identifying the purpose of a test is the first step in deciding if the test has a valid use in your program. Research the following language exams and indicate their purpose (i.e., placement, diagnostic, proficiency, achievement):

- STAMP (www.avantassessment.com)
- DIALANG (www.lancs.ac.uk/researchenterprise/dialang/about)
- WebCAPE (www.aetip.com)
- TFI (www.ets.org/tfi)
- PET, FCE, CAE, and CPE (www.cambridgeesol.org/exams/index.html)

The Center for Applied Linguistics (2007) maintains a searchable database of language tests at www.cal.org/CALWebDB/FLAD that contains information on more than 200 assessment tools.

CREATING COMPUTER-BASED TESTS

As technology advances, CBTs and WBTs have become synonymous for many instructors. The facility with which instructors can create WBTs today is astounding compared to only a few years ago. It would be impossible to list all the tools available to instructors for creating WBTs. The most appropriate place to look for the latest, most reliable tools is a prominent CALL journal such as *Language Learning and Technology* (llt.msu.edu), *CALICO* (calico.org), or *ReCALL* (www.eurocall-languages.org). Unlike in the early 1990s, when instructors needed significant knowledge in coding languages (i.e., javascript, CGI, .asp, .cfm), most instructors today need only visit an online service such as Quia.com, hot potatoes (hotpot.uvic.ca) or Quizstar (quizstar.4teachers.org) and use the teacher-made exercises available to the public or simply register and begin entering questions and answers. Learning management systems (LMSs) also offer the ability to create online quizzes and surveys, including pools of items. Instructors can also use software such as *Respondus*® (if their institution has a license) that takes quizzes written in Microsoft Word and uploads them to a Blackboard, Moodle, or Desire2Learn site. An off-line aid to online tests is helpful for most and indispensable for those with slower or unreliable internet connections because it reduces the number of clicks and minimizes the redundancy required for most online quiz making.

The systems for creating a test are similar, so once instructors learn to use one system it is relatively easy to shift to a different system. Instructors choose an item type, enter the item and available responses (e.g., multiple choice, matching), and then designate the correct response. Instructors can do a number of activities with online quiz-making software. This section discusses how to create surveys, exercises, and tests for use in the foreign language classroom.

Surveys

Surveys can be a useful source of information for instructors who want to gauge the abilities or attitudes of their students. Surveys are generally low-stakes measures, which means that the need for security is low, there is no time limit, and the focus of the exercise is on the program more than on the evaluation of students. Surveys can be created using a wide variety of tools, and instructors should consider what they want to do with the results before choosing a delivery method. For instructors who prefer qualitative responses and have relatively few students, email or a nontraditional format may be the best option. Instructors can send out an email to all students with the prompts and students need only respond and send the email back to the instructor (or use Wimba with email for oral responses). Additionally, voicethread.com allows students to record their responses to a picture or an audio prompt, and instructors need only log in and listen to the responses. In fact, instructors may use any of the asynchronous tools mentioned in Chapter 8 to create an online survey.

One of the major drawbacks with this form of surveying students is that it does not lend itself to data aggregation. Instructors must listen to each audio file or read each email and tally the results on their own. The data are richer, but instructors with large classes may find it difficult to review the results from such a survey.

Clickers, also called student response systems (SRS), audience response systems (ARS), or personal response systems (PRS), offer an excellent, real-time method of surveying students in class and aggregating data on a PowerPoint slide. Clickers are available to most institutions from middle school through graduate school. Many universities require students buy their own clickers the same way they buy their books. Clickers range from $10 to more than $100 depending on the model and the available responses (i.e., y/n, multiple choice, text entry). Instructors must have a receiver that plugs into the USB port of their computer and then produces a polling slide (using PowerPoint, typically) according to the instructions from the accompanying software. Students enter their responses on their clickers when the instructor opens polling, and then the results display in real time on the graph or slide created by the instructor. Although clicker systems are intuitive, they differ in important ways. It is worthwhile to consult with the institutional technology support personnel to become acquainted with the tools.

Clickers bring some key features to the classroom. First, they provide a method for individuals to participate anonymously. Second, they add a game approach to the classroom that may raise engagement levels. Finally, clickers are an excellent method of checking comprehension, monitoring motivation and attitude, and taking attendance. Clickers tend to be more useful in large classes where instructors may not have the opportunity to call on students individually.

In lieu of surveys or clickers, instructors can monitor classroom activity in a large classroom or presentation by using a backchannel, which is a conversation that takes place while the presenter or instructor is speaking to the class. Students make comments online while listening to the professor (e.g., to check facts, give opinions, ask questions). Atkinson (2009) argues that the use of backchannels extends the reach of ideas, improves communication, and increases the sense of community. A backchannel can take place over cell phones, Twitter, or sites specifically designed for backchannel conversations, such as todaysmeet.com (which includes Twitter hash tags). To take advantage of a backchannel, the classroom must offer wifi and students must have a computer available to them. A backchannel may be more effective in a culture- or literature-focused class because language-focused classes tend to consist of more group and pair work and face-to-face conversations. Backchannels tend to be an alternative to these conversations and to passing notes.

Outside of class, instructors can ask students to complete surveys on the web for feedback on presentations, coursework, homework, or any item an instructor wants to monitor in class. Instructors can make surveys to be used during presentations using urtak.com (for wifi-enabled spaces), and the results are posted in real time, much like with clickers. Nonetheless, it may be more efficient to ask students to complete certain types of surveys (e.g., midterm class evaluations) outside of class to allow for more thoughtful responses. The most popular sites for making online surveys are surveymonkey.com and questionpro.com. These sites are simple and intuitive and offer tutorials. The survey URLs are easily distributed via asynchronous or synchronous CMC and results are easily aggregated.

Surveys tend to be useful as low-stakes information-gathering tools. They may be particularly suited to activities that encourage students to self-assess and identify areas for improvement and goals for the class. Most surveys tend to maintain a certain amount of response validity; that is, students respond with authentic answers rather than guessing or being facetious. Nonetheless, instructors should be conscious that concerns with validity and security grow as the stakes are raised for quizzes and tests.

Exercises

Exercises, quizzes, and tests are easily produced using a variety of sites. Some of these sites offer free software for creating activities for upload (e.g., hotpot. uvic.ca, malted.cnice.mec.es), whereas others allow registration and direct

---

TASK 9.4

Use one of the sites listed here to create a survey. Send the link to at least five people to elicit a response or, if you teach a class, ask your class to complete the survey:

- www.surveymonkey.com
- questionpro.com
- freeonlinesurveys.com
- www.kwiksurveys.com
- www.zoomerang.com

creation on the web (e.g., quia.com, challenge.zoho.com, quizstar.4teachers. org). Most of these sites offer access to activities created by other instructors and uploaded for open access. To maintain quality control, it is wise to review activities carefully before assigning them to students. Online exercises can be useful to review, reinforce, informally assess, or identify gaps in the L2.

Instructors can use many of these sites in conjunction with each other or with other useful blogs, video feeds, or other content sites. The increasingly common use of information (e.g., video, text, audio) on a web site that is taken directly from other sites is called a mashup. Mashups are implemented using a scripting language such as php or asp. Scores of sites allow mashups (open. dapper.net, mashmaker.intel.com, www.xfruits.com); instructors new to mash-ups are advised to start with the *Rich Internet Applications* from the Center for Language Education and Research (CLEAR). CLEAR provides a mashup maker for education (clear.msu.edu/teaching/online/ria) that enables instructors to create web pages that include text areas, an audio dropbox, and embedded elements. The text area supports foreign language fonts and provides an area for instructions and the prompt. The audio dropbox allows students to record themselves (with no additional software) and saves the audio in a secure loca-tion designated by the instructor who sets up the audio dropbox. Embedded elements can include photos, videos, twitter feeds, videos, blog posts, or even entire web pages. In fact, CLEAR offers an unparalleled suite of internet applications for educational purposes.

Tests

Teachers may find that it is so easy and rewarding to create tests that they lose sight of the purpose of the assessments. A major point to consider for any test or exercise development is task authenticity (Chapelle & Douglas, 2006). Authenticity refers to the fact that the skills students use to complete the test or task are similar to those they would need to complete real-life tasks. For example, some natural reading behaviors include skimming, scanning, highlight-ing, note taking, skipping ahead, and rereading. An authentic computer-based test should build in the need to use these skills. Many instructors may have dif-ficulty assuming that discrete-point tests (e.g., true/false, multiple choice) cause students to use the same skills they would use for completing real-life language tasks. These instructors would most likely prefer alternative testing (see Chapter 10). Nonetheless, a variety of discrete-point tests purport to measure global language skills (DLAB, MLAT) and appear to do so with significant statistical reliability. Even though discrete-item testing may not be the best measure of overall language ability, many institutions may require machine-scorable tests because of multiple sections of the same level. A few of the testing options available online allow for item banking, particularly LMSs, which allow instruc-tors to create a bank of test items of nearly unlimited size. Instructors can cre-ate a bank of items and then design a test that uses certain item types (true/false, multiple choice) or a certain number of items (as a random block) to be included in the test that the students take. In the test options section of the LMS, instructors can set the following options: the number of items, the order in which to display them (random or sequential), the time allotted for the test, the opportunity for multiple attempts on an item, and the feedback given to students (score, submitted answers, correct answers). This resource is particularly useful for instructors who teach the same content for a number of semesters or years. Once the test bank is created, instructors can add or subtract items as necessary. The computer will continue to select items from the bank, and the test will evolve because of the continuing influx of items. Another benefit that LMSs offer is that the score from the test goes directly into the online grade book so students know their score immediately and there is no risk of copying the score incorrectly.

Despite its many advantages, online testing also has some disadvantages. Technical problems can be a significant source of difficulty (although this is less and less of a concern). If learners are disconnected from the site for a test they will take only once, they will be unable to return to complete the test without instructor intervention. Having the score sent directly to the online grade book is beneficial only if instructors use the online grade book. Fonts can be an issue if students are unfamiliar with their system. For example, if students are unable to produce appropriate letters (e.g., hablo vs. habló), their responses are counted as incorrect in many cases. Instructors should also be attentive to the difficulty levels of different versions of the same test; with tests that are randomly generated from the item bank, there is no guarantee that all tests will be equivalent in difficulty level.

Automatic Scoring of Tests

Item-response theory (IRT), or latent-trait theory, is probably the most important development in psychometrics of the past century (Henning, 1987). IRT is used to develop CATs, which improve both the efficiency and effectiveness of testing by administering shorter tests tailored to each student. CAT provides shorter tests by reducing the number of items needed to arrive at a score. With IRT, the only items that really matter in determining the test score are those whose difficulty level matches the ability of the test taker. For example, if a person's ability is 6 (on a 10-point scale), the items that have the most measurement power are those with a difficulty level of 5, 6, and 7, because theoretically the test taker would answer correctly all items with a difficulty level of 1 to 4 and be unable to respond to items at difficulty 8 to10 (in a very simplistic world). Thus, the individual whose ability level is 6 would need to answer only a subset of questions between levels of 5 and 7 on a CAT. The uninformative items can easily be deleted from a computerized test but cannot be immediately removed from a paper-and-pencil test.

The development of tests with a CAT format requires professional expertise and substantial resources. The most prominent CAT in foreign language is the TOEFL test (www.ets.org/toefl), which tests English language ability and is often used as an entrance requirement for non-native speakers of English to study in American universities. WebCape (aetip.com), a CAT for placement purposes at the college level, is available for English, French, German, Russian, and Spanish, with a Chinese version under development at the time of this writing.

The Standards-based Measurement of Proficiency, or STAMP test (avantassess-ment.com), targets novice to intermediate learners and is available for French, German, Italian, Japanese, Spanish, and Chinese and is designed to measure proficiency levels based on ACTFL's performance guidelines. Finally, DIALANG (www.lancs.ac.uk/researchenterprise/dialang/about), as mentioned earlier, uses self-assessment along with adaptive assessment for diagnostic purposes.

Almost all of the CATs available to language teachers are delivered and rated by the computer. These are called indirect tests because they do not directly test the construct that they claim to test. For example, a multiple choice test can only test for writing and speaking indirectly because test takers will neither write nor speak natural language while taking the test. CATs are generally discrete-point tests because the algorithms used to determine the next item rely on a binary result from the previous item (i.e., right/wrong). However, many of the tests available on a local level (e.g., in a single class) use semi-direct methods that allow a variety of other responses. Semi-direct computer-assisted tests use the computer to elicit responses that are subsequently evaluated by humans (e.g., Computerized Oral Proficiency Instrument [COPI]; PRAXIS II). As noted in the previous section, it has been difficult if not impossible for computers to assign a score to an essay or other constructed-response test. Yet, recent technological and theoretical advances have made computer scoring of constructed-response items possible.

Constructed-Response Tests

Newer constructs of writing, improvements in models of natural language processing, and operationalization of desirable textual response have allowed for advances in a number of technological tools that automatically assess constructed-response tests (i.e., essay and short-answer exams). This technology has existed since the mid-1960s (Page, 1966); however, the technology and research have not reached the point where these tools are widely available in languages other than English. Nonetheless, many of them can conceivably be available in the near future for the more commonly taught languages such as Spanish and Chinese. These automatic grading applications use semantic analysis techniques that were originally designed for information retrieval (e.g., summarizing, finding documents on the web, rating relevance of documents). Two tools are of particular popularity, E-rater (Attali & Burstein, 2006) and the Intelligent Essay Assessor, or IEA (Landauer, Laham, & Foltz, 2003).

E-rater has been used by ETS since 1999 to score a variety of standardized test essays. E-rater rates writing samples by comparing them to manually graded training essays. A few hundred manually graded essays are fed into the computer and converted into word frequency vectors. The computer identifies the most pertinent aspects (called proxes) to help determine the grade and then applies these proxes to the subsequent essays (this process is called content vector analysis). The difficulty for E-rater and second language essays is identifying the several hundred graded essays that provide the proxes.

IEA uses a different process from E-rater to assess essays; it is called latent-semantic analysis (LSA). Manually graded papers are not needed; rather, a collection of documents has been separated into meaningful terms (often thousands to millions of terms) called a semantic space. LSA compares word and terms and their use within a corpus of documents similar to E-rater, but LSA can generalize across synonyms such that terms like *China, chinese,* and *mandarin* would yield the same assessment for the essay. An example of how this works can be seen by typing in "~spanish" into Google's search engine. The results will include keywords such as *spanish, spain, mexico, madrid,* and *español,* without regard to capitalization of letters. LSA is particularly useful in AP exams where essays are evaluated not only on the quality of the writing but also the background knowledge on the topic that supports the essay. The content of the essay can be assessed better using LSA because a variety of terms in the text can still signal a successful response to the prompt.

Anyone who has used multiple sentences in a search engine has performed a similar analysis to what E-rater or IEA does. The user inputs the target document (i.e., the search terms). A search engine searches available documents to see which documents most appropriately match the target document. The documents are then ranked in order of how well their pertinent aspects (proxes) match the proxes (search terms) in the target document. In the case of essay rating, the search terms are the "good" essays and the searched documents are the essays to be graded and ranked.

The most notable benefits of computer-assisted scoring include instructor effort, time, and rater reliability. Instructors can save considerable effort and time when a computer evaluates a student's performance. Likewise, instructors and students can have immediate results on any CBTs they take. Computer-based constructed assessment tools also enable specific feedback for a given test (e.g., "you are good with present tense narration; you should work on past-tense description"). Even the machine-scored essays could eventually generate summaries that enable better writing and encourage writers to focus on particular aspects of their writing. Finally, and perhaps most important, automatic grading permits high levels of reliability. Inter-rater reliability tends to be satisfactory above 90%. That is to say that when human raters agree on a rating 90% of the time, they are said to be reliable raters. Unlike humans who show inconsistencies, machines will assign the same essay the same score 100% of the time, given identical starting material.

Unfortunately, these resources are not yet available for languages other than English or at the institutional level, and there is little research on L2 learner essays to allow instructors to profit from it. However, because constructed-response grading procedures use many of the same algorithms as widely available technology (e.g., search engines, summarizers), it is not unrealistic to assume that these tools will be available in the near future.

Disadvantages in CALT

Both commercial and instructor-designed CALTs have a number of disadvantages. The time it takes to create an online test is significantly longer than the time it takes to create a paper-and-pencil test because test makers must also code the responses with the questions in CBTs. Software such as *Respondus* has facilitated the shift from pencil-and-paper to CBTs but even that limits the platform to a particular LMS. Additionally, automated scoring of constructed-response tests is simply unavailable to most L2 instructors for two reasons. First, the complexity of LSA applications is currently such that it is prohibitive for most colleges and schools (both for technical knowledge and textual requirements—thousands of documents). Second, the amount of data necessary to set baseline information is not available in languages other than English. One would need several hundred essays on one topic to train the scoring application. By the time most instructors have graded 150 essays, there are not too many more in their classes who have written on the same topic at the same level.

Nonetheless, it is worth noting that the technology is developing rapidly and is already widely used for standardized tests (and by web designers and librarians for automatic ranking of search results). Moreover, the training data for these essay scores would need to be recalibrated only for topic and not for syntax or grammar, which could eventually make the rating systems available at the level of the individual instructor and in any language. The use of a consistent baseline data set for grammar and syntax would also enable instructors to show progress over time in writing (particularly across an entire curriculum). At the heart of the matter is how the constructs developed for automatic scoring may actually change the nature of the writing task; the washback effects of automatic grading may impact significantly the way we teach writing and what we expect good writing to be.

THE FUTURE OF CBT

In this section, we explore the future possibilities of CBT and what instructors can expect as technological advancements allow for greater detail and varying perspectives on assessment and language. We analyze the technological advances and psychometric improvements that will modify the construct of language testing, particularly the ability to test for multidimensional skills without conflating the construct, the ease of including authentic material and tasks, the capacity to use the computer to create questions, and the proliferation of WBTs for distance education.

One of the major disconnects between language learning and language testing has been the concept of unidimensionality and multidimensionality. Language, by nature, is multidimensional. That is to say, one uses a variety of skills. As Chalhoub-Deville (2001) states, "the [language] construct comprises a variety of interacting components that include knowledge of the language system, knowledge of the world, knowledge of the particular situation of language use, and a variety of strategies and processing skills needed to access, plan, and execute the communicative intents" (p. 474). With the quantity of information that can be stored in computers and the ability to accumulate those data, future tests may focus more on behaviors that are indicative of proficiency. For example, future tests of reading could examine note taking, rereading, scanning, and other practices that are important reading skills. They will need to do this in conjunction with other skills because reading is seldom an activity conducted in seclusion. In addition to deciphering written texts, reading generally includes writing or speaking to someone about what one has read. The TOEFL iBt (TOEFL internet-based test), released in 2005, has attempted to do this by combining reading, writing, listening, and speaking skills to examine the test takers' ability to take notes, get the gist, paraphrase, reference a text, and infer in order to determine how a text and a lecture are related, for example.

Where computers have been and will be used to score responses, they will be increasingly used to create questions. Response generative modeling, or RGM (Bejar, 1993; Bennett, 1999), can be used to produce items to accompany prototypical responses. Prototypical responses are fed into a database that then generates alternate tasks that would produce similar language. With this tool, test makers can use the computer to generate test items. The type of automated item generation that would be available through RGM would enable simulations, role plays, static interviews (i.e., students respond to a set of questions), and even interactive conversations (i.e., the computer asks follow-up questions). This type of generative model could easily be combined with speech recognition and IRT models to develop diagnostic tests that determine which types of items prove to be more difficult (e.g., speaking, listening, cultural) for a given individual. These types of assessments will be of particular use to instructors who can assign work that targets each student's weaknesses.

Another continual improvement that will enhance CBTs is the inclusion of authentic material in both the prompt and the response. The STAMP test shows progress in this direction in that the test items do not use realia from the target culture, but most of the questions exhibit falsalia, test material that is inauthentic but designed to look authentic. Available tests increasingly use listening modules but do not show significant use of videos or mashups. As LSA tools and RGM improve, it will be increasingly easy to produce prompts for authentic (and current) videos as well as automatically correct, and give partial credit for, constructed responses produced both orally and textually. It will still be many years before oral exams can be administered and evaluated using computers. Speech recognition is far from being able to diagnose errors in non-native speaker pronunciation, for example. However, the combination of speech recognition, LSA, and RGM shows promise for evaluating spoken responses on a semantic and syntactic level.

Web-based testing will increase as the demand for distance education and online courses increases. These modes of delivery for language education will continue to proliferate and will need to be supported by efficient, standardized, and continuous assessment. A number of colleges and institutions are moving away from seat time requirements to proficiency requirements for acceptance to the university, graduation, completion of a course, or for certification purposes. Hence, the need will increase to provide regular diagnostic tests to group students into homogenous groups, to identify gaps in knowledge, and to determine the most efficient curriculum for each learner. Notwithstanding, technical concerns may continue to haunt CALT on the side of both the student and the instructor.

TECHNICAL CONSIDERATIONS

The technical impediments to online assessment have diminished significantly over the past decades. Today, with support from LMSs and various other third-party sites, instructors can create exercises, quizzes, and exams with very little technical know-how. Some of the major considerations are the amount of support from institution, the amount of control over posting or modifying content, and the amount of time it requires to maintain the online assessment portion of a section or group.

The amount of support from the institution can smooth the path for students or make it excruciating. Many students may not require assistance, but it may be necessary to ensure that students know how to use peripherals for recording and listening to audio or video. An efficient help desk can enable students to retrieve or reset passwords for LMSs, clear clogged email accounts, or instruct students about where to get the necessary peripherals such as a recorder or a clicker. Instructors may also need help dealing with lost data, digitization of recordings for the sake of realia, or training sessions for available technology (i.e., clickers, LMSs, data aggregation).

Language program directors who are responsible for multi-section courses will need to consider how well they can manage other instructors teaching sections at the same level. LMSs can be structured for individual instructors, team instructors, or sections led by teaching assistants (TAs), and each of these allows for certain control over all courses. LPDs may not want to have this much direct responsibility if they have a language center with a TA dedicated to deal with technology issues. It may be important in smaller colleges that the instructor be able to override test-taking limitations when a proctor (e.g., lab assistant, TA) is unavailable. For example, if a student is taking an online exam and disconnects from the server, only the person with administrative rights can reset the test so that the student can continue. Hence, it may be helpful in some instances for the LPD to have administrative control over all sections.

Finally, instructors should be aware of how much time and energy is required to integrate a sequence of computer-based assessment measures into the curriculum. If the test scores are entered directly into an online grade book, most students expect to be able to see all of their grades including those that are not entered directly into the grade book (e.g., participation, homework, projects). Instructors will need to update the online grade book frequently and often on a daily basis, if students expect full disclosure of all grades in the online gradebook.

As with nearly any implementation of technology, instructors should first determine the resources available to them, including the human resources. Although CBT provides many advantages in delivery, presentation, scoring, and washback, the human aspect of all implementations must compensate for a perceived change in the norm. As CBT, and particularly WBT, becomes the norm, students, instructors, and administrators will see fewer drawbacks and will be able to rely on user familiarity to minimize the drawbacks that accompany the technology.

Practical Work

1. Online quizzes are relatively simple to construct and a number of sites facilitate the process. Choose one of the following sites and use it to make a quiz or questionnaire. Try to embed video and audio in your quiz and provide some specialized feedback for correct and incorrect answers. Evaluate your quiz for its construct validity. Does it test what you think students should be learning? Would it provide positive washback?
   - Blackboard, Moodle, or NiceNet.org
   - www.quia.com
   - challenge.zoho.com
   - hotpot.uvic.ca
   - quizstar.4teachers.com
2. Take the sample Stamp test (www.avantassessment.com/stamp). Describe five positive and five negative characteristics of the test.
3. Take the Dialang test (www.lancs.ac.uk/researchenterprise/dialang/about) for the language that you speak. Take it again for a tertiary language. Did you find significant differences in how you approached the tests? Would you use the Dialang test at your institution? When? For what purpose?

Suggestions for Further Reading

Bailey, K. M. (1998). *Learning about language assessment: Dilemmas, decisions, and directions*. Boston: Heinle & Heinle.

Carr, N. (2006). Computer-based testing: Prospects for innovative assessment. In L. Ducate & N. Arnold (Eds.), *Calling on CALL: From theory and research to new directions in foreign language teaching* (pp. 289–312). San Marcos, TX: CALICO.

Center for Applied Linguistics. (2007). *Foreign language assessment directory*. Available at www.cal.org/CALWebDB/FLAD

Chapelle, C. A., & Douglas, D. (2006). *Assessing language through computer technology*. Cambridge, Eng.: Cambridge University Press.

Erben, T., Ban, R., & Castañeda, M. (2009). *Teaching English language learners through technology*. New York: Routledge.

Kane, M. T. (2006). Validation. In R. L. Brennan (Ed.), *Educational measurement* (4th ed., pp. 17–64). Westport, CT: American Council on Education/Praeger.

Messick, S. (1989). Validity. In R. Linn (Ed.), *Educational measurement* (3rd ed., pp. 13–103). Washington, DC: American Council on Education/Macmillan.

Roever, C. (2001). Web-based language teaching. *Language Learning and Technology* 5(2), 84–94.

CHAPTER 10

Alternative Assessment: Projects, Performances, and ePortfolios

OVERVIEW

In the term *alternative measurements of student ability*, the word *alternative* generally suggests a counterpoint to traditional or standardized tests. Although alternative assessment takes many forms, it has been most closely associated with projects, performances, and portfolios, and sometimes with only one of these forms. Shaklee and Viechnicki (1995), for example, suggest that portfolio assessment and nontraditional assessment are essentially synonymous. Nonetheless, projects, performances, and portfolios are the three basic types of alternative assessment and may be essential for guiding students beyond the intermediate level and into advanced-level production. This chapter focuses on the advantages and disadvantages of projects, performances, and electronic portfolios (ePortfolios), and how best to implement alternative approaches in the curriculum. An essential ingredient to all forms of alternative assessment is a consistent method of evaluation. This chapter also examines the creation and use of checklists or rubrics to help instructors provide consistent ratings among students, to elicit feedback from others, to enable students to assess their own evidence of learning, and to delineate the tasks that contribute to the overall activity/product. Formats for projects, performances, and ePortfolios are numerous, and this chapter aims to illustrate the benefits and limitations of a variety of forms of digital expression available to instructors and students.

TRADITIONAL VS. ALTERNATIVE APPROACHES

A few major points distinguish traditional assessment from alternative assessment. The most prominent is that traditional testing requires the learner to produce very little, and what is produced is similar among students (e.g., true/false, fill-in-the-blank, multiple-choice, drag-and-drop, short answer). Alternative assessment requires the production of substantial amounts of language, which may be significantly different among learners. Project-based learning and performance-based learning, both abbreviated PBL, emphasize production in the language in a variety of forms.

Another important feature of PBL (and growing trend) is the integration of assessment and teaching. As the focus of language learning has shifted from a mastery of forms to the ability to use the language in context, the goals of assessment have shifted, and evaluation methods have moved from standardized testing to performance assessment. More recent emphases in assessment have strived to associate assessment practices with performance-based teaching that occurs in the classroom (e.g., Adair-Hauck, Glisan, Koda, Swender, & Sandrock, 2006). Alternative approaches to assessment help create a more direct link between instruction and assessment. This approach also reflects modern developments in dynamic assessment, a procedure that assumes that teaching and assessment are two sides of the same coin and aims to improve the overall performance of the individual rather than simply measure it (Poehner, 2008).

Projects have been used for a number of years in the arts, the sciences, and the social sciences. For example, students often have lab work to do in the natural sciences, or they may be required to write letters to elected officials as part of a project in the social sciences. Weinstein (2006) states that "project-based learning is an approach in which learners investigate a question, solve a problem, plan an event, or develop a product" (p. 161). PBL has become increasingly popular as technology has facilitated longer-term projects or recorded performances with real-world audiences and consequences. It has also been referred to as PrOCall or project-oriented computer-assisted language learning (Jeon-Ellis, Debski, & Wigglesworth, 2005).

These types of assessment derive tasks for testing from authentic activities that must be performed in the target language; they include a final product or performance. The products may range from simple skits in class to several editions of an online magazine, podcast, or vodcast that includes multiple sites in the target countries. Regardless of its complexity or the length of time required for a project, PBL has some compelling features that apply to language learning:

- Contextualizing language tools by tying grammatical forms to functions, vocabulary to need, and critical thought to language use
- Focusing on authentic communication with a clear connection to the real world
- Incorporating effective use of technology
- Requiring student decision making and self-assessment
- Providing interdisciplinary/multidisciplinary lessons
- Promoting curricular articulation in that it involves students in sustained effort over time
- Encouraging collaboration
- Creating a learning environment that is more stimulating and real world–based than traditional learning environments (Albanese & Mitchell, 1993)

Although PBL has many advantages, it also has several disadvantages, the most notable being the significant amount of time required to implement it. All of the options discussed here (performances, projects, and ePortfolios) require more time to implement and assess than traditional measures. Moreover, because alternative methods of assessment may require changes in teaching style and teaching methodology, instructors may think that they cannot teach for both traditional testing and alternative assessment. Moreover, PBL may appear to be an inefficient method if instructors view projects as additional work beyond the perceived essential curriculum (e.g., activities imposed by high-stakes testing or multi-section exams required by departments). Students may also feel distracted and ineffective if they view PBL as extracurricular or unrelated to the central content of a course (Beckett, 2002). In most cases, to take advantage of the benefits of PBL, the projects must be fully integrated into the curriculum, so that students see a clear connection between the real-life products they create, the task they must accomplish in order to do well in the course, and the activities they engage in as part of the course.

Additionally, these types of assessment have inherent subjectivity issues with regard to how the final assessment is determined. In many cases, the rater tends toward subjective evaluation rather than being held to a widely accepted standard. There are no commonly shared criteria for what constitutes a satisfactory project. The instructor (or students) must determine these criteria, which do not always prove to be reliable across students and courses and from year-to-year, particularly when instructors must compare highly dissimilar products (e.g., written text vs. multimedia). Law and Ecke (1995) also mention several reliability/subjectivity issues related to alternative assessment that have yet to be refuted (e.g., teachers often give credit when credit is not merited, instructors may coach some students but not others).

Instructors can mitigate the subjectivity issues by using rubrics and by clarifying the evaluation process and criteria. When students are aware of the specific criteria that describe an acceptable performance/product, and when these criteria can be applied to all student creations for a specific project, the subjectivity tends to be better controlled than when the criteria are not explicit to both students and teachers. In most cases, these concerns are weighed against positive effects mentioned earlier to determine the benefits or drawbacks of using alternative assessment.

All forms of alternative assessment can capitalize on the advantages of technology provided by media (i.e., text, audio, video, multimedia), availability (i.e., available anywhere, at anytime, to anyone, and always changing), and flexibility (i.e., allowing for multiple forms of representation, expression, and engagement). Nevertheless, technology plays a different role in projects and performances than it does in ePortfolios. Projects and performances generally exploit technology for the purposes of collaborating, investigating, authoring, and presenting, whereas ePortfolios take advantage of the social and data-driven aspects of technology such as aggregating a collection of materials (e.g., projects and performances) that are born digital (i.e., created initially as digital documents), eliciting feedback from others through tagging and commenting, and encouraging student self-assessment by allowing constant updating. The following sections present examples of how various forms of technology can support performances and facilitate projects and how these projects can be presented online as ePortfolio. These projects may include digitally born representations such as videos of skits, online tutorials, presentations using PowerPoint, in lingua tours at local museums in .mp3 format, or vodcasts on a variety of topics. The ePortfolio can include these projects and performances as well as accompanying self-, peer-, or instructor evaluations.

The following discussion introduces a highly focused approach to assessment that serves as a prototype for performance assessments. The next section discusses the use of projects and identifies some important elements in the design, execution, and assessment of project-based learning. Finally, the advantages and disadvantages of ePortfolios are discussed.

INTEGRATED PERFORMANCE ASSESSMENT

Integrated performance assessment (IPA) is a means of assessing student performance in the language while taking into consideration the relationship between the students' classroom experiences and their performance on the assessment (Glisan, Adair-Hauck, Koda, Sandrock, & Swender, 2003). IPA is somewhat limited in scope, concentrating mainly on student progress on interpretive, interpersonal, and presentational tasks in a specific thematic unit. The IPA makes enormous strides toward meeting current demands in assessment practices. Adair-Hauck et al. (2006) note four current language assessment practices that are increasingly supported by research: (1) the use of performance-based and authentic tasks, (2) the sharing of criteria and exemplars with students before the assessment, (3) feedback to improve learner performance, and (4) feedback to improve instruction in learning (p. 361). The IPA aims to adhere to these four trends by providing a systematic method of measuring students' progress toward the standards (National Standards, 1999, 2006).

The IPA posits three interrelated tasks that examine the three modes of communication, interpretive, interpersonal, and presentational (Glisan et al., 2003): (1) Students are exposed to new and comprehensible vocabulary through an interpretive task, (2) they use this information in an interpersonal task, and (3) they summarize their learning with a presentational task. For example, if students are studying interrogative questions and the vocabulary focuses on leisure activities, students might read, listen to, or watch an authentic text about sports. This would be followed by a comprehension task such as identifying the healthiest sport or the most expensive sport. This portion might easily include using survey tools discussed in Chapter 9. Interactive language tasks are the primary means by which interpersonal communication can be accomplished. Some examples of interpersonal activities that use technology might include interviewing another person via Skype about their likes and dislikes; writing an email, text message, or instant message to a keypal to describe differences between daily habits; interviewing a native speaker (recorded on video and shown to class), or any combination of the above (e.g., an asynchronous video introduction or a recorded Skype interview). The interpersonal tasks can concentrate on activities that students already do on a regular basis such as using Twitter to identify good hangouts around town; updating one's status on a social networking site; or, for the theme mentioned earlier, joining a social networking group and finding people who have similar interests in leisure activities. The presentational task is generally the final performance and can include an array of activities such as a PowerPoint presentation, radio broadcast, or web page.

Scoring for IPAs is done using a longitudinal rubric for the tasks at each level (novice, intermediate, and pre-advanced ranges; ACTFL, 1998) and for each mode (interpretive, interpersonal, presentational). The longitudinal nature of the rubrics allows instructors to identify change over time on similar tasks. The rubrics also provide important feedback to both the learner (to identify strengths and weaknesses) and the instructor (to improve instruction). In fact, Adair-Hauck et al. (2006) found that 83% of the participants in their study indicated that implementation of the IPA had a positive aspect on their teaching, a desirable washback effect. A washback effect occurs when teachers do something they wouldn't normally do because of the test.

The IPA appears to have some positive aspects, particularly in terms of consciousness-raising for practicing instructors. The IPA focuses on linking classroom experiences and assessments while using one to strengthen the other. For example, students can be coached or helped at any point during the assessment in order to improve their overall performance. Students are frequently exposed to a variety of model performances so they can identify those that meet the criteria identified in the rubric, thereby encouraging self-assessment.

Finally, for many instructors, the IPA does not require extensive change from their current practices or necessitate significant time to implement. In this way, the IPA responds to criticisms mentioned earlier that instructors might not have the time or resources to implement alternative assessment. For instructors who are limited in time or overly structured in their curriculum and evaluation procedures, the IPA appears to be a simpler alternative method of assessing student progress without requiring a significant overhaul of the curriculum or the teaching methodology.

PROJECTS

Projects, in general, tend to be more involved and ambitious in scope than the IPA as far as what they require from the students and the instructor. In fact, from a curricular standpoint, the advantages and disadvantages appear to be two sides of the same coin. Using projects makes planning the day-to-day classes more straightforward because one project could easily take several weeks to complete and when the goal is clearly defined, the steps to get there become more apparent. By the same token, the production of a project may overshadow the content to be acquired. For example, students may spend more time recording, rerecording, and adding special effects to a podcast than they do producing the content for the project.

Integrating PBL is generally viewed as a three-step process that includes planning, production, and evaluation (Fried-Booth, 1997). PBL is much like painting a room: the more time spent preparing, the better the final product will be. Of concern during the first phase, planning, are identifying the objectives, back planning (i.e., planning from the last step to the first step), and preparing the students. The second phase, production, includes cyclical feedback to improve the process and final product and organizing the final performance/ presentation. The third phase, evaluation, relies on efficient and positive feedback from multiple sources and project extension.

Planning

The planning phase consists of two major phases. First, instructors prepare the project by identifying the end product and planning the activities for the unit based on the anticipated final product. Second, instructors prepare the students by presenting a clear purpose (from the students' perspective) and eliciting commitment from them. Once the instructor has determined the purpose and design of the project, planning from the final step to the first step can help ensure that students have the knowledge, tools, and support needed to create a final project that is useful and motivating and enables them to meet the objectives for the course or unit.

START WITH THE END IN MIND   During the planning phase, instructors should focus on creating a clear vision of what the final project should look like and on back planning. Planning from the last step to the first involves determining why students are doing a project (i.e., identify the objectives), clarifying what the final project should look like (i.e., create an evaluation rubric), detailing the aspects of the final project (e.g., how many words or pictures? how long?), and then deciding which activities or procedures will lead most effectively toward that goal. For example, if the goal is to enable students to express their opinions about and to describe music, instructor may decide to use a radio show project that features music from the target culture that students select, introduce, and comment on. In this case, the instructor should devote class time to all of the components of the project: exposure to popular music, practice with the language used to introduce and review music, familiarity with the technological tools used to record voice and/or produce audio files, and clarity concerning the format (e.g., web page, audio recording, mashup) to display the introductions and reviews. Instructors may also wish to have students air their program on a local public access radio station. The important steps for this phase are (1) identify the objectives, (2) identify the final product and create the rubric, and (3) back plan the activities starting with the final presentation.

Identify the objectives   The objectives should guide the entire project from its initial conception to the final feedback given to the students. Instructors should start with the standards and objectives for their class (see Chapter 6). Although it may seem unusual that instructors would attempt a project without identifying the desired outcomes, it is important to make these objectives explicit to all participants. The objectives can easily be stated as "can do" statements: "Students can describe their family (home, neighborhood, vacation, etc.)" or "Students can ask and answer questions concerning life for immigrant minorities." Next, instructors identify the overall project to be accomplished (e.g., a web page or podcast describing their family, a Google maps tour, a photo story, an interview with native speakers, a collection of immigrant stories). Table 10.1 offers a selection of possible projects.

Identify the final product and create the rubric   Although it may seem counterintuitive to begin planning by starting with the evaluation in mind, this method makes it much easier to explain the project to the students in the initial stages, particularly when it is tied to clearly identified objectives. By starting with the end in mind, instructors can gain a clearer idea of what steps to take to ensure that students are able to accomplish the goal. For example, if the project is to interview native speakers, it will be important to know what the project will look like upon completion. What kind of questions are they supposed to be asking (again reaffirming the objective of the project)? Will there be an oral or written presentation of responses or both? How long will the presentation be? Will there be an accompanying PowerPoint? Will there be a communal web site

---

TABLE 10.1 Possible projects

Short updates
- Online journals and diaries (blogs)
- Cell phone diaries
- Twitter status updates
- Social bookmarking

Short-to-medium presentations
- Résumés and CVs
- Online scrapbooks
- Online art galleries
- Poems and word art
- Digital stories and books
- eBook creation
- PowerPoint presentations

Research projects
- Interviews
- Newsletters and brochures
- Movie and restaurant reviews
- Reports and surveys
- Wikipedia entries
- Wiki site on a preferred topic
- Letter or email exchanges

Maps and models
- Google Earth tour of cities
- Plan a trip to a country
- Dialect maps
- Famous monument locations

Audio recordings
- Radio shows
- Podcasts
- Read aloud stories

Videos projects
- Skits and plays
- Song and dance
- Readers' theater
- Mime

Multimedia
- Photo stories and photo albums
- Virtual tours at local art museums
- Podcasts and vodcasts
- Screen casts and mashups
- Animations and cartoons

TASK 10.1

Using suggestions from Table 10.1 or your own interests, identify a possible project that might meet the objectives stated here. Share your results with others. An example follows.

Objective: Students can describe weather and local events.

Project: Students put together a morning show for different areas of the target language country or countries.

1. Students can order food in a restaurant or shop.
2. Students can ask and give directions.
3. Students can describe their daily routines.
4. Students can express their likes and dislikes (e.g., about sports, music, movies).
5. Students can describe their childhood.
6. Students can express goals, wishes, desires, and dreams.
7. Students can compare cultural products between L1 and L2.
8. Students can express opinions about familiar topics.

on which students can aggregate their results? Will the interviews be filmed or recorded? Will they be posted online? Will these interviews be part of a multi-year project? Do students work individually, in groups, or in pairs? How/when will each aspect of the project be evaluated?

When attempting to identify all of the pieces of the final project, instructors should gain a better idea of what is feasible in the amount of time they can allot to the project. Instructors may also find that significant guidance is needed as the students begin the project. The final project may not look exactly like what the instructor imagined initially, but it is important to flesh out a tentative vision of what is expected.

The next step, creating the rubric, can help instructors answer important questions about the quality and quantity of each aspect of the project. Using the earlier example: How much information should students get from each interview? What should be the focus of the conversation? Are there required and elective aspects of the interviews? Should there be requirements for length, use of outside sources (i.e., web sites, books) or number of questions asked? How will teamwork be evaluated? How will the presentation be evaluated (e.g., language, content, comprehensibility, design, oral presentation, originality, ability to work with others)?

It is important to remember that, at this point, the rubric is tentative. As instructors continue to plan the project, they may find that some aspects will need to be eliminated because of a variety of constraints (e.g., time, logistics, resources). The rubric may therefore change before it is given to the students as part of the initial instructions for the project. Rubrics are discussed in more detail later, including their benefits and the nuts and bolts of creating them.

Plan the days backwards starting with the final project/performance   Once the objectives are clear, a final project has been described, and a tentative rubric has been created, instructors can begin to plan the classes leading up to the project. Back planning from the final performance/project is relatively simple. Instructors should identify items that need to be addressed for each subsequent day to proceed. For example, to complete a video project that features stories from native speakers in the community, students need to know how to present their video (e.g., PowerPoint? YouTube?). Before presenting their video, they need to know how to edit it, and even before editing, they need to know how to record the video. Before recording, they need, most probably, to have a consent form in order to record and post the video. In order to get signed consent forms, they would need to know how to find/address/contact native speakers. Before meeting with the native speakers, they would need to know which questions to ask and how to ask them (including interview techniques) with appropriate practice in class. Students would know which questions only if the objectives and the purpose of the interview were clear to them. The purpose of the interview can be clarified as instructors show examples (if available) or model them in class. And so, in many cases, the beginning of a project is a model of the final product. The process of back planning will be significantly different for each project, but nonetheless as complex. The important point about back planning a project is that it facilitates instruction because each day/ week prepares students for the next step. Instructors should also back plan to make sure that the students have enough time and resources to produce a good project.

PREPARING THE STUDENTS   Once the project is planned, instructors can begin preparing students by making the purpose and the plan transparent, eliciting commitment from them, providing sufficient resources and support, and facilitating group interactions. A transparent plan and student commitment to the project are inextricably linked. Uden and Beaumont (2006) underscore that commitment to a project is not likely to occur when students are unsure of the goals or purpose of the project/performance, the method for creating the project, and how the project will be evaluated. In addition to being technically prepared for the activity, students must also be prepared to work in groups and have sufficient skills in information literacy to produce a project that is meaningful for the entire group.

Identify a clear purpose and transparent plan   A transparent plan includes making sure that students know why they are doing the project and how it will benefit them. These benefits should coincide to some extent with the expectations of the students in terms of their goals for the course (i.e., students should perceive class activities as enabling their language learning). Disparity of expectations between instructor and students concerning project work has been shown to result in frustration for both (Beckett, 2002). For example, if the objectives for a unit are to describe places or people, a project could be to create a target language web page for the institution. The purpose of such a project would be to show an insider's view of what the school or institution is like from a student's perspective (this is a variant of the cities project in which students describe their town online). To make the plan clear, activities would presumably include discussions concerning typical content for a web page, characteristics (e.g., design, content) of the current web page for the institution (and if it meets the expectations of what should be on an institutional web page), characteristics of a target language web site differences, pertinent information from a student perspective, and, possibly, characteristics of unacceptable institutional web sites. It may also help to know what will happen to their project: Will the project be housed on the institution's server and be available to target language speakers (i.e., like a translation of the institutional page)? Is the project being done in conjunction with another institution to share students' insights about each others' institutions/cultures? Will students make an oral presentation about the site they have created? Instructors should strive to clarify their vision concerning the creation, presentation, and future of the project.

Elicit commitment from students Commitment from students may be problematic to obtain, and not all approaches to encouraging commitment will be effective with all groups of students. A productive approach is to allow students leeway in defining the parameters of their projects, encourage expansion on aspects that are of particular interest to them, and give them an active role in designing the assessment criteria for the project and the technology they use. Students may be more committed to a project in which they can collaborate with the instructor in setting the parameters of the project, such as how many pages/sites should they write, how many images should they include, how many references/links are required, and how it will be presented. Likewise, when students are encouraged to expand on particular aspects, they generally take a decisive stance on their topic, which promotes critical thinking (Marx et al., 1994), increases motivation (Collins & Halverson, 2009), and empowers students to appropriate the project for their own purposes (Gardner, 1995; Gonglewski & DuBravac, 2006), thus increasing commitment to the project and to the group (Palloff & Pratt, 2007). Finally, when students are given the opportunity to define the assessment criteria, the end result becomes more concrete, thus making it easier for them to commit because they have a clear idea of the purpose and expected outcome of the project (Beckett, 2002).

Provide sufficient resources/support Instructors must also ensure that students have sufficient resources to complete the task and are prepared to work in groups if that is required. While doing the project, instructors can encourage positive activity by (1) making sure that students have access to the appropriate technologies, (2) ensuring that students know which applications to use and how to use them, (3) clarifying each student's role in the team, and (4) facilitating continual communication within the teams.

Instructors may be tempted to assume that because the students are digital natives, they can use the applications with minimal support, yet many digital natives are still not familiar with the specific tools needed for a project (e.g., MovieMaker, iMovie, Audacity). As with any technology, instructors should plan to have an icebreaker task to ensure that students are familiar with the technology to be used. Furthermore, students may not know how to work in groups and may benefit from training and additional social structure to help them navigate group work dynamics. An icebreaker task can help scaffold them to the point at which they can begin to work in groups.

Facilitate group interactions   PBL relies heavily on a group's ability to work as a team. Students may be resistant to working in teams for a variety of reasons (e.g., previous bad experiences, preference for working alone). Teams often do not function well because of varying expectations of the group members (Johnson & Johnson, 2005), and most teams need assistance to communicate well and work collaboratively. After setting clear expectations early, instructors should help learners clarify their role and facilitate the division of labor appropriately (Clarke, 2008). To alleviate stress within the groups and inhibit group dysfunctions, instructors should take steps to ensure that students know how to distribute responsibility, organize workload and follow-up, and provide useful feedback to one another. Regular checklists can encourage students to communicate regularly concerning the project. A short worksheet with simple items may also help (e.g., What is your responsibility? What is your partner's responsibility? Check with your partner to make sure you have similar answer).

Instructors should establish the groups early and allow ample time to organize the project and accompanying tasks, their time, and the distribution of work. Limited time for structuring the tasks for the group can cause apathy from group members, a limited scope of investigation, or hesitancy among group members who dare not be creative because the parameters of the task are not sufficiently specific or clear. Allowing ample time for organization permits the instructor to address harmful group dynamics (e.g., a dominating or a detached student), to lead students to appropriate the project for their own purposes, and to reiterate the overall objective of the project.

Group dynamics, according to Dörnyei and Murphey (2003), can determine the success or failure of the learning processes in the classroom. These group dynamics are important both in courses that meet face-to-face (F2F) as well as those that are hybrid or completely online. Mason and Rennie (2008) posit little difference in group dynamics between F2F communication and online relationships. Hence, whether the communication, organization, planning, or execution happens online or F2F, instructors should be prepared to facilitate communication and help perpetuate good group dynamics among students. Efforts to sustain healthy group dynamics should continue throughout the production phase of the project.

Production

The production phase includes cyclical feedback from the instructor and the organizing of the final project. Feedback can also come from other sources (e.g., comments on a blog, email messages, peer editing forms). It is during this phase that students begin to record, upload, and display their work. Some level of assessment occurs at this stage, although it may not be formal. For example, peers may encourage students to redo certain aspects of the project, or instructors may need to guide students toward improving pieces of the project. The purpose of continual feedback during the production stage is to improve students' overall performance, encourage self-assessment, and promote process-oriented approaches to learning. Organizing the presentation of the project is also included here because the presentation is, in most cases, the crowning activity for the project and it may take several days for all students to present their projects.

During the planning stage, instructors should have given students checklists and rubrics to enable them to monitor their progress as they complete the project. Instructors can engage others in the evaluation process throughout the production stage using shareable media (e.g., social networks, public blogs, online video/image repositories). For example, short rubrics that include four simple indicators can be used for peer evaluation: I understand the project easily, I understand most of the project, I understand some of the project, or I don't really understand what you have done. Instructors can also involve outside participants (i.e., other classes, parents, friends) by soliciting feedback via posted comments of work published on the web. The internet should be used judiciously to showcase student work, depending on the age of the students, but in many cases parents, peers, and friends are eager to provide positive feedback. This type of feedback is facilitated in the online version of LinguaFolio (LinguaFolio.uoregon.edu, discussed later in this chapter) that includes methods for self- and other evaluation (including peers and eventually parents). Shareable presentations and accompanying checklists or rubrics help clarify the tasks in the project and serve to provide substantial feedback along the way to improve the end product (Shrum & Glisan, 2010).

The project can be presented in a variety of forms, including live oral reports; recorded audio, video, and multimedia presentations; or screen casts for blended learning environments. When organizing the performance, instructors should be mindful of time and space constraints, evaluation concerns, and how feedback will be reported. The initial instructions should include duration limits (e.g., a 2- to 5-minute presentation); an additional 5 to 10 minutes per presentation will allow for setup, follow-up, and transition to the next group. Considering the amount of time that students spend preparing and completing the assignment, it is unwise to rush students through their project presentations. If lack of time and lengthy presentations are concerns, instructors can elect a timekeeper for the activity or make a clock visible to the entire class. Instructors must make sure that sufficient time is allotted for the presentation of all groups or individuals and the presentations may often span several days.

Much has been written about the general learning differences between contemporary youth and older generations (Collins & Halverson, 2009; Sharpe, Beetham, & de Freitas, 2010). An important characteristic of contemporary youth is the relational aspects that surround learning activities (McNeely, 2005). For many of today's youth, learning is more of a social experience than an individual activity. Hence, presentations are enhanced by extending them to the society outside the school or institution. They may be done in class for peers or outside of class in a public arena (i.e., at a café, on YouTube, or as

TASK 10.2

Projects can often become more social by simply adding a task or tweaking an existing task. Explain how the following projects can become more social for students. An example follows.

Objective: Students produce a video of a skit.

Example: Videos are posted on YouTube. Students must post comments using the superlative such as, "This is the funniest video" or "This is the longest video." All groups must come to a consensus on the superlatives.

1. Students do PowerPoint presentations on holidays in the target culture.
2. Students produce travel brochures for specific cities in the target culture.
3. Students keep an online journal.
4. Students create digital stories about their youth.
5. Students produce restaurant reviews for their cities.

a webinar). Feedback can also come from in-class participants as well as the public at large for presentations in the public sphere. For example, a project for which students write their own poetry and read it at a local café is enhanced when they can plan the presentation (e.g., make flyers, invite friends), receive feedback in a variety of ways (comments on a blog, posts on a Facebook wall, or comment cards available at the presentation), and share the results with other participants.

Evaluation

The third phase, evaluation, relies on efficient and positive feedback from multiple sources and should promote project extension. This interpretation and reporting of results can come from four basic sources: self, instructors, peers, and others. As mentioned earlier, efficient feedback is facilitated with checklists and rubrics. Project extension occurs when students continue to work on the project by sharing it with others, revising it, or combining it with other projects.

The methods of interpreting and reporting results can be as varied as the projects themselves. The feedback to the student ideally includes more than a percentage or letter grade and normally comes from several sources. Arguably, the most important assessment that students receive for their project is the self-assessment. With the help of checklists of "can-do" statements, students can easily assess their projects and their progress. Emphasis on can-do statements (Gouiller, 2007; National Council for State Supervisors for Languages, 2012) has facilitated feedback that highlights learners' abilities rather than what they have failed to do and encourages students to assess their own performance and identify goals for improvement. Detailed feedback with rubrics (e.g., meets expectations) has been shown to improve overall performance (Adair-Hauck et al., 2006).

The instructor generally contributes feedback in the form of a rubric, often with additional comments that identify strengths or areas for improvement. Peers, with the help of the instructor, can provide feedback in the form of rubrics, checklists, or comments. Furthermore, other individuals (such as parents, administrators, students in other classes, or other teachers) can easily provide feedback in the form of comments; Web 2.0 applications (blogs, wikis, YouTube, etc.) usually allow visitors to post comments. Other services enable anyone to comment on any page (e.g., Diigo's diigolet, Firefox's Internote BounceApp.com).

Extending the project enables students to repeat positive experiences in other arenas. For example, a project in which students compare French homes with American homes by combining (known as mashing) audio overlay and textual markup with online photos from France and the United States (e.g., apartments, single-dwelling houses, and town homes in urban and rural settings) would take a significant amount of time and might spark interest in both the technology and the content. If students demonstrate increased motivation and enthusiasm in such a project, they might be interested in another that uses and integrates the material from their housing project to study transportation, for example, by using the same tools to examine another cultural phenomenon (e.g., cars, buses, trains, tramways).

Projects can assume a variety of forms that may or may not include technology (however, technology seems to exploit the advantages of PBL). Instructors should be aware of how best to prepare and plan, implement and support, and evaluate and extend the project not only through the class but also throughout the curriculum. These extensions can include additional episodes (e.g., of a vodcast, podcast, or webzine) or projects that use similar technologies on additional topics (e.g., blog journals on specific topics, mashups to compare cultural phenomena, or social bookmarking projects to explore perspectives on content). Finally, for those who promote PBL, assessment and teaching are two sides of the same coin. The preparation and production of projects facilitates what Ellis (2003) calls incidental formative assessment that arises from "instructional conversations" that make it indistinguishable from good teaching (p. 314).

ePORTFOLIOS

Both performances and projects can become part of an ePortfolio stored both for a single course and for a series of courses (e.g., all courses included in a major, those required for certification). Portfolio grading has been popular in studio art programs around the country and came into fashion before the turn of the millennium in English writing and composition departments as an acceptable method of assessment (Katz, 1988; Moya & O'Malley, 1991; Purves & Quattrini, 1997; Valencia, 1990). High school and middle school language classes have long used portfolios as a way of evaluating projects and assessing the process of language learning. Nevertheless, language departments in colleges and universities throughout the United States have proven less eager to incorporate portfolio assessment into the curriculum. Although various second language (L2) composition courses in the university setting have periodically championed portfolio grading, the cause has not consistently spread across foreign language programs.

Different types of ePortfolios have different purposes and goals. It is important to distinguish the purpose of the ePortfolio before assignments are made. Some ePortfolios include only the best of what has been done throughout the semester, others focus on multiple drafts to show progress on a given writing task, and still others focus on the variety and scope of the work done in class. In general, ePortfolios have two main purposes: learning and accountability. The learning ePortfolio functions as a method of documenting a student's learning experience or progress in certain areas (e.g., speaking, strategy use, meeting standards, IPA results), and this has been the trend in the L2 curriculum. An accountability ePortfolio is usually summative in nature and provides a final picture of the accomplishments of a semester, term, or year. The main difference between a learning ePortfolio and an assessment ePortfolio lies in the audience. A learning ePortfolio is addressed to everyone, reflects the identity of the student who creates it, and is constantly under construction; an accountability ePortfolio is addressed to the instructor (or committee); reveals the documented progress or final state of the required skills; and must represent a final, finished product for evaluative purposes.

This section focuses on a learning ePortfolio. We begin by discussing LinguaFolio which is the premier tool designed for documenting language learning experiences. The advantages of LinguaFolio are both technological and curricular. We then discuss the content and particular advantages provided by an ePortfolio. Finally, we describe how to go about assembling an ePortfolio and what practices can facilitate ePortfolio creation for students.

LinguaFolio

LinguaFolio was created by the National Council of State Supervisors for Language (NCSSFL) initially in a paper format, but it also exists in an online format (LinguaFolio.uoregon.edu). The online version and the paper version are nearly identical. On the online version, students can access the three basic components of LinguaFolio from the main menu: the biography, the passport, and the dossier. Each component serves a different function. In the biography, students write their background (e.g., languages studied, heritage status, age) and intercultural activities (called *interculturality* on the online version), which includes any encounters they have with the target culture. In the passport section, students put formal assessments and self-assessments. The passport section includes a collection of checklists whereby learners can identify abilities and goals. They can also begin to upload evidence to accompany the successfully completed items from the checklist. For example, if the checklist says, "I can greet people in a polite way using single words and memorized phrases," learners may choose to upload a video of their greeting a native speaker using formulaic speech. Each of the items in the checklist is broken down into smaller tasks. For example, the task just noted can be separated into "I can say hello to my teacher," "I can say hello to someone I do not know," or "I can say hello to an adult," among others. Uploaded evidence is stored in the dossier. The dossier can support a wide variety of image, sound, and video formats, as well as Web 2.0 sources (e.g., blogs, wikis, Twitter, Facebook).

LinguaFolio is an excellent model for language teachers for two significant reasons. First, it overcomes the technical difficulties that teachers and administrators have of where to store students' work and how to train individuals for the technical aspects of ePortfolios. This advantage is less impressive when you consider that many individuals are already well versed in the technology-related practices required by LinguaFolio (e.g., posting comments, uploading/downloading files, filling in online forms, or even posting video from a mobile device). The second reason, and by far the most astounding advantage of LinguaFolio, is that it forces instructors to focus on portfolio grading as a conversation about learning rather than a one-way presentation. Students take ownership of their learning ePortfolios; ePortfolio development is no longer the routine assignment whereby instructors tell students which items to put in the ePortfolio; learners are responsible for determining which goals to focus on, whether or not they have achieved these goals, and what evidence supports that achievement. LinguaFolio requires instructors to approach portfolio assessment from a collaborative, documentation-of-learning approach rather than a summative, accountability approach to learning.

Because LinguaFolio restricts what instructors can do to some extent, it may be frustrating to those who view it as a method of accountability or as a replacement for standardized tests. However, LinguaFolio provides a flexible tool that can be used in a variety of settings (immersion, language for specific purposes, K–8, 9–12, postsecondary, or postgraduate) and provides longitudinal support to language learners. Learners are responsible for their development, and teachers, instructors, and professors can articulate proficiency demands using a common language. This articulation aims to propel learners to higher levels of proficiency (NCCSFL, 2011). LinguaFolio offers many advantages to document learning, but these student-centered advantages should be weighed against the institutional requirements of accountability and evaluation.

Contents

After the purpose of the ePortfolio has been identified (e.g., to document learning, to provide accountability), the instructor and/or student must decide what goes into an ePortfolio. Traditionally, the contents of a portfolio stemmed from the class content and so depended on the course focus or level. Modern learning ePortfolios can contain any communicative activity in which a student engages and can include a wide variety of formats: audio/video recording, slideshows, screencasts, photostories, chat transcripts, personalized portals, RSS feeds, SMS/IM exchanges, blog/microblog/web site/discussion posts, mobile phone diaries, wiki sites, webzines, profile or group pages (e.g., Facebook, LinkedIn), online games, mashups (e.g., Google Earth Presentations), eBooks, or podcasts, to name only a few.

Additionally, formal assessment materials for a portfolio have generally included items handed back to the student such as entry/exit assessments, progress reports, observations, peer evaluations, checklists, feedback from presentations, journals, video/audio tapes, or final papers or projects. Today, most documents are created digitally to begin with (i.e., born digital) or they are Web 2.0 pieces and can simply be links to items already found online. With material already online, the contents can easily represent multiple capabilities rather than specific abilities, developments, or preferences. Instructors may want to decide on the contents before the assembly begins. LinguaFolio is an excellent model for this because precise items are not required; rather, any evidence that justifies a can-do statement is acceptable. Students can justify that they can greet someone by posting video or audio, telling a story, or showing a picture. Table 10.2 compares the old and new expectations of what belongs in an ePortfolio.

The positive aspects of ePortfolios are too numerous to provide an in-depth description of all of them, but a few of the key advantages are listed here:

- ePortfolios promote task authenticity. Bonk and Cunningham (1998) argue that students write for real audiences and not just the instructor.
- ePortfolios provide positive example to others in the class of what constitutes good work. This may be of particular use to those having difficulty conceptualizing the task.
- ePortfolios facilitate storage, recording, and possibly presentation.
- Stored student performances focus attention on the task of using the language rather than having linguistic knowledge (i.e., completing a test).

TABLE 10.2 Old and new models of portfolio contents

Old model	New model
Includes items handed back to the student	Includes anything born digital
• entry/exit tests	• learner biography
• student progress reports	• links to online projects
• teacher observations	• links to feedback/survey results
• comments from peers	• links to posts/status updates
• checklists	• links to blogs/wikis/web sites
• journals/logs	• links to online rating (like/dislike)
• videos and audiotapes	• links to posted videos/audios
• presentations, transcripts	• social bookmarks
• email messages	• screen shots and/or transcripts
• final projects	• links to uploaded/shared media
Carefully classified for readability/evaluation	Tagged and commented
• arranged as per instructors directive	• structured by popularity/tags/searchable
• designed to show progress over time	• designed to show current activities
Must meet requirements by the instructor	Guided by self-evaluation and can-do
• instructor lists minimum requirements	• students determine what constitutes learning
• instructor supplies rubric and evaluates portfolio in consultation with student	• Self and peer assessment play key roles

- ePortfolio assessments allow for multiple approaches to a problem; a concentration on the individual needs and interests of the students; and higher-level skills of socialization, functional proficiency, and the ability to integrate information.
- ePortfolios generally have no negative washback effects (Moya & O'Malley, 1991).
- ePortfolios facilitate a focus on process over product. The nature of the web (and thereby ePortfolios) is constant change and evolution. Writing on the web for the web emphasizes that texts are never completely finished because writers always have the ability to edit their work even after turning it in.
- ePortfolios integrate easily throughout the curriculum. In most cases, ePortfolios are completed in a single course, rather than throughout the curriculum (Batson, 2010). Creating ePortfolios can help students have a running record of everything they have accomplished in the language.

Assembling the ePortfolio

Similar to working on projects and performances, attention to a few key guidelines can enable instructors to take advantage of the benefits of ePortfolios. The guidelines are simple and include the icebreaker task for the ePortfolio, collaboration, and modeling. These guidelines can promote student engagement, encourage social approaches to learning, and facilitate creativity.

As with most activities that include technology, an icebreaker task helps students prepare for an activity while enabling the instructor to identify individuals who may have difficulty accomplishing the final project. The icebreaker task for ePortfolios should be simple but relevant and measurable to ensure that students have the technological prowess to continue to develop the ePortfolio throughout the semester or curriculum without constant intervention from the instructor. One possible assignment is an introductory statement of expectations for the course. An expectations assignment lets the instructor know that students have begun their ePortfolio and that they have identified a location where they can compile the additional assignments to include in their ePortfolio. The icebreaker task could also be a profile page, a table of contents, or a learning biography (as in LinguaFolio). The instructor can, at this point, create a central site to link to each student's ePortfolio.

Although most portfolios are used for individualized assessment, ePortfolios enable collaboration because all students can access others' pieces. LinguaFolio, for example, allows learners to make their evidence available to other students in order to receive feedback from them. The final product for some ePortfolio entries may appear like a Facebook wall on which a learner's post is supported by abundant feedback from peers. Collaborations require social time and support to encourage interaction. Regular time dedicated to ePortfolio development throughout the semester can help students interact, focus on their goals, add new items to the ePortfolio, and improve previous items.

Finally, each ePortfolio provides positive examples to others concerning how certain tasks can be done. Instructors can also provide examples of the types of evidence that can be included in ePortfolio. Many students may not have created ePortfolios before, or they may be unclear on the purpose or use of ePortfolios. Simply providing model items in the ePortfolio may ease many of the students' doubts and uncertainties. The model can be created by the instructor or taken from one used in previous years, but it should be in a recognizable form such as a Facebook page, LinkedIn site, or portal page with which students are familiar. By using common formatting and design and a well-known platform, instructors help students view the ePortfolio as a simple, regular activity, rather than extra projects for the course.

Finally, rubrics and checklists not only help assess the ePortfolio, they help define it and clarify exactly what belongs in it. Checklists and rubrics are discussed in depth in the next section in relation to projects, performances, and ePortfolios.

CHECKLISTS AND RUBRICS

Regardless of the form of the alternative assessment (performance, project, or ePortfolio), checklists or rubrics are indispensable. This section discusses the difference between checklists and rubrics, how to develop them, and how and when to use them. Checklists and rubrics have two distinct advantages: (1) they allow instructors to be more objective in their evaluation procedures, and (2) they allow instructors to include others in the evaluation process without extensive training on the grading process.

The major difference between checklists and rubrics is the number of performance indicators per category. Rubrics generally offer various levels of performance (e.g., on a scale of 0–4), whereas checklists normally indicate whether an item is present or absent. Checklists are particularly useful for students to know exactly what is expected in a project and can often detail the steps that students must take to complete the project (e.g., "Your presentation must include the following items: one picture, three videos, etc."). Figure 10.1 shows a comparison of a checklist and a rubric.

Checklist for beginning language	Rubric for beginning language		
Check the items that you can do:	Check the items that you can do:		
☐ I can greet people.		I can	With help	My goal
☐ I can count money.				
☐ I can tell time.	I can greet people.	☐	☐	☐
☐ I can identify classroom objects.	I can count money.	☐	☐	☐
☐ I can say goodbye.	I can tell time.	☐	☐	☐
	I can identify classroom objects.	☐	☐	☐
	I can say goodbye.	☐	☐	☐

FIGURE 10.1 Checklist and rubric comparison

Rubrics are usually laid out in a grid style that gives specific indicators rather than the three global indicators shown in Figure 10.1. Figure 10.2 shows a typical rubric for a project. The categories are listed along the left side (Content, Presentation, Workload, Attractiveness, Requirements), and each category has four possible levels. Instructors can use the rubric to determine how each aspect of the project (in this case a multimedia project) meets the standards.

The rubric shown in Figure 10.2 is an analytic rubric. Analytic rubrics break the project into components that can be assessed separately. Rubrics are relatively easy to develop, and a number of excellent sites on the web facilitate rapid rubric development (e.g., Kathy Schrock's guide www.schrockguide.net/assessment-and-rubrics.html, Rubistar.4Teachers.org, www.Rubrics4Teachers .com). Rubistar, for example, allows instructors to log in, choose the type of activity (e.g., video, web site, multimedia, digital storytelling), and then decide on the key elements (e.g., presentation, grammar, content, organization) depending on the type of activity. Rubistar makes a variety of suggestions for key elements and descriptors for each category. Instructors can modify the rubric by translating it into the target language, modifying the points, or creating additional categories. Once the instructor is satisfied with the rubric, it can be printed, downloaded, or saved online for students, parents, and cooperating teachers.

Finally, checklists and rubrics are particularly helpful when they accompany examples of good student work. Students can make greater sense of performance indicators when they can see concrete examples of how each description is realized. Curtain and Dahlberg (2010) suggest using a variety of examples that are very different from one another in order to encourage individual creativity.

TASK 10.3

Using one of the web sites listed here, create a rubric for a final project, performance, or ePortfolio. Make sure to title your rubric so it is clear what type of object you are assessing.

rubistar.4teachers.org

www.rubrics4teachers.com

www.rubricbuilder.on.ca

www.teach-nology.com/web_tools/rubrics

www.schrockguide.net/assessment-and-rubrics.html

TECHNICAL CONSIDERATIONS

This section focuses on the technical considerations for ePortfolios; the previous chapters discussed the various technologies used in creating the pieces for the ePortfolio (e.g., Chapter 7 examined synchronous tools; Chapter 8 looked at asynchronous tools). ePortfolio formats range widely and depend on available

CATEGORY	4	3	2	1
Content	Covers topic in-depth with details and examples. Subject knowledge is excellent.	Includes essential knowledge about the topic. Subject knowledge appears to be good.	Includes essential information about the topic but there are 1–2 factual errors.	Content is minimal OR there are several factual errors.
Presentation	I understood most of the presentation.	I understood a lot of the presentation.	I understood about half of the presentation.	I didn't really understand much.
Workload	The workload is divided and shared equally by all team members.	The workload is divided and shared fairly by all team members, although workloads may vary from person to person.	The workload was divided, but one person in the group is viewed as not doing his/her fair share of the work.	The workload was not divided OR several people in the group are viewed as not doing their fair share of the work.
Attractiveness	Makes excellent use of font, color, graphics, effects, etc. to enhance the presentation.	Makes good use of font, color, graphics, effects, etc. to enhance the presentation.	Makes use of font, color, graphics, effects, etc. but occasionally these detract from the presentation content.	Uses font, color, graphics, effects, etc. but these often distract from the presentation content.
Requirements	All requirements are met and exceeded.	All requirements are met.	One requirement was not completely met.	More than one requirement was not completely met.

From Rubistar.4teachers.org

FIGURE 10.2 Typical rubric for a multimedia project

resources, student computer skills, and instructor needs. When deciding on the best electronic format for student ePortfolios, instructors should consider the following technical concerns: ease of use for students, sense of ownership, ease of access for readers, availability of templates, aggregatable data, amount of storage, and frequency of data backups/reliability of the server. Ease of use for students means that they should have little difficulty accessing, storing, deleting, and modifying their ePortfolio items. Sense of ownership means that students feel like their ePortfolio is a representation of themselves and not just another assignment. If the rest of the class will also read the assignment, ease of access for others becomes more important. If the instructor is the only reader, then easy access may not be a dominant concern. A variety of templates that support multimedia files (e.g., audio, video, slide presentations) can help students improve the appearance of their online work. Blackboard, for example, allows students to select templates for job portfolios, school portfolios, and course portfolios using the same documents that are modified depending on the template used. The ability to aggregate certain data may be extremely useful for instructors who need to show consistent progress of students diachronically (e.g., across semesters, before and after study abroad) or on a large scale (e.g., among several classes). The amount of available storage will also be a factor if students are creating and posting numerous multimedia files, because these files tend to be large. Finally, instructors should try to select a server that is backed up regularly (nightly or weekly at the least) to make sure that students do not lose files. The final decision about which technology is best will depend on the purpose and use of the ePortfolio, the instructor's and the students' familiarity with the technology, and the students' ability to access the technology. The following discussion addressed various platforms for ePortfolios and the advantages and disadvantages of each.

ePortfolios can be stored on various platforms including the following:

- Files on portable storage such as a DVD or flashdrive
- Files in the cloud or on a web site such as Dropbox, Box.net, Yahoo, Google docs, or personal web sites
- Blogs and microblogs
- Wikis
- Learning management systems (LMSs)
- Social networking sites

The simplest form of an ePortfolio is a collection of files saved on portable storage such as a DVD or a flashdrive. The files can be hyperlinked from a *Welcome Page* or *Table of Contents* document such as an MSWord document, a spreadsheet, a web page, or PowerPoint. This type of structure is generally easy for students to learn, encourages a sense of ownership, and supports multimedia, but it has limitations on access for readers, available templates, and regular backups. Because the information is not on the web, it is available only to those who have access to the physical storage (e.g., flashdrive, zipped files). The templates usually rely on what the instructor supplies, and the backup schedule depends on the students' diligence to save their work regularly. Files on portable storage are limited to the size of the disc (4.7GB) or flashdrive (320GB and rising) and do not allow instructors to aggregate data from others in similar classes or to compare accomplishments among students without considerable difficulty.

ePortfolios created as web sites are an improvement on static files located on portable storage. A number of web site creation tools exist such as Google sites (or Google docs), Tripod.com, Zoho.com, Bravenet.com, or others mentioned in Chapter 2. Web pages have some of the same advantages as portable media ePortfolios: they are easy for students to learn, they encourage a sense of ownership, and they support multimedia. Web sites or cloud resources are better than flashdrives because they provide greater access to readers and usually offer templates and regular backups of the information. Like portable media, cloud or web sites do not offer the ability to aggregate the data and may have significant space limitations (even Google limits documents to 5GB as of 2012). Instructors and students can circumvent these limitations by using cloud storage services (e.g., YouTube for videos, PhotoBucket/Picasa for pictures, eSnips.com for audio files, Box.net, SkyDrive.com and FlipDrive.com. for large document files), but there are less complex alternatives. A notable advantage with the web site creation tools or cloud services is that they allow students to create items for upload or create them directly on the site. Students do not need their own computer or flashdrive to continue to work on a project. This can be particularly useful when a substitute teacher is needed or if students forget to bring papers to class. LinguaFolio online (LinguaFolio.uoregon.edu) fits into this group of ePortfolio formats.

The third group of ePortfolio formats includes blogs and microblogs. The advantage of using a blog or microblog is the intuitive posting. Very few, if any, services are easier to learn to use than blogs and microblogs. Most blogs are fully customizable, which gives users a good sense of ownership. Blogging sites also offer the option to make the blog public or private for the benefit of readers and provide a wide variety of templates. All blogs and several microblogs support multimedia with few limits on storage and frequent backups. In fact, it is often safer to keep your journal online than on your computer (or backup drive) simply because your files would still be safe in case of fire, earthquake, flood, or theft if they are maintained in the cloud. Blogs and microblogs are aggregateable. For example, Twitter is inherently an aggregate of all the people you follow. Likewise, blogs generally contain an RSS feed that could be easily aggregated using a reader such as Google Reader or Bloglines.com. In this way, instructors would be able to see the content from a variety of places all in one place. The content would be structured chronologically rather than logically, which may be a problem only if instructors require a specific order to the ePortfolio contents.

The wiki format for ePortfolios maintains most of the advantages mentioned previously. They are easy to learn and easy to access. Wikis support multimedia, offer numerous templates, have plentiful storage, and back up regularly (and even let you return to previous versions after having saved changes). Wikis usually foster a sense of ownership because individuals can customize much of their experience and share with others without significant problems. Wikis can cause difficulties for instructors because they have no inherent structure and the data are not aggregatable. Hence, it may be difficult if not impossible for instructors to know if and when an assignment is added to the ePortfolio, and it is equally difficult for instructors to be able to compare multiple ePortfolios at once.

Not surprisingly, LMSs offer formats that maintain significant advantages for student ePortfolios. These systems along with those services that specifically target online ePortfolios (e.g., Epsilen.com, foliotek.com, eFolioMinnesota. com, Nuventive.com) tend to meet all the necessary criteria. Both Blackboard's ePortfolio and Moodle's Moofolio offer wizards and templates to facilitate learning and permissions to control access to readers and support a wide variety of multimedia. The storage and backup are dependent on the administrators of the particular institution hosting the site, but storage is normally plentiful and, at a minimum, backups occur every 24 hours. The data can be aggregated for the instructors so they can see multiple ePortfolios at once for grading purposes and can search all students' ePortfolios for specific items. Students can create multiple ePortfolios for different classes but include identical elements without the need for redundant posting of materials. The major drawback of LMS ePortfolios is that students cannot normally take their ePortfolio with them. In other words, LMS-based ePortfolios do not necessarily foster ownership because the materials are not easily accessed beyond the institution. There are some exceptions whereby universities continue to grant access to individuals, and both Moodle and Blackboard allow students to burn their ePortfolios to portable media such as a flashdrive. For the most part, however, students complete the ePortfolio for one particular class and then do nothing else with it (Batson, 2010).

Finally, social networking sites provide a solid foundation for ePortfolio development. Social networking sites are, by nature, ePortfolios of the user's life that include photos, videos, personal and professional information, and updates while enabling sharing and evaluation of contributions. Social networking sites range from highly personal ones such as Facebook.com, Orkut.com, and Bebo .com, to more professional sites such as LinkedIn.com, Xing.com, and Naymz .com. These services are extremely easy to learn, and many of them are intuitive and may also offer tutorials and reminders (e.g., "You haven't completed a portion on your profile"). They are aimed at making data accessible to readers and support standard multimedia formats. Some sites allow for templates and customization of design, whereas others provide a common interface. Most social networking sites provide sufficient storage and back up data regularly. As with many of the previous formats, social networking sites do not allow (or encourage) the aggregation of data from multiple member pages. The main advantage of using social networking sites for ePortfolio development is that most participants already produce portfolio-type entries for their network without identifying their work as an ePortfolio-building activity. It is also arguable that social networking sites foster a sense of ownership that is unparalleled in other forms. A potential drawback of using social networking sites is that

TASK 10.4

How does LinguaFolio compare to the other platforms mentioned? Using the criteria mentioned earlier for your comparison:

- Ease of use
- Sense of ownership
- Ease of access
- Availability of templates
- Aggregatable data
- Amount of storage
- Reliability of the server

students may not want to have their language class interfere with their personal expression. However, that is exactly the goal for most language teachers—to create lifelong learners of the language who use the language outside of the class and beyond their time spent in class.

As has been argued in this chapter, alternative assessments have numerous advantages. Regardless of the format for the alternative assessment or the technological tools used to complete the project, performance, or ePortfolio, a few simple rules can improve the planning, production, and feedback of the final product. First, planning should begin with the end product and back plan to the first day of the project. The planning phase also includes preparing students by familiarizing them with the technology, the language task, and the self-assessment tools. The production phase of alternative assessment includes continual, dynamic feedback so students can repair and improve while completing the project. Finally, the evaluation phase includes feedback from multiple sources (self, peer, instructor, parents, others) and uses multiple formats (checklists, rubrics, comments, votes, etc.). It is the consistent execution of these three phases that allows instructors to take advantage of the benefits offered by technology and alternative assessment.

Practical Work

1. Using the integrated performance assessment as a prototype, plan a lesson or series of lessons in which you detail the interpretive, interpersonal, and presentational tasks for a given content area. How will you know if the students have achieved the objectives?
2. Identify a project you want to do with your students. Some examples may include a literary magazine, a radio show, a podcast, or a video project. Choose the theme and articulate each step of the project from the presentation to the students to the feedback provided to them after the project is complete. What types of technology are required (e.g., video cameras, audio recordings, design programs for the computer)?
3. Begin a professional ePortfolio for yourself using a social networking site such as LinkedIn.com or Xing.com. Include links to your online work and your students' online work, including blogs, videos, Twitter account, and web sites.

4. Open an account at LinguaFolio.uoregon.edu and complete the biography and some of the passport sections. How do you think this helps describe your language learning? How does it differ from what you expected?

5. Some alternative forms of assessment that were not mentioned in this chapter are open-ended questions, exhibits, and demonstrations. Why do you think that these weren't discussed in this chapter? How can each of these be used in the L2 curriculum?

Suggestions for Further Reading

Barrett, H. (2010). E-portfolio portal. Available at ElectronicPortfolios.com

Curtain, H., & Dahlberg, C. A. (2010). *Language and children, making the match: New language for young learners, grades K–8* (4th ed.). Boston: Pearson.

Glisan, E., Adair-Hauck, B., Koda, K., Sandrock, P., & Swender, E. (2003). *ACTFL Integrated Performance Assessment*. Yonkers, NY: ACTFL.

Jeon-Ellis, G., Debski, R., & Wigglesworth, G. (2005). Oral interaction around computers in the project-oriented CALL classroom. *Language Learning & Technology 9*(3), 121–145.

Johnson, D., & Johnson, R. (2005). *Joining together: Group theory and group skills* (9th ed.). Boston: Allyn & Bacon.

Palloff, R. M., & Pratt, K. (2007). *Building online learning communities: Effective strategies for the virtual classroom*. San Francisco, CA: Jossey-Bass.

Zubizarreta, J. (2004). *The learning portfolio: Reflective practice for improving student learning*. San Francisco: Jossey-Bass.

CHAPTER 11

The Future of CALL

OVERVIEW

This volume has examined technology in the second language (L2) curriculum by discussing four areas of computer-assisted language learning (CALL): electronic media evaluation and use, L2 learning and teaching, computer-mediated communication (CMC), and assessment. This chapter reviews current developments in these areas with an eye toward how these trends in technology and world language education influence future directions in CALL. The most recent developments in CALL are driven by the "social turn" in both second language acquisition (SLA; Block, 2003; Ellis, 2003; Firth & Wagner, 1997; Thorne, 2008) and computing. Social behavior will increasingly impact how instructors choose and use electronic materials. Whereas instructors will continue to share resources via social networks and personal learning networks (PLNs), computers will draw on user behavior data to suggest sites and activities. Human-to-human communication via computer is complemented more and more by machine-to-machine communication and decision making (e.g., automatically ordering supplies when sensors indicate low levels, changing the language on a mobile device according to the GPS sensor, or determining the most appropriate homework according to the results from the most recent test) thus exemplifying the evolution from Web 1.0 toward Web 3.0 applications. The increase in machine-to-machine decision making has been facilitated by data creation and management that will eventually have an influence on localization of applications.

Social uses of technology have influenced the types of tasks in which learners engage both within and beyond the classroom. Gaming is increasingly recognized as a viable method of learning. Moreover, CALL will support language maintenance (and not simply language learning) to a greater extent as well as facilitating lifelong learning of languages and cultures. The social emphasis in technology and learning has also shaped how and why people speak to each other and what technology they use to learn or maintain languages. Communication trends include the ubiquity of mobile devices and the use of electronic books (including textbooks) that will continue to influence literacy practices. Finally, as stated in Chapter 10, although standardized testing is on the rise for languages, learning assessment practices will continue to encourage self-assessment and social validation through peer networks. Instructors should strive to be aware of these trends and identify a toolbox of resources to facilitate language learning activities among students.

TRENDS IN EVALUATION

Much of Chapter 2 addressed how language instructors can find and make use of technological resources for teaching. Social input will increasingly inform instructors' decisions about which tools to use. Current trends indicate growth in crowdsourcing, viral activities, and social rankings. Crowdsourcing is the act of taking a job traditionally accomplished by a single individual and outsourcing it to a group of people via an open call for input. This model of activity stems from open source software practices in which a variety of individuals contribute code to produce a free application. Crowdsourcing has been used for many different commercial products including beer (samueladams.com), clothing (threadless.com), vehicles (local-motors.com), restaurants (http://www.facebook.com/media/set/?set=a.115969038463663.15153.108821665845067), and reference materials (wikipedia.com, urbandictionary.com). In all of these cases, the product is defined by an entity (a person, a group, a sponsor), the call is made, and others contribute solutions. Crowdsourcing works because the product is well defined by the initiator and the responses go directly to the initiator. Language teaching suffers from a lack of agreement concerning how and why language learning happens. As such, crowdsourcing could work for language educators through their particular social networks because these would presumably include like-minded individuals (see Chapter 8). The initiator will not have to filter out suggestions that do not align with his or her underlying language learning assumptions. Moreover, because crowdsourced solutions come directly to the initiator, teachers are not required to search for the answers; the answers come to them. Attempts have been made to produce repositories of good language learning sites and activities. Merlot.org, for example, is a wonderful tagged, commented, and rated repository for online language learning resources, but it is underutilized by language instructors who must still search for, evaluate, and adapt activities for their local needs and objectives. Crowdsourcing materials development and evaluation allows instructors to select from a list rather than search through databases.

The sharing of electronic materials can occur on request such as crowdsourcing or from unsolicited suggestions, as shown by the phenomenon of viral videos. A viral video is one that has become popular through internet sharing.

The video becomes viral because so many users find it interesting and repost the link to various sites or email it to their friends. Sharing of useful sites and activities is most likely to occur on social networks or through PLNs. As mentioned in Chapters 6 and 8, instructors learn about new resources and activities through their PLNs. These resources become available only to those connected to the professional network, so it will be increasingly important for instructors to participate in a well-connected PLN composed of like-minded individuals (see Chapter 3).

Finally, evaluation of CALL resources will be facilitated through social bookmarking on sites such as delicious.com, digg.com, and stumbleupon.com. Instructors bookmark good sites or activities that they find online. Members of their social group can see the popularity of these sites among their peers. The evaluation of sites and activities will increasingly become socially driven. Friends will suggest popular and useful sites or these sites will simply rise to the top of a computer-created suggestion list because their usefulness has been shown through visits or recommendations. Instructors who increase their connections in PLNs will be able to receive the most updated information about effective resources and their uses.

INTERNET TRENDS

Internet analysts have been avidly watching the evolution from static Web 1.0 applications, characterized by unidimensional information flow, to social Web 2.0 applications, characterized by social interconnectivity. The move toward Web 3.0 applications, in which machines play a role in decision making, does not entail a loss of Web 1.0 applications, just as Web 2.0 did not do away with static web pages and presentational web sites. Similarly, Web 3.0 will not make the internet any less social (Web 2.0), but rather Web 3.0 applications will capitalize on the social aspects of the internet and allow computers to facilitate internet activity through data management and interconnectedness of devices.

As discussed in Chapter 3, the versioning of the web (1.0, 2.0, and 3.0) refers more to human use of the web rather than to the web itself. Web 1.0 applications tend to provide static, read-only pages, from which users find and consume information from reputable sources. Web 2.0 applications tend to be interactive and allow users to both read and write on the web. In the case of Web 2.0, users find, consume, produce, evaluate, and share information with other users. Web 3.0 applications extend beyond Web 2.0 uses because the computer becomes a user in the production and evaluation of information. Web 3.0 applications can be seen in social networking friend suggestions (facebook. com, goodreads.com), product suggestions depending on past purchases or wish lists (iTunes, Amazon), or restaurant suggestions depending on your location and past interests (urbanspoon.com, yelp.com). Web 3.0 may take a while to reach academia for teaching purposes, but when it does, it could easily play a role in how homework is assigned. For example, students could take pre- and posttests that allow the computer to determine which types of activities provide the most efficient help, feedback, or practice for individual students. The

computer will simply monitor the types of activities that foster the most noticeable benefits for each learner and be able to suggest activities based on past
performance. Further, using information from previous classes, friends, or other
online activities, computers could make suggestions about how best to prepare
for upcoming tests or which activities a learner should practice to satisfy benchmarks set by the institution or instructor. Web 3.0 also facilitates mobile learning, in which computers could make suggestions of what to study according to
location, available time, or time of day.

Web 3.0 applications require significant data management. Data must be
collected (e.g., age, location, preferences, friends, interests) and then applied
to specific users. User data are increasingly easy to collect and store because
users typically log in to sites through which the server can track behavior to
keep a record of interests. Using mobile apps, services can track the location of
students and the times when they are most active. Given students' histories, current interests, friends, and preferred activities, universities may one day suggest
a schedule of courses rather than have students seek out their own courses.
Computers may also prepare language vocabulary lists for individuals according
to preferences, interests, or friends. The data collected from a variety of sources
(time spent studying, scores on tests, heritage) could be used to assess students'
language skills over time and compare their progress to national trends, local
scores, or individual development measures.

TASK-RELATED TRENDS

Consumer trends online have leaned toward two main concepts: gaming and
app-lification. Gaming refers more to the stance that students take toward learning and the program of study than to the technical aspects of computer games.
The gaming approach means that users accomplish tasks to win awards, gain
a reputation, or earn points in competition with other students. A number of
sites have begun incorporating a gaming atmosphere. Foursquare.com, a social
connection and venue recommendation site, enables users to meet with friends
via updates from their friend list or to get recommendations about a venue from
others who frequent it. Foursquare incorporates gaming concepts by allowing
users to earn badges or recognition for logging in and posting their whereabouts
with a tip about the site. LinkedIn.com has incorporated some gaming aspects
to its social networking site. As users prepare their online profiles, the system
rates the completion of the task and notifies them of the next steps to take to
complete their profile, such as "add your education," "import your résumé," or
"ask for a recommendation." Moreover, users are informed as their connections
improve their portfolio, such as "Giada is connected to Sean," "Xiaoliang has
joined the group X," and "Ali received a recommendation." These continuous
updates serve three purposes: they identify tasks to accomplish, they share past
accomplishments with others, and they enable users to compete to accomplish
additional tasks—all characteristics of online gaming.

Gaming concepts will eventually enhance language learning activities, particularly because language learning is such a long-term endeavor. For

example, LinguaFolio could incorporate badges or awards for a variety of activities such as points for the number of can-do statements, credit for frequent logins, recognition for comments solicited from others, or prestige for comments posted on others' LinguaFolio sites. Recognition for achievements in language learning becomes more meaningful when it is shared among a social group. Developments in apps and widgets permit these accomplishments to be communicated through a variety of platforms. The social aspect of gaming is most visible in massively multiplayer online role-playing games (MMORPGs). Although MMORPGs have become popular among teens, few language learning software applications have capitalized on this popularity. EnterZon.com, is one of the few examples of a multiplayer online game used for learning Chinese. Students enter China at the Beijing airport and must complete tasks in order to win prizes and progress through the game. Students progress from easy tasks that have few steps to tasks that are more complicated and difficult. Users who complete tasks are rewarded with Zon dollars based on the difficulty of the task. Zon dollars can be used to buy food, bus tickets, or other necessities. Learners interact with nonplaying characters and other players to accomplish tasks, earn dollars, and share these accomplishments with others in the game.

App-lification, the second major trend in online behaviors, is the use of apps in mobile devices to accomplish tasks such as social networking, entertainment, or productivity. Numerous apps have already been created for language learning, such as phrasebooks, stroke order practice for Asian languages, and flashcards. These apps encourage multimodal ubiquitous learning, called m-learning (micro learning or mobile learning). M-learning combined with CALL is called MALL (mobile-assisted language learning). MALL had been hindered by poor technology (sound quality, screen size, and connection speed) and lack of access for all students to a mobile device such as a smartphone or tablet. Advances in technology have overcome audio, video, and connectivity issues, and ownership of mobile devices is on the rise. The use of MALL can only grow as the supply and functionality of mobile devices increase. MALL offers advantages over CALL in regard to collaboration, portability, localization, and individualization of activities through the use of apps.

Commercial companies create a number of language learning apps (e.g., Rosetta Stone, Transparent Language), and there are many free learning apps (e.g., cloudbank, quizlet). It is unclear, however, how apps can or should be used in classrooms; many of them lack a solid theoretical foundation on how languages are learned. Nonetheless, because apps support peer-to-peer networks for information sharing, social networking, and contextualization, they could easily satisfy student and instructor needs for comprehensible and meaningful language. For example, MicroMandarin (Edge, Searle, Chiu, Zhao, & Landay, 2011) uses geolocation to supply users with appropriate vocabulary for their location; if they are in a restaurant, they have immediate access to food and drink vocabulary; if they are in a train station, the app supplies vocabulary related to travel and purchasing tickets. Indeed, app-lification has enabled the growth of ubiquitous language learning that is projected to continue.

Consistent with the trend toward interconnecting devices, the development of apps enables users to create personal learning environments (PLEs). A PLE is a web-based portal that is fully customized for the user through the use of apps or widgets. Some examples include iGoogle or MyYahoo! These PLEs could be composed of learning management systems (LMSs), portions of LMSs, calendars, newsfeeds, writing tools, media players, or file storage, to name only a few tools. PLEs offer advantages over LMSs because instructors can incorporate all of the tools available in a LMS plus social networking among numerous third-party apps. This capability has implications for language instructors who wish to include the asynchronous and synchronous tools described in Chapters 7 and 8 (Twitter, wikis, discussion boards, etc.). Moreover, instructors design LMSs, whereas individuals design a PLE to fulfill personal goals and then modify it according to their needs. As discussed in Chapter 10, the shift of ownership to the student is an important step in increasing motivation and encouraging life-long learning of the target language.

Lifelong learning and language maintenance will continue as goals for students, and learners will use their PLEs and social networks to accomplish these goals. Rather than use language experiences only to learn a language, lifelong learners seek out language experiences to maintain or improve their language skills. The solidification of an online identity through PLEs can facilitate this improvement.

TRENDS IN COMMUNICATION

Telecommunications—in particular, CMC—is a rapidly changing field. The market has driven much of the development, particularly in the field of mobile technologies (e.g., smartphones, pads, and tablets). These developments have yet to be directly applied to language instruction but will someday influence how these devices are used for language learning and maintenance. Today, most mobile devices have a multitude of sensors, including light sensors for cameras, sound-canceling sensors, GPS (location sensors), accelerometers (motion sensors), and pressure sensors. From an economic standpoint, demand drives supply, and supply drives unintended uses. For communications, demand has increased the supply of smartphones and tablets. Increased supply of mobile technologies, in addition to stronger processing and additional sensors, will continue to open up new and unintended uses for communication technology in both audio and multimedia forms.

As discussed in the previous section, apps have enabled devices to communicate with one another. These applications can make informed decisions on a range of topics such as when to take medications (Vitality.net), when not to drive (AntiSleepPilot.com), or even when meat is cooked (iGrillInc.com). With advances in speech recognition and GPS sensors, students could do sociolinguistic projects in which they examine pronunciation variation according to geography, style or register. The use of GPS sensors also allows devices to switch to the target language within the confines of the classroom (or any other space) or during certain times of the day. Apps will eventually be able to keep track of how frequently multilingual users speak a certain language during the day to help them decide which language needs more maintenance over a specific period of time.

In conjunction with the increase in mobile technologies, electronic books and eTextbooks sales will continue to increase, a phenomenon that will give rise to more interconnectivity between books and book rentals. Currently, most eBooks are written for print and are then made available in electronic format. Electronic books, in general, make little use of social networking, multimedia, or interoperability among devices. Moreover, only a few sites represent the majority of texts that are written for online consumption (e.g., wikipedia. com, huffingtonpost.com, cnet.com). Most newspapers, journals, and books are excluded from this list because they are simply digital editions of the print versions. Most material that is both created and consumed online stems from social networking (e.g., Facebook, blogs, wikis).

Despite the amount of social networking material, many eBook readers have emerged over the past several years such as the Kindle, the Nook, and the iPad. In fact, Amazon consistently sells more eBooks than hardcover books (Tweney, 2010); eBooks, however, still appear the same as printed materials with some added electronic enhancements (bookmarking, highlighting, and transferability among devices). There are a number of services that publish eBooks (e.g., kdp.Amazon.com, lulu.com, SmashWords.com) but they rarely offer advantages beyond traditional features of print books (e.g., static print, simulated page turning). The increase in availability may encourage experimentation (as with all new technology) to include the use of multimedia, glosses, socially generated footnotes and commentaries, and interoperability with other devices. For example, if users are reading about health in a textbook that is designed as an eBook first and foremost, they will be able to identify recent online news stories that contain similar or supplemental information, thereby accessing multiple contextualized examples of the language they are studying.

Like reading, writing has evolved with developments in mobile technology. As discussed in previous chapters, texting has largely replaced email for one-to-one communication. Furthermore, users are no longer limited to simple text messages; smartphones have cameras, and much of what users need to do can be accomplished through the cloud for which users do not even send messages to each other. Instead, members of a social group post links to the online video, audio, or multimedia content; a service sends a message that new content has been added; and participants access the new content at their convenience. These methods of communication are prevalent in Facebook, Twitter, and wikis. By being aware of the literacy habits and behaviors of students, language instructors can help them engage in language-oriented social activities using social networking practices and CMC.

Writing exchanges with members of other cultures have traditionally been done by establishing tandem partners between groups of English language learners abroad and target language learners locally. The notable problem with these tandem exchanges is that many students write as an assignment from the teacher rather than as a personal commitment to their partners in the other culture. A number of newer sites target learners who want to engage socially with speakers of other languages (e.g., LiveMocha. com, iTalki.com, Byki.com). These sites enable learners to choose the interactions they wish to pursue by allowing them to find friends and by making friend suggestions of speakers of the target language. Future endeavors in language instruction must focus on the issue of helping students realize the importance of communicating with others in the target language. Indeed, this is no small task, given the emphasis on short-term courses, assessment, and accountability.

TRENDS IN ASSESSMENT

Current assessment trends include increases in online testing, peer-assessment, and self-assessment. The advent of national standards and the drive for accountability have lured numerous institutions into online testing. Others have been pushed into it because of online courses that require online testing. Advances in technology have enabled secure and reliable access to the tests, with the assurance that all elements will function appropriately (e.g., audio, video, internet connections). The initial movement into high-stakes testing at the K–12 level is led by a few states such as Virginia and Delaware, but it will still be many years before high-stakes online testing becomes widely available in a variety of languages. Nonetheless, several states have already begun to use the STAMP test for measurement purposes, and it may be only a matter of time before postsecondary institutions use online testing as the delivery mode for outcomes assessment for individual and programmatic purposes.

Peer assessment will increase as a result of the inclusion of social networks in language teaching and will take the form of online comments on projects or feedback from activities such as LinguaFolio entries. As discussed in Chapter 10, portfolio assessment will not grow until instructors and students see it as beneficial documentation of learning and until students take ownership of their portfolios. Other trends that may help speed the adoption of portfolios are the inclusion of gaming characteristics—wherein students record accomplishments as a method of advancing and gaining awards or recognition—and peer interaction is encouraged and commonplace (as one sees in professional portfolios such as LinkedIn).

Self-assessment has been on the rise and will be facilitated through LinguaFolio-type evaluations. Beginning with their early language learners, instructors and programs have emphasized can-do statements and self-assessment. As these students continue to learn languages, it is anticipated that they will maintain the expectation for formal self-assessment and then transfer the behaviors learned in the K–12 setting to the postsecondary level. Self-assessment has not been utilized extensively at the postsecondary level, but it will become more important as language students include their own evaluations as part of their online identities. These self-assessments will be facilitated through online portfolios and the students' creation of online identities and presentation of self via Facebook, LinkedIn, or other portals.

Developments and current trends in technology discourage research that compares face-to-face instruction with computer-based instruction because the option of teaching without technology will become less attractive as technological resources grow in number and accessibility. Rather, instructors must learn to exploit the technology in sound methodological ways to assist language learning. Throughout this book, readers have been encouraged to acquire tools and become familiar with available technology to determine the best uses of that technology for their particular context. It would not be fruitful to use all of the types of technology discussed in this book, because many of them are redundant. For example, using both Twitter and a discussion board for out-of-class discussions may be confusing to students when both services satisfy the same function. The goal in using CALL is to identify the most efficient tools for the instructor and students depending on their experiences and environment.

The role of the instructors is to evaluate and frame language learning experiences within the local context. It was once thought that computers would replace teachers. We now know that computers cannot replace teachers, but teachers who use computers will eventually replace those who do not. The field of CALL is constantly evolving and so, whereas this volume provides an introduction to the field, instructors should stay attuned to and up-to-date with products and practices in electronic media, second language teaching and learning, communication, and assessment to make the most of CALL.

APPENDIX A

Overview of Evaluation Criteria

Chapelle (2001)

Language learning potential	Sufficient opportunity to focus on form
Learner fit	Difficulty level
	Task appropriateness
Meaning focus	Learner's focus on meaning of language
Authenticity	Correspondence of CALL task to L2 task outside of classroom
	Identifiable connection for students
Impact	Student learning
	Instructor use
	Interaction with technology
Practicality	Hardware
	Software
	Personnel

Hubbard (2006)

Technical considerations	Function
Operational considerations	Activity type (tasks)
	Presentational scheme (flow)
Teacher fit	Language teaching approach
Learner fit	Learner variables
	Syllabus
Implementation schemes	Integration into the curriculum
	Learner training
Appropriateness	Teacher fit/learner fit
	Costs and benefits

Susser and Robb (2004)

Module 1: Language acquisition	Language learning potential
	Learner fit
	Meaning focus
	Authenticity
	Positive impact
	Practicality

(Continued)

Module 2: ESL materials design	Meaningful and contextualized presentation
	Systematic presentation
	Underlying grammar rule displayed
	Sufficient number of items
	Variety of items
	Meaningful items
	Well-written items free of typographical and other errors
	Appropriate variety of English used
	Appropriate vocabulary and subject matter for the target audience
	Culturally appropriate content
Module 3: Learner profile and learning styles	Purpose
	Language level
	Ability to handle metalanguage
	Technical ability
	Receptivity to change
Module 4: Courseware and multimedia instructional design	Interface
	Navigation
	Text quality
	Graphics and sound
	Interactivity
Module 5: Online courseware instructional design	Theoretical implementation
	Facilitation
	Management
	Support for interactivity
	Adaptivity to users' history and preferences
	Multimedia
	Accessibility
	Web-centric

WORKS CITED

Adair-Hauck, B., Glisan, E., Koda, K., Swender, E., & Sandrock, P. (2006). The integrated performance assessment (IPA): Connecting assessment to instruction and learning. *Foreign Language Annals, 39*, 359–382.

Ahern, N. R. (2005). Using the Internet to conduct research. *Nurse Researcher, 13*(2), 55–70.

Albanese, M. A., & Mitchell, S. (1993). Problem-based learning: A review of literature on its outcomes and implementation issues. *Academic Medicine, 68*, 52–81.

Aljaafreh, A., & Lantolf, J. P. (1994). Negative feedback as regulation and second language learning in the zone of proximal development. *The Modern Language Journal, 78*, 465–483.

American Council on the Teaching of Foreign Languages (ACTFL). (1998). *ACTFL performance guidelines for K–12 learners*. Yonkers, NY: Author.

American Council on the Teaching of Foreign Languages (ACTFL). (2002). *Program standards for the preparation of foreign language teachers*. Alexandria, VA: ACTFL. Retrieved from www.actfl.org/files/public/ACTFLNCATEStandardsRevised713.pdf

Andrade, H., & Valtcheva, A. (2009). Promoting learning and achievement through self-assessment. *Theory into practice, 48*(1), 12–19.

Angell, J., DuBravac, S., & Gonglewski, M. (2008). Thinking globally, acting locally: Selecting textbooks for college-level language programs. *Foreign Language Annals, 41*, 562–572.

Apple.com (2012). *The Mac app store*. Retrieved from http://www.apple.com/macosx/whats-new/app-store.html

Arnold, N., & Ducate, L. (2006). CALL: Where are we and where do we go from here? In L. Ducate & N. Arnold (Eds.), *Calling on CALL: From theory and research to new directions in foreign language teaching* (pp. 1–20). San Marcos, TX: CALICO.

Arnold, N., Ducate, L., & Lomicka, L. (2007). Virtual communities of practice in teacher education. In M. A. Kassen, R. Z. Lavine, K. Murphy-Judy, & M. Peters (Eds.), *Preparing and developing technology-proficient L2 teachers* (pp. 103–132). *CALICO Monograph Series*, vol. 6. San Marcos, TX: CALICO.

Atkinson, C. (2009). *The backchannel: How audiences are using Twitter and social media and changing presentations forever*. Berkley, CA: New Riders.

Attali, Y., & Burstein, J. (2006). Automated essay scoring with e-rater® V. 2. *Journal of Technology, Learning, and Assessment, 4*(3). Retrieved from http://ejournals.bc.edu/ojs/index.php/jtla/article/view/1650

Ayoun, D. (2001). The role of negative and positive feedback in the second language acquisition of passé composé and imparfait. *Modern Language Journal, 85*, 226–243.

Bachman, L. (1990). *Fundamental considerations in language testing.* Oxford, Eng.: Oxford University Press.

Bailey, K., Madden, C., & Krashen, S. (1974). Is there a "natural sequence" in adult second language learning? *Language Learning, 21*, 235–243.

Baker, F. B. (1989). Computer technology in test construction and processing. In R. L. Linn (Ed.), *Education measurement* (3rd ed., pp. 409–428). New York: Macmillan.

Bardovi-Harlig, K., & Comajoan, L. (2008). Order of acquisition and developmental readiness. In B. Spolky & F. M. Hult (Eds.), *Handbook of educational linguistics* (pp. 383–397). Oxford, Eng.: Blackwell.

Baron, N. (2008). *Language in an online and mobile world.* Oxford, Eng.: Oxford University Press.

Batson, T. (2010). Is portfolio evidence useful? *Campus Technology, 23*(9). Retrieved from campustechnology.com/Articles/2010/05/19/Is-Portfolio-Evidence-Useful.aspx

Bauman, J. (2000). Extend class discussion activities via cyberspace. In K. Ryan (Ed.), *Recipes for teachers* (pp. 54–55). Tokyo: Japan Association for Language Teaching.

Beauvois, M. H. (1992). Computer-assisted classroom discussion in the foreign language classroom: Conversation in slow motion. *Foreign Language Annals, 5*, 455–465.

Beauvois, M. H. (1994). E-talk: Attitudes and motivation in computer-assisted classroom discussion. *Computers and the Humanities, 28*, 177–190.

Beauvois, M. H. (1997a). Computer-mediated communication: Technology for improving speaking and writing. In M. D. Bush & R. M. Terry (Eds.), *Technology-enhanced language learning* (pp. 165–184). Lincolnwood, IL: National Textbook Company.

Beauvois, M. H. (1997b). Write to speak: The effects of electronic communication on the oral achievement of fourth semester French students. In J. A. Muyskens (Ed.), *New ways of learning and teaching: Focus on technology and foreign language education* (pp. 93–115). Boston: Heinle.

Beauvois, M. H. (1998). Conversation in slow motion: Computer-mediated communication in the foreign language classroom. *The Canadian Modern Language Review, 54*, 198–217.

Beckett, G. H. (2002). Teacher and student evaluations of project-based instruction. *TSL Canada Journal/Revue TESL du Canada, 19*(2), 52–66.

Bejar, I. I. (1993). A generative approach to psychological and educational measurement. In N. Frederiksen, R. J. Mislevy, & I. I. Bejar (Eds.), *Test theory for a new generation of tests* (pp. 323–357). Hillsdale, NJ: Lawrence Erlbaum.

Bell, P. K., & Collins, L. (2009). "It's vocabulary"/"it's gender": Learner awareness and incidental learning. *Language Awareness, 18*(3/4) 277–293.

Belz, J. A. (2002). Social dimensions of telecollaborative foreign language study. *Language Learning & Technology, 6*(1), 60–81. Retrieved from llt.msu.edu

Belz, J. A., & Müller-Hartmann, A. (2003). Teachers as intercultural learners: Negotiating German-American telecollaboration along the institutional fault line. *Modern Language Journal, 87*, 71–89.

Belz, J. A., & Thorne, S. L. (2005). *Internet-mediated intercultural foreign language education*. Boston: Thomson-Heinle.

Bennett, R. E. (1999). Using new technology to improve assessment. *Educational Measurement: Issues and Practice, 18*, 5–12.

Berne Convention for the Protection of Literary and Artistic Works (Paris Text 1971). Retrieved from www.wipo.int/treaties/en/ip/berne/trtdocs_wo001.html

Berne Convention Implementation Act of 1988, Pub. L. No. 100–568, 102 Stat. 2853 (1988).

Bikowski, D., & Kessler, G. (2002). Making the most of discussion boards in the ESL classroom. *TESOL Journal, 11*(3), 27–30.

Birdsong, D. (Ed.). (1999). *Second language acquisition and the critical period hypothesis*. Mahwah, NJ: Lawrence Erlbaum.

Birdsong, D. (2006). Age and second language acquisition and processing: A selective overview. *Language Learning, 56*, 9–49.

Birdsong, D., & Paik, J. (2008). Second language acquisition and ultimate attainment. In B. Spolsky & F. M. Hult (Eds.), *The handbook of educational linguistics* (pp. 242–236). Oxford, Eng.: Blackwell.

Blake, R. (2000). Computer mediated communication: A window on L2 Spanish interlanguage. *Language Learning & Technology, 4*(1), 120–136. Retrieved from llt.msu.edu

Blake, R. (2008). *Brave new digital classroom technology and foreign language learning*. Washington, DC: Georgetown University Press.

Block, D. (2003). *The social turn in second language acquisition*. Washington, DC: Georgetown University Press.

Blyth, C. (1999). *Untangling the web: Nonce's guide to language and culture on the Internet*. New York: Nonce.

Bohlke, O. (2003). A comparison of student participation levels by group size and language stages during chatroom and face-to-face discussions in German. *CALICO Journal, 21*, 67–87.

Bonk, C., & Cunningham, D. (1998). Searching for learner-centered, constructivist, and sociocultural components of collaborative educational learning tools. In C. Bonk & K. King (Eds.), *Electronic collaborators* (pp. 25–50). Mahwah, NJ: Laurence Erlbaum.

Bragger, J. D., & Rice, D. B. (1998). Connections: The National Standards and a new paradigm for content-oriented materials and instruction. In J. Harper, M. Lively, & M. Williams (Eds.), *The coming of age of the profession: Issues and emerging ideas for the teaching of foreign languages* (pp. 191–217). Boston: Heinle.

Braine, G., & Yorozu, M. (1998). Local area network (LAN) computers in ESL and EFL writing classes: Promises and realties. *JALT Journal, 20*, 47–59.

Brandl, K. (2008). *Communicative language teaching in action: Putting principles to work*. Upper Saddle River, NJ: Pearson.

Breen, M. (1987). Learner contributions to task design. In C. Candlin & D. Murphy (Eds.), *Language learning tasks* (pp. 23–46). Englewood Cliffs, NJ: Prentice Hall.

Brooks, F., & Donato, R. (1994). Vygotskyan approaches to understanding foreign language learner discourse during communicative tasks. *Hispania,* 77, 262–274.

Bruce, B., Peyton, J. K., & Batson, T. (Eds.). (1993). *Network-based classrooms: Promises and realities.* Cambridge, Eng.: Cambridge University Press.

Burr, W. E., Dodson, D. F., & Polk, W. T. (2006). *Electronic authentication guideline, recommendations of the National Institute of Standards and Technology.* Retrieved from www.nist.gov/manuscript-publication-search.cfm?pub_id=151295

Burston, J. (2006). Working toward effective assessment of CALL. In R. P. Donaldson & M. A. Haggstrom (Eds.), *Changing language education through CALL* (pp. 249–270). New York: Routledge.

Bush, M. D. (1997). Implementing technology for language learning. In M. D. Bush & R. Terry (Eds.), *Technology-enhanced language learning* (pp. 287–349). Lincolnwood, IL: National Textbook Company.

Bush, M. D., & Terry, R. M. (Eds.). (1997). *Technology-enhanced language learning.* Lincolnwood, IL: National Textbook Company.

Butler, Y. G., & Lee, J. (2010). The effects of self-assessment among young learners of English. *Language Testing* 27(1), 5–31.

Campaign Monitor. (2011). *Email client popularity: June 2011.* Retrieved from www.campaignmonitor.com/stats/email-clients/

Campbell, R., & Wales, R. (1970). The study of language acquisition. In J. Lyons (Ed.), *New horizons in linguistics* (pp. 242–260). Harmondsworth, Eng.: Penguin.

Canale, M. (1983). From communicative competence to communicative language pedagogy. In J. Richards & R. Schmidt (Eds.), *Language and communication* (pp. 2–27). London and New York: Longman.

Canale, M., & Swain, M. (1980). Theoretical bases of communicative approaches to second language teaching and testing. *Applied Linguistics, 1,* 1–47.

Candlin, C. (1987). Toward task-based learning. In C. Candlin & D. Murphy (Eds.), *Language learning tasks* (pp. 5–22). Englewood Cliffs, NJ: Prentice Hall.

Carr, N. (2006). Computer-based testing: Prospects for innovative assessment. In L. Ducate & N. Arnold (Eds.), *Calling on CALL: From theory and research to new directions in foreign language teaching* (pp. 289–312). San Marcos, TX: CALICO.

Carroll, J. B., & Sapon, S. (2002). *Modern language aptitude test: Manual 2002 edition.* Bethesda, MD: Second Language Testing, Inc.

CDW–G. (2010). *21st-century classroom report.* Retrieved from webobjects.cdw.com/webobjects/media/pdf/newsroom/CDWG-21st-Century-Classroom-Report-0610.pdf

Cech, C. G., & Condon, S. L. (1998). Message size constraints on discourse planning in synchronous computer-mediated communication. *Behavior Research Methods, Instruments, & Computers, 30,* 255–263.

Celce-Murcia, M., Dörnyei, Z., & Thurrell, S. (1995). Communicative competence: A pedagogically motivated model with content specifications. *Issues in Applied Linguistics, 6,* 5–35.

Center for Applied Linguistics. (2007). *Foreign language assessment directory*. Retrieved from www.cal.org/CALWebDB/FLAD

Chalhoub-Deville, M. (2001). Technology in standardized language assessments. In R. B. Kaplan (Ed.), *The Oxford handbook of applied linguistics* (pp. 471–484). Oxford, Eng.: Oxford University Press.

Chapelle, C. (1999). Theory and research: Investigation of "authentic" language learning tasks. In J. Egbert & E. Hanson-Smith (Eds.), *CALL environments: Research, practice and critical issues* (pp. 101–115). Alexandria, VA: TESOL.

Chapelle, C. A. (2001). *Computer applications in second language acquisition: Foundations for teaching, testing, and research*. Cambridge, Eng.: Cambridge University Press.

Chapelle, C. A., & Douglas, D. (2006). *Assessing language through computer technology*. Cambridge, Eng.: Cambridge University Press.

Chastain, K. (1976). *Developing second language skills: Theory to practice* (2nd ed.). Chicago: Rand McNally.

Chávez, C. L. (1997). Students take flight with Daedalus: Learning Spanish in a networked classroom. *Foreign Language Annals, 30*, 27–37.

Chen, Y. (2005). The emergence of links between lexical acquisition and object categorization: A computational study. *Connection Science, 17*, 381–397.

Chomsky, N. (1965). *Aspects of the theory of syntax*. Cambridge, MA: MIT Press.

Chumbow, S. B. (1981). The mother tongue hypothesis in a multilingual setting. In J.-G. Savard & L. Laforge (Eds.), *Proceedings of the 5th Congress of the International Association of Applied Linguistics* (pp. 42–55). Québec: Laval University Press.

Chun, D. M. (1994). Using computer networking to facilitate the acquisition of interactive competence. *System, 22*, 17–31.

Clark, C. L. (2000). *Working the web: A students' research guide* (2nd ed.). Orlando, FL: Harcourt.

Clarke, A. (2008). *E-learning skills* (2nd ed.). New York: Palgrave Macmillan.

Collins, A., & Halverson, R. (2009). *Rethinking education in the age of technology: The digital revolution and schooling in America*. New York: Teachers College Press.

comScore. (2011). *Press release: comScore releases February 2011, U.S. search engine rankings*. Retrieved from www.comscore.com/Press_Events/Press_Releases/2011/3/comScore_Releases_February_2011_U.S._Search_Engine_Rankings

Cook, V. (1991). *Second language learning and teaching* (2nd ed.). Oxford, Eng.: Oxford University Press.

Copyright Office. (2003). *Copyright law of the United States and related laws contained in Title 17 of the United States code* (Circular 92). Washington DC: U.S. Government Printing Office.

Copyright Office. (2009). *Fair use* (FL–102). Washington DC: U.S. Government Printing Office.

Corbett, J. (2010). *Intercultural language activities with CD*. Cambridge, Eng.: Cambridge University Press.

Crookes, G., & Gass, S. (Eds.). (1993). *Tasks in a pedagogical context: Integrating theory and practice*. Clevedon, UK: Multilingual Matters.

Crystal, D. (2001). *Language and the internet*. Cambridge, Eng.:Cambridge University Press.

Curtain, H., & Dahlberg, C. A. (2010). *Language and children, making the match: New language for young learners, grades K–8* (4th ed.). Boston: Pearson.

Curtis, A., & Roskams, T. (1999). Language learning in networked writing labs: A view from Asia. In J. A. Inman & D. N. Sewell (Eds.), *Taking flight with OWLs: Examining electronic writing center work* (pp. 29–39). Mahwah, NJ: Lawrence Erlbaum.

Darhower, M. (2002). Interactional features of synchronous computer-mediated communication in the intermediate L2 class: A sociocultural case study. *CALICO Journal, 19*, 249–277.

Davies, G., Walker, R., Rendall H., & Hewer, S. (2012). Introduction to computer assisted language learning (CALL). Module 1. 4. In G. Davies (Ed.) *Information and communications technology for language teachers (ICT4LT)*. Slough, Eng.: Thames Valley University. Retrieved from www.ict4lt.org/en/en_mod1-4.htm

Davis, B., & Thiede, R. (2000). Writing into change: Style shifting in asynchronous electronic discourse. In M. Warschauer & R. Kern (Eds.), *Networked-based language teaching: Concepts and practice* (pp. 87–120). Cambridge, Eng.: Cambridge University Press.

de Freitas, S., & Conole, G. (2010). The influence of pervasive and integrative tools on learners' experiences and expectations of study. In R. Sharpe, H. Beetham, & S. de Freitas (Eds.), *Rethinking learning for a digital age: How learners are shaping their own experiences* (pp. 15–30). New York: Routledge.

Delcloque, P. (2000). *The history of computer-assisted language learning web edition*. Retrieved from www.ict4lt.org/en/History_of_CALL.pdf

Desmarais, L. (1998). *Les technologies et l'enseignement des langues*. Montréal: Éditions Logiques.

Dewey, J. (1916/1966). *Democracy and education. An introduction to the philosophy of education*. New York: Free Press.

DIALANG. (2002). [Computer Software] Retrieved from www.lancs.ac.uk/researchenterprise/dialang/dialang.zip

Dickinson, M., Eom, S., Kang, Y., Lee, C. M., & Sachs, R. (2008). A balancing act: How can intelligent computer-generated feedback be provided in learner-to-learner interactions. *Computer Assisted Language Learning, 21*, 369–382.

Digital Millennium Copyright Act of 1998, Pub. L. No. 105–304, 112 Stat. 2860, 2887 (1998).

Dodge, B. (1995). WebQuests: A technique for internet-based learning. *The Distance Educator, 1*, 10–13.

Dodge, B. (1997*). Some thoughts about WebQuests*. Retrieved from webquest.sdsu.edu/about_webquests.html

Dodge, B. (2001). FOCUS—Five rules for writing a great WebQuest. *Learning & Leading with Technology, 28*(8), 6–9, 58.

Doering, A., & Veletsianos, G. (2008). Hybrid online education: Identifying integration models using adventure learning. *Journal of Research on Technology in Education, 41*(1), 23–41.

Donato, R. (1994). Collective scaffolding in second language learning. In J. P. Lantolf & G. Appel (Eds.), *Vygotskian approaches to second language research* (pp. 33–56). Norwood, NJ: Ablex.

Dörnyei, Z. (2005). *The psychology of the language learner: Individual differences in second language acquisition*. Mahwah, NJ: Lawrence Erlbaum.

Dörnyei, Z., & Murphey, T. (2003). *Group dynamics in the language classroom*. Cambridge, Eng.: Cambridge University Press.

Dörnyei, Z., & Ushioda, E. (2011). *Teaching and researching motivation* (2nd ed.). London and New York: Longman.

Doughty, C. (2003). Instructed SLA: Constraints, compensation, and enhancement. In C. J. Doughty & M. H. Long (Eds.), *The handbook of second language acquisition* (pp. 256–310). Oxford, Eng.: Blackwell.

Doughty, C. J., & Long, M. H. (Eds.). (2003). *The handbook of second language acquisition*. Oxford, Eng.: Blackwell.

DuBravac, S. (2004). L2 task design for electronic media. In M. Singhal (Ed.), *Proceedings of the First International Conference on Second and Foreign Language Teaching and Research* (pp. 173–180). Retrieved from www.readingmatrix.com/onlineconference/proceedings2004.html

DuBravac, S., Gonglewski, M., & Angell, J. (2008, March). *Podcasting projects made simple*. Presentation at the Northeast Conference on the Teaching of Foreign Languages, New York.

Dudeney, G. (2000). *The Internet and the language classroom: A practical guide for teachers*. Cambridge, Eng.: Cambridge University Press.

Duff, P. A. (2007). Second language socialization as sociocultural theory: Insights and issues. *Language Teaching, 40*, 309–319.

EA Games. (2007). *The Sims* [Computer Software]. Surrey, UK: Electronic Arts Limited.

Edge, D., Searle, E., Chiu, K., Zhao, J., & Landay, J. A. (2011). MicroMandarin: Mobile language learning in context. *CHI 2011*. Vancouver, BC, Canada. Retrieved from research.microsoft.com/en-us/people/daedge/micromandarinpublished.pdf

Ellis, R. (1986). *Understanding second language acquisition*. Oxford, Eng.: Oxford University Press.

Ellis, R. (1994). *The study of second language acquisition*. Oxford, Eng.: Oxford University Press.

Ellis, R. (2003). *Task-based language learning and teaching.* Oxford, Eng.: Oxford University Press.

Ellis, R. (2008). *The study of second language acquisition* (2nd ed.). Oxford, Eng.: Oxford University Press.

Ellis, R. (2012). *Language teaching research and language pedagogy.* West Sussex, UK: Wiley-Blackwell.

fhsoftware. (2000). Hyperchat Suite [Computer application] Retrieved from http://tucows.newnova.com/win2k/preview/37527.html

Firth, A., & Wagner, J. (1997). On discourse, communication, and (some) fundamental concepts in SLA research. *Modern Language Journal, 81*, 285–300.

Fitze, M. (2006). Discourse and participation in ESL face-to-face and written electronic conferences. *Language Learning & Technology, 10*(1), 67–86. Retrieved from llt.msu.edu

Franklin, L. (2007). Online resources in language teacher education. In M. A. Kassen, R. Z. Lavine, K. Murphy-Judy, & M. Peters (Eds.), *Preparing and developing technology-proficient L2 teachers: CALICO Monograph Series* (vol. 6, pp. 103–132). San Marcos, TX: CALICO.

Fried-Booth, D. (1997). *Project work.* Oxford, Eng.: Oxford University Press.

Furstenberg, G. (1994). *À la rencontre de Philippe* [Videodisc program for Macintosh environment]. New Haven, CT: Yale University Press.

Gardner, D. (1995). Student produced video documentary provides a real reason for using the target language. *Language Learning Journal, 12*, 54–56.

Gardner, H. (1983). *Frames of the mind: The theory of multiple intelligences.* New York: Basic Books.

Gardner, H. (1993). *Multiple intelligences: The theory in practice.* New York: Basic Books.

Gardner, H. (1999). *Intelligence reframed: Multiple intelligences for the 21st century.* New York: Basic Books.

Gass, S., & Mackey, A. (2007). Input, interaction, and output in second language acquisition. In B. VanPatten & J. Williams (Eds.), *Theories in second language acquisition: An introduction* (pp. 175–200). Mahwah, NJ: Lawrence Erlbaum.

Gass, S., & Selinker, L. (2008). *Second language acquisition: An introductory course.* New York: Routledge.

Gibs, J. (2009). Is social media impacting how much we email? *Neilsen News: Online + Mobile,* Retrieved from http://blog.nielsen.com/nielsenwire/online_mobile/is-social-media-impacting-how-much-we-email/

Glenn, J. M. (2000). Teaching the net generation. *Business Education Forum, 54*(3), 6–14.

Glisan, E., Adair-Hauck, B., Koda, K., Sandrock, P., & Swender, E. (2003). *ACTFL Integrated Performance Assessment.* Yonkers, NY: ACTFL.

Godwin-Jones, R. (2006). Tag clouds in the blogosphere: Electronic literacy and social networking. *Language Learning & Technology, 10*(2), 8–15. Retrieved from llt.msu.edu

Gonglewski, M. R. (1999), Linking the Internet to the National Standards for Foreign Language Learning. *Foreign Language Annals, 32*, 348–362.

Gonglewski, M., & DuBravac, S. (2006). Multiliteracy: Second language literacy in themultimedia environment. In L. Ducate & N. Arnold (Eds.), *Calling on CALL: From theory and research to new directions in foreign language teaching* (pp. 43–68). San Marcos, TX: CALICO.

Gonglweski, M., Meloni, C., & Brant, J. (2001). Using e-mail in foreign language teaching: Rationale and suggestions. *The Internet TESL Journal, 7*(3). Retrieved from iteslj.org

Gonzales, C. (1999). WebQuests. In S. Smith & E. Monsevais (Eds.), *Integrating technology in the classroom*. Retrieved from www.cahe.nmsu.edu/USWEST/Chapter%204.html

González-Bueno, M. (1998). The effects of electronic mail on Spanish L2 discourse. *Language Learning & Technology, 1*(2), 50–65. Retrieved from http://llt.msu.edu

González-Bueno, M., & Perez, L. C. (2000). Electronic mail in foreign language writing: A study of grammatical and lexical accuracy, and quantity of language. *Foreign Language Annals, 33*, 189–197.

Gouiller, F. (2007). *Council of Europe tools for language teaching: Common European framework and portfolios.* Paris: Didier.

Grabe, M., & Grabe, C. (2001). *Integrating technology for meaningful learning* (3rd ed.). Boston: Houghton Mifflin.

Granger, S. (2002). *The simplest security: A guide to better password practices.* Retrieved from www.symantec.com/connect/articles/simplest-security-guide-better-password-practices

Greenfield, R. (2003). Collaborative e-mail exchanges for teaching secondary ESL: A case study in Hong Kong. *Language Learning & Technology, 7*(1), 46–70. Retrieved from llt.msu.edu

Gresso, H., & Lomicka, L. (1999). Intercultural communities: Rethinking Célestin Freinet. In D. Alley & C. M. Cherry (Eds.), *Dimension 1999* (pp. 1–12). Valdosta, GA: SCOLT Publications.

Hall, J. K. (2001). *Methods for teaching foreign languages: Creating a community of learners in the classroom.* Upper Saddle River, NJ: Merrill/Prentice Hall.

Hall, J. K., & Verplaetse, L. S. (Eds.). (2000). *Second and foreign language learning through classroom interaction.* Mahwah, NJ: Lawrence Erlbaum.

Harrington, C. F., Gordon, S. A., & Schibik, T. J. (2004). Course management system utilization and implications for practice: A national survey of department chairpersons. *Online Journal of Distance learning Administration, 7*(4). Retrieved from www.westga.edu/~distance/ojdla/

Harrison, R. & Thomas, M. (2009). Identity in online communities: Social networking sites and language learning. *International Journal of Emerging Technologies and Society 7*(2), 109–124.

Hartman, K., Neuwirth, C., Kiesler, S., Sproull, L., Cochran, C., Palmquist, M., & Zubrow, D. (1991). Patterns of social interaction and learning to write: Some effects of network technologies. *Written Communication, 8*, 19–113.

Hata, M. (2003). Literature review: Using computer-mediated communication in second language classrooms. *Osaka Keidai Ronshu, 54*(3), 115–125.

Hellermann, J., & Vergun, A. (2007). Language which is not taught: The discourse marker use of beginning adult learners of English. *Journal of Pragmatics, 39*, 157–179.

Henning, G. (1987). *A guide to language testing: Development, evaluation, research.* Boston: Heine.

Hertel, T. J. (2003). Using an e-mail exchange to promote cultural learning. *Foreign Language Annals, 36*, 386–396.

Hirotani, M. (2005). *The effects of synchronous and asynchronous computer-mediated communication (CMC) on the development of oral proficiency among novice learners of Japanese* (Doctoral dissertation, Purdue University). Retrieved from http://search.proquest.com/docview/305388079/previewPDF?accountid=11836

Horwitz, E. K. (2008). *Becoming a language teacher: A practical guide to second language learning and teaching.* Boston: Pearson.

Hubbard, P. (1992). A methodological framework for CALL courseware development. In M. C. Pennington & V. Stevens (Eds.), *Computers in applied linguistics: An international perspective* (pp. 39–65). Clevedon, UK: Multilingual Matters.

Hubbard, P. (2006). Evaluating CALL software. In L. Ducate & N. Arnold (Eds.), *Calling on CALL: From theory and research to new directions in foreign language teaching* (pp. 313–338). San Marcos, TX: CALICO.

Hyltenstam, K., & Abrahamsson, N. (2003). Maturational constraints in SLA. In C. J. Doughty & M. H. Long (Eds.), *The handbook of second language acquisition* (pp. 539–588). Oxford, Eng.: Blackwell.

Hymes, D. (1972). On communicative competence. In J. P. Pride & J. Holmes (Eds.), *Sociolinguistics* (pp. 269–293). Harmondsworth, UK: Penguin.

ICANN (2011). ICANN Approves Historic Change to Internet's Domain Name System | Board Votes to Launch New Generic Top-Level Domains. Retrieved from www.icann.org/en/news/announcements/announcement-20jun11-en.htm

internetworldstats.com. (2012a). *Internet world stats usage and population statistics.* Minwatts marketing group. Retrieved from www.internetworldstats.com/stats.htm

internetworldstats.com. (2012b). *Top ten internet languages.* Minwatts marketing group. Retrieved from www.internetworldstats.com/stats7.htm

ISTE. (2007a). *The ISTE NETS and Performance Indicators for Students (NETS–S).* Retrieved from www.iste.org/Libraries/PDFs/NETS_for_Student_2007_EN.sflb.ashx

ISTE. (2007b). *NETS for Students 2007 Profiles.* Retrieved from www.iste.org/standards/nets-for-students/nets-for-students-2007-profiles.aspx

ISTE. (2008). *The ISTE NETS and Performance Indicators for Teachers (NETS–T).* Retrieved from www.iste.org/Libraries/PDFs/NETS_for_Teachers_2008_EN.sflb.ashx

Jamieson, J., Chapelle, C., & Preiss, S. (2005). CALL evaluation by developers, a teacher and students. *CALICO Journal, 23*(1), 93–138.

Jeon-Ellis, G., Debski, R., & Wigglesworth, G. (2005). Oral interaction around computers in the project-oriented CALL classroom. *Language Learning & Technology* 9(3), 121–145. Retrieved from llt.msu.edu

Jepson, K. (2005). Conversations—and negotiated interaction—in text and voice chat rooms. *Language Learning & Technology, 9*(3), 79–98. Retrieved from llt.msu.edu

Johnson, D. L. (1998). Rethinking the teacher as developer model. *Computers in the Schools, 14*(3/4), 1–4.

Johnson, D., & Johnson, R. (2005). *Joining together: Group theory and group skills* (9th ed.). Boston: Allyn & Bacon.

Johnson, J. S., & Newport, E. L. (1989). Critical period effects in second language learning: The influence of maturational state on the acquisition of English as a second language. *Cognitive Psychology, 21*, 60–99.

Kane, M. T. (2006). Validation. In R. L. Brennan (Ed.), *Educational measurement* (4th ed.; pp. 17–64). Westport, CT: American Council on Education/Praeger.

Kasper, L. (2000). New technologies, new literacies: Focus discipline research and ESL learning communities. *Language Learning & Technology* 4(2), 105–128. Retrieved from llt.msu.edu

Kassen, M. A., & Lavine, R. Z. (2007). Developing advanced level foreign language learners with technology. In M. A. Kassen, R. Z. Lavine, K. Murphy-Judy, & M. Peters, M. (Eds.), *Preparing and developing technology-proficient L2 teachers. CALICO Monograph Series* (vol. 6, pp. 233–264). San Marcos, TX: CALICO.

Kassen, M. A., Lavine, R. Z., Murphy-Judy, K., & Peters, M. (Eds.), (2007*). Preparing and developing technology-proficient L2 teachers. CALICO Monograph Series* (vol. 6). San Marcos, TX: CALICO.

Katz, A. (1988). The academic context. In P. Lowe Jr. & C. W. Stansfield (Eds), *Second language proficiency assessment: Current issues* (pp. 178–201). Englewood Cliffs, NJ: Prentice Hall/ Regents.

Kelm, O. (1992). The use of synchronous computer networks in second language instruction: A preliminary report. *Foreign Language Annals*, 25, 441–454.

Kendall, C. (1995). Individual electronic mail with native speakers. In M. Warschauer (Ed.), *Virtual connections: Online activities and projects for networking language learners* (pp. 109–115). Honolulu: University of Hawai'i Press.

Kern, R. (1995). Redefining the boundaries of foreign language literacy. In C. Kramsch (Ed.), *Redefining the boundaries of language study* (pp. 61–98). Boston: Heinle.

Kern, R. (1996). Computer-mediated communication: Using e-mail exchanges to explore personal histories in two cultures. In M. Warschauer (Ed.), *Telecollaboration in foreign language learning* (pp. 105–119). Honolulu: University of Hawai'i Press.

Kern, R. (1997). Technology, social interaction, and FL literacy. In J. Muyskens (Ed.), *New ways of learning and teaching: Focus on technology and foreign language education* (pp. 57–92). Boston: Heinle.

Kern, R., & Warschauer, M. (2000). Theory and practice of network-based language teaching. In M. Warschauer & R. Kern (Eds.), *Network-based language teaching: Concepts and practice* (pp. 1–19). New York: Cambridge University Press.

Kiesler, S., Siegel, J., & McGuire, T. W. (1984). Social psychological aspects of computer-mediated communication. *American Psychologist, 39,* 1123–1134.

Kinginger, C. (2002). Defining the zone of proximal development in US foreign language education. *Applied Linguistics, 23,* 240–261.

Kinginger, C., Gourves-Hayward, A., & Simpson, V. (1999). A tele-collaborative course on French–American intercultural communication. *French Review, 72,* 853–866.

Kitade, K. (2000). L2 learners' discourse and SLA theories in CMC: Collaborative interaction in internet chat. *Computer Assisted Language Learning, 13,* 143–166.

Kivela, R. (1996). Working on networked computers: Effects on ESL writer attitude and comprehension. *Asian Journal of English Language Teaching, 6,* 85–93.

Kjisik, F., Voller, P., Aoki, N., & Nakata, Y. (Eds.) (2009). *Mapping the terrain of learner autonomy: Learning environments, learning communities and identities.* Tampere, Finland: Tampere University Press.

Klapper, J. (2005). Assessment in modern languages. In J. A. Coleman & J. Klapper (Eds.), *Effective learning and teaching in modern languages* (pp. 80–89). New York: Routledge.

Kötter, M. (2003). Negotiation of meaning and codeswitching in online tandems. *Language Learning & Technology, 7*(2), 145–172. Retrieved from llt.msu.edu/

Kötter, M. (2006). Language education and networked online environments (MOOs). In R. P. Donaldson & M. Haggstrom (Eds.), *Changing language education through CALL* (pp. 169–196). New York: Routledge.

Kramsch, C., & Thorne, S. (2002). Foreign language learning as a global communicative practice. In D. Block & D. Cameron (Eds.), *Globalization and language teaching* (pp. 83–100). New York: Routledge.

Krashen, S. (1982). *Principles and practice in second language acquisition.* New York: Pergamon Press.

Krashen, S. (1985). *The input hypothesis: Issues and implications.* New York: Longman.

Krashen, S. (2004). The power of reading (2nd ed.). Portsmouth, NH: Heinemann.

Krashen, S., Long, M., & Scarcella, R. (1979). Age, rate and eventual attainment in second language acquisition. *TESOL Quarterly, 9,* 573–582.

Lai, C., & Zhao, Y. (2006). Noticing and text-based chat. *Language Learning & Technology, 10*(3), 102–120. Retrieved from llt.msu.edu

Lai, E. (2009). *To woo partners, cloud computing vendors show them the money: Deals, discounts used to attract partners to sell vendor's services.* Retrieved from www.infoworld.com/d/cloud-computing/woo-partners-cloud-computing-vendors-show-them-money-426

Lamy, M.-N., & Klarskov Mortensen, H. J. (2011). Using concordance programs in the modern foreign languages classroom. Module 2.4 in G. Davies (Ed.), *Information and communications technology for language teachers (ICT4LT).* Slough, Thames Valley University [Online]. Retrieved from www.ict4lt.org/en/en_mod2-4.htm

Landauer, T. K., Laham, D., & Foltz, P. W. (2003). Automatic essay assessment. *Assessment in Education: Principles, Policy & Practice, 10*, 295–308.

Lantolf, J. P. (2000). Introducing sociocultural theory. In J. P. Lantolf (Ed.), *Sociocultural theory and second language learning* (pp. 1–26). Oxford, Eng.: Oxford University Press.

Lantolf, J. P. (2006). Sociocultural theory and L2. *Studies in Second language Acquisition, 28,* 67–109.

Lantolf, J. P., & Appel, G. (Eds.). (1994). *Vygotskian approaches to second language research*. Norwood, NJ: Ablex.

Lantolf, J. P., & Pavlenko, A. (1995). Sociocultural theory and second language acquisition. *Annual Review of Applied Linguistics, 15,* 108–124.

Lantolf, J. P., & Thorne, S. L. (2006). *Sociocultural theory and the genesis of second language development*. Oxford, Eng.: Oxford University Press.

Law, B., & Eckes, M. (1995). *Assessment and ESL*. Manitoba, Canada: Peguis Publishers.

Le MOOFrançais.(1999). Retrieved from www.umsl.edu/~moosproj/moofrancais.html

Lee, J. F. (2000). *Tasks and communicating in language classrooms*. New York: McGraw-Hill.

Lee, J. F., & VanPatten, B. (2003). *Making communicative language teaching happen* (2nd ed.). Boston: McGraw-Hill.

Lee, J., & Valdman, A. (Eds.). (1999). *Form and meaning: Multiple perspectives*. Boston: Heinle.

LeLoup, J., & Ponterio, R. (2003). Second language acquisition and technology: A review of the research. *Eric Digest*, EDO-FL-03-11.

Lenhart, A., Ling, R., Campbell, S., & Purcell, K. (2010). *Teens and mobile phones. Pew Internet and American Life Project*. Retrieved from pewinternet.org/Reports/2010/Teens-and-Mobile-Phones.aspx

Leont'ev, A. N. (1978). *Activity, consciousness, and personality*. Englewood Cliffs, NJ: Prentice Hall.

Levy, M. (1997). *Computer-assisted language learning: Context and conceptualization*. Oxford, Eng.: Clarendon Press.

Levy, M. (2007). Research and technological innovation in CALL. *Innovation in Language Learning and Teaching, 1*(1), 180–190.

Levy, M., & Stockwell, G. (2006). *CALL dimensions: Options and issues in computer-assisted language learning*. Mahwah, NJ: Lawrence Erlbaum.

Liaw, M.-L., & Johnson, R. J. (2001). E-mail writing as a cross-cultural learning experience. *System, 29,* 235–251.

Liskin-Gasparro, J. (1984). The ACTFL proficiency guidelines: Gateway to testing and curriculum. *Foreign Language Annals, 17,* 475–489.

Liu, M., Moore, Z., Graham, L., & Lee, S. (2002). A look at the research on computer-based technology use in second language learning: Review of literature from 1990 to 2000. *Education Review Journal, 34,* 250–273.

Lomicka, L., & Lord, G. (Eds.). (2009). *The next generation: Social networking and online collaboration in foreign language learning*. San Marcos, TX: CALICO.

Lomicka, L. (2006). Understanding the other: Intercultural exchange and CMC. In L. Ducate & N. Arnold (Eds.), *Calling on CALL: From theory and research to new directions in foreign language teaching* (pp. 211–236). San Marcos, TX: CALICO.

Lomicka, L., Lord, G., & Manzer, M. (2003). Merging foreign language theory and practice in designing technology-based tasks. In C. M. Cherry & L. Bradley (Eds.), *Models for excellence in second language education: Dimension 2003* (pp. 37–52). Valdosta, GA: SCOLT Publications.

Long, M. (1985a). A role for instruction in second language acquisition: Task-based language training. In K. Hyltenstam & M. Pienemann (Eds.), *Modeling and assessing second language acquisition* (pp. 77–99). Clevedon, UK: Multilingual Matters.

Long, M. (1985b). Input and second language acquisition theory. In S. Gass & C. Madden (Eds.), *Input in second language acquisition* (pp. 377–393). Rowley, MA: Newbury House.

Long, M. (1996). The role of the linguistic environment in second language acquisition. In W. Ritchie & T. Bhatia (Eds.), *Handbook of second language acquisition* (pp. 413–468). New York: Academic Press.

Lorenz, C. (2007). The death of email: Teenagers are abandoning their Yahoo! and Hotmail accounts. Do the rest of us have to? *Slate.com*. Retrieved July 1, 2010, from http://www.slate.com/id/2177969/

Luke, C. (2006). Situating CALL in the broader methodological context of foreign language teaching and Learning: Promises and possibilities. In N. Arnold & L. Ducate (Eds.), *Calling on CALL: From theory and research to new directions in foreign language teaching* (pp. 21–42). San Marcos, TX: CALICO.

Mabrito, M. (1991). Electronic mail as a vehicle for peer response: Conversations of high- and low-apprehensive writers. *Written Communication, 8*, 509–532.

Manteghi, C. (1995). The collaborative fairy tale. In M. Warschauer (Ed.), *Virtual connections: Online activities and projects for networking language* (pp. 20–21). Honolulu: University of Hawai'i Press.

Marjanovic, O. (1999). Learning and teaching in a synchronous collaborative environment. *Journal of Computer Assisted Learning, 15*, 129–138.

Marx, R. W., Blumenfeld, P. C., Krajcik, J. S., Blunk, M., Crawford, B., Kelly, B., & Meyer, K. M. (1994). Enhancing project-based science: Experiences of four middle grade teachers. *Elementary School Journal, 94*, 517–538.

Mason, R., & Rennie, F. (2008). *E-learning and social networking handbook: Resources for higher education*. New York: Routledge.

McCourt, C. A. (2009). Pragmatic variation among learners of French in real-time chat communication. In R. Oxford & J. Oxford (Eds.), *Second language teaching and learning in the net generation* (pp. 143–153). Honolulu: University of Hawai'i Press.

McLaughlin, B. (1987). *Theories of second language learning*. London: Arnold.

McNeely, B. (2005). Using technology as a learning tool, not just the cool new thing. In D. G. Oblinger & J. L. Oblinger (Eds.), *Educating the net generation* (4. 1–4. 10). Washington, DC: Educause. Retrieved from www.educause.edu/books/educatingthenetgen/5989

Meloni, C. (1995). The cities project. In M. Warschauer (Ed.), *Virtual connections: Online activities and projects for networking language learners* (pp. 211–215). Honolulu: University of Hawai'i Press.

Meloni, C. (1997). Armchair travelers on the information superhighway. In T. Boswood (Ed.), *New ways of using computers in language teaching*. Alexandria, VA: TESOL.

Meskill, C., & Anthony, N. (2005). Foreign language learning with CMC: Forms of online instructional discourse in a hybrid Russian class. *System, 33,* 89–105.

Messick, S. (1989). Validity. In R. Linn (Ed.), *Educational measurement* (3rd ed.; pp. 13–103). Washington, DC: American Council on Education/Macmillan.

Messick, S. (1996). *Standards-based score interpretation: Establishing valid grounds for valid inferences.* Proceedings of the joint conference on standard setting for large-scale assessments, sponsored by the National Assessment Governing Board and the National Center for Education Statistics. Washington, DC: Government Printing Office.

Meunier, L. E. (1997). Personality and motivational factors in computer-mediated foreign language communication. In J. A. Muyskens (Ed.), *New ways of learning and teaching: Focus on technology and foreign language education* (pp. 145–197). Boston: Heinle.

Midgley, K., Holcomb, P. J., & Grainger, J. (2009). Masked repetition and translation priming in second language learners: A window on the time-course of form and meaning activation using ERPs. *Psychophysiology, 46,* 551–565.

Mitchell, R., & Myles, F. (2004). *Second language learning theories* (2nd ed.). London: Arnold.

Moehle-Vieregge, L., Bird, S. R., & Manthegi, C. (1997). *Surf's up! Website workbook for German*. Gilford, CT: Audioforum.

Moehle-Vieregge, L., James, R. A., & Chuffle, E. (1997). *Surf's up! Website workbook for Spanish*. Gilford, CT: Audioforum.

Moehle-Vieregge, L., Lyman-Hager, M., DuBravac, S., & Bradley, T. (1997). *Surf's up! Website work book for French*. Gilford, CT: Audioforum.

Mohan, B., & Luo, L. (2005). A systemic functional linguistics perspective on CALL. In J. Egbert & G. Mikel (Eds.), *CALL research perspectives* (pp. 87–96). Mahwah, NJ: Lawrence Erlbaum.

Morris, M. (2006). Addressing the challenges of program evaluation: One department's experience aftertwo years. *Modern Language Journal, 90,* 585–588.

Moya, S. S., & O'Malley, J. M. (1991). A portfolio assessment model for ESL. *The Journal of Educational Issues of Language Minority Students, 13*(Spring), 13–36.

Mullen, T., Appel, C., & Shanklin, T. (2009). Skype-based tandem language learning and Web 2.0. In M. Thomas (Ed.), *Handbook of research on Web 2.0 and second language learning* (pp. 101–118). Hershey, PA: IGI Global.

MundoHispano: The Spanish learning MOO (n.d.). Retrieved from http://www.umsl. edu/~moosproj/mundo.html

Muñoz, C. (2006). The effects of age on foreign language learning: The BAF project. In C. Muñoz (Ed.), *Age and the rate of foreign language learning* (pp. 1–40). Clevedon, UK: Multilingual Matters.

Murray, D. E. (2000). Protean communication: The language of computer-mediated communication. *TESOL Quarterly, 34*, 397–421.

Murray, L. (1997). Advanced CALL to WALL? *Francophonie, 16*, 18–32.

Musumeci, D. (1997). *Breaking tradition: An exploration of the historical relationship between theory and practice in second language teaching.* Boston: McGraw-Hill.

Mynard, J. (2002). Making chat activities with native speakers meaningful for EFL learners. *The Internet TESL Journal, 8*(3). Retrieved from iteslj.org/

National Council of State Supervisors for Languages. (2012). *LinguaFolio.* Retrieved from www.ncssfl.org/LinguaFolio/index.php?linguafolio_index

National Standards in Foreign Language Education Project. (1996). *National standards for foreign language learning: Preparing for the 21st century.* Lawrence, KS: Allen Press.

National Standards in Foreign Language Education Project. (1999). *Standards for foreign language learning in the 21st century.* Lawrence, KS: Allen Press

National Standards in Foreign Language Education Project. (2006). *Standards for foreign language learning in the 21st century.* Lawrence, KS: Allen Press, Inc.

Newburger, E. C. (2001). *Home computers and Internet use in the United States: August 2000.* Washington DC: U.S. Census Bureau. Retrieved from www.census.gov/ prod/2001pubs/p23-207.pdf

Nie, N., & Erbring, L. (2000). *Study of the social consequences of the Internet.* Stanford Institute for the Quantitative Study of Society (SIQSS) publications.

Nielsen. (2011). *State of the media 2010: U.S. audiences and devices.* Retrieved from http://blog.nielsen.com/nielsenwire/wp-content/uploads/2011/01/nielsen-media-fact-sheet-jan-11. pdf

Norton, B. (2000). *Identity and language learning: Gender, ethnicity and educational change.* Harlow, Eng.: Pearson Education Limited.

Nunan, D. (1988). *The learner-centered curriculum.* Cambridge, Eng.: Cambridge University Press.

Nunan, D. (1989). *Designing tasks for the communicative classroom.* Cambridge, Eng.: Cambridge University Press.

Nunan, D. (1999). *Second language teaching and learning.* Boston: Heinle.

Nunan. D. (2004). *Task-based language teaching.* Cambridge, Eng.: Cambridge University Press.

O'Dowd, R. (2003). Understanding the "other side": Intercultural learning in a Spanish–English e-mail exchange. *Language Learning & Technology, 7*(2). Retrieved from llt. msu.edu/

O'Dowd, R., & Ritter, M. (2006). Understanding and working with "failed communication" intelecollaborative exchanges. *CALICO Journal, 23*(3), 623–642.

Oblinger, D. G., & Oblinger, J. L. (Eds.). (2005). *Educating the net generation.* Washington, DC: Educause. Retrieved from www.educause.edu/books/educatingthenetgen/5989

Odlin, T. (2003). Cross-linguistic influence. In C. J. Doughty & M. H. Long (Eds.), *The handbook of second language acquisition* (pp. 436–486). Oxford, Eng.: Blackwell.

Odlin, T. (2005). Cross-linguistic influence and conceptual transfer: What are the concepts? *Annual Review of Applied Linguistics, 25,* 3–25.

Ogunrombi, S. A., & Adio, G. (1995). Factors affecting the reading habits of secondary school students. *Library Review, 44*(4), 50–57.

Omaggio-Hadley, A. (1993). *Teaching language in context* (2nd ed.). Boston: Heinle.

Omaggio-Hadley, A. (2001). *Teaching language in context* (3rd ed.). Boston: Heinle.

Online Publishing Association. (2009). *Online Publishers Association study shows consumers exposed to display advertising are more engaged and spend more money online.* Retrieved from onlinepubs.ehclients.com/images/pdf/1059_W_TheSilentClick_OPA.pdf

Ortega, L. (1997). Processes and outcomes networked classroom interaction: Defining the research agenda for L2 computer-assisted classroom discussions. *Learning Language & Technology, 1*(1): 82–93.

Ortega, L. (2005). What do learners plan? Learner-driven attention to form during pre-task planning. In R. Ellis (Ed.), *Planning and task performance in a second language* (pp. 77–110). Philadelphia: John Benjamins.

Ortega, L. (2009). *Understanding second language acquisition.* London: Hodder.

Page, E. B. (1966). The imminence of grading essays by computer. *Phi Delta Kappan, 48,* 238–243.

Palloff, R. M., & Pratt, K. (2007). *Building online learning communities: Effective strategies for the virtual classroom.* San Francisco, CA: Jossey-Bass.

Paramskas, D. (1999). The shape of computer mediated communication. In K. Cameron (Ed.), *CALL: Media, design and applications* (pp. 13–34). Lisse, Netherlands: Swets & Zeitlinger.

Pavlenko, A. (1999). New approaches to concepts in bilingual memory. *Bilingualism, Language and Cognition, 2,* 209–230.

Pelletieri, J. (2000). Negotiation in cyberspace: The role of chatting in the development of grammatical competence in the virtual foreign language classroom. In M. Warschauer & R. Kern (Eds.), *Network-based language teaching: Concepts and practice* (pp. 59–86). Cambridge, Eng.: Cambridge University Press.

Penfield, W., & Roberts, L. (1959). *Speech and brain mechanisms.* Princeton, NJ: Princeton University Press.

Pérez-Llantada, C. (2009). Textual, genre and social features of spoken grammar: A corpus-based approach. *Language Learning & Technology, 13*(1), 40–48. Retrieved from llt.msu.edu

Peters, E., Hulstijn, J., Sercu, L., & Lutjeharms, M. (2009). Learning L2 German vocabulary through reading: The effect of three enhancement techniques compared. *Language Learning, 59*, 113–151.

Phillips, J., & Draper, J. (Eds.). (1999). *The five Cs: The standards for foreign language learning work text*. Boston: Heinle.

Piaget, J. (1970). *Structuralism*. New York: Harper & Row.

Piaget, J. (1979). *The development of thought*. New York: Viking.

Pica, T. (2008). Task-based teaching and learning. In B. Spolsky & F. M. Hult (Eds.), *The handbook of educational linguistics* (pp. 525–538). Oxford, Eng.: Blackwell.

Pienemann, M. (2003). Language processing capacity. Social context. In C. J. Doughty & M. H. Long (Eds.), *The handbook of second language acquisition* (pp. 679–714). Oxford, Eng.: Blackwell.

Plummer, T. J. (1988). Cognitive growth and literary analysis: A dialectical model for teaching literature. *Die Unterrichtspraxis, 21*, 68–80.

Poehner, M. E. (2008). *Dynamic assessment: A Vygotskian approach to understanding and promoting second language development*. Berlin: Springer Publishing.

Prensky, M. (2001). Digital natives, digital immigrants part 1. *On the Horizon, 9*(5), 1–6.

Pulido, D. (2007). The relationship between text comprehension and second language incidental vocabulary acquisition: A matter of topic familiarity? *Language Learning, 57*, 155–199.

Purves, A. C., & Quattrini, J. A. (1997). *Creating the literature portfolio: A guide for students*. Lincolnwood, IL: NTC Publishing.

Radicati, S. (Ed.). (2009). *Email statistics report 2009–2013: Executive summary*. Palo Alto, CA: Radicati Group.

Radicati, S. (Ed.). (2010). *Microsoft exchange server and Outlook market analysis 2010–2014: Executive summary*. Palo Alto, CA: Radicati Group.

Ramanathan, V. (2003). Written textual production and consumption in vernacular- and English-medium settings in Gujarat, India. *Journal of Second Language Writing, 12*, 125–150.

Redecker, C., Ala-Mutka, K., & Punie, Y. (2010). *Learning 2.0 – The Impact of Social Media on Learning in Europe (JRC Technical Notes)*. Luxemburg, Luxemburg: Office for Official Publications of the European Communities. Retrieved from http://ftp.jrc. es/EURdoc/JRC56958.pdf

Reeder, K., Heift, T., Roche, J., Tabyanian, S., Schlickau, S., & Gölz, P. (2004). Toward a theory of evaluation for second language learning media. In S. Fotos & C. Browne (Eds.), *New perspectives on CALL for second language classrooms* (pp. 255–278). Mahwah, NJ: Lawrence Erlbaum.

Reynolds, C. R., Livingston, R. B., & Willson, V. (2009). *Measurement and assessment in education* (2nd ed.). Upper Saddle River, New Jersey: Pearson Education.

Ribble, M. (2010). *Nine elements of digital citizenship*. Retrieved from www. digitalcitizenship.net/Nine_Elements.html

Richards, J. C. (2006). *Communicative language teaching today.* Cambridge, Eng.: Cambridge University Press.

Richardson, W. (2009). *Blogs, wikis, podcasts, and other powerful web tools for classrooms* (2nd ed.). Thousand Oaks, CA: Corwin Press.

Robb, T. N. (1996). E-mail keypals for language fluency. *Foreign Language Notes, 38*(3), 8–10. Retrieved from www.cc.kyoto-su.ac.jp/~trobb/keypals.html

Robinson, P. (2002). Learning conditions, aptitude complexes and SLA: A framework for research and pedagogy. In P. Robinson (Ed.), *Individual differences and instructed language learning* (pp. 113–135). Amsterdam: John Benjamins

Robinson, P. (2005). Aptitude and second language acquisition. *Annual Review of Applied Linguistics 25,* 46–73.

Robinson, P., & Ellis, N. C. (Eds.). (2008). *Handbook of cognitive linguistics and second language acquisition* (pp. 456–488). New York: Routledge.

Roever, C. (2001). Web-based language teaching. *Language Learning & Technology, 5*(2), 84–94. Retrieved from llt.msu.edu

Roscorla, T. (2011). The impact of iPads on K–12 schools. *Converge,* Retrieved May 15, 2012 from http://www.convergemag.com/classtech/Impact-iPad-K12-Schools.html

Rother, C. (2005). Teachers talk tech. *T.H.E. Journal, 32*(3). Retrieved from thejournal.com/Articles/2005/10/01/Teachers-Talk-Tech.aspx

Rubin, D. L. (1993). Listenability = oral-based language + considerateness. In A. Wolvin & C. Coakley (Eds.), *Perspectives on listening* (pp. 261–282). Beverly Hills, CA: Sage.

Rudner, L. & W. Schafer (2002). *What Teachers Need to Know About Assessment.* Washington, DC: National Education Association. Retrieved 1 June 2012 from http://echo.edres.org:8080/nea/teachers.pdf

Salaberry, M. R. (1996). A theoretical foundation for the development of pedagogical tasks in computer mediated communication. *CALICO Journal, 14*(1), 5–34.

Salaberry, M. R. (2000). L2 morphosyntactic development in text-based computer-mediated communication. *Computer Assisted Language Learning, 13,* 5–27.

Santore, F., & Schane, S. (2000). *Open sesame: Your guide to exploring foreign language resources on the World Wide Web.* Boston: Heinle.

Savignon, S. J. (1972). *Communicative competence: An experiment in foreign language teaching.* Philadelphia: Center for Curriculum Development.

Saville-Troike, M. (2006). *Introducing second language acquisition.* Cambridge, Eng.: Cambridge University Press.

Schaumann, C., & Green, A. (2003). Enhancing the study of literature with the web: Collaborative projects for advanced German. In L. Lomicka & J. Cooke-Plagwitz (Eds.), *The Heinle series in language instruction: Vol.1. Teaching with technology* (pp. 79–93). Boston: Heinle.

Schmidt, R. W. (1987). Sociolinguistic variation and language transfer in phonology. In G. Ioup & S. Weinberger (Eds.), *Interlanguage phonology* (pp. 356–377). Rowley, MA: Newbury House.

Schmidt, R. W., & Frota, S. N. (1986). Developing basic conversational ability in a second language: A case study of an adult learner of Portuguese. In R. Day (Ed.), *Talking to learn* (pp. 237–326). Rowley, MA: Newbury House.

Schumann, J. (1978). *The pidginization process: A model for second language acquisition*. Rowley, MA: Newbury House.

Schwartz, M., Kozminsk, E., & Leikin, M. (2010). Socio-linguistic factors in second language lexical knowledge: The case of second-generation Russian-Jewish immigrants in Israel. *Language, Culture, and Curriculum, 22*, 15–28.

Schwienhorst, K. (2008). *Learner autonomy and CALL environments*. New York: Routledge.

Selinker, L. (1972). Interlanguage. *International Review of Applied Linguistics, 10*, 209–231.

Shaklee, B. D., & Viechnicki, K. J. (1995). A qualitative approach to portfolios: The early assessment for exceptional potential model. *Journal for the Education of the Gifted, 18*, 156–170.

Sharpe, R., Beetham, H., & de Freitas, S. (Eds.). (2010). *Rethinking learning for a digital age: How learners are shaping their own experiences*. New York: Routledge.

Shield, L. (2003). MOO as a language learning tool. In U. Felix (Ed.), *Language learning online: Towards best practice* (pp. 97–122). Lisse, The Netherlands: Swets & Zeitlinger.

Shin, D.-S. (2006). ESL students' computer-mediated communication practices: Context configuration. *Language Learning & Technology, 10* (3), 65–84. Retrieved from llt. msu.edu

Shrum, J., & Glisan, E. (2010). *Teacher's handbook: Contextualized language instruction* (4th ed.). Boston: Heinle.

Siegel, J. (2003). Social context. In C. J. Doughty & M. H. Long (Eds.), *The handbook of second language acquisition* (pp. 178–223). Oxford, Eng.: Blackwell.

Skehan, P. (1989). *Individual differences in second-language learning*. London: Arnold.

Skehan, P. (1996). A framework for the implementation of task-based instruction. *Applied Linguistics, 17*, 38–62.

Skinner, B. F. (1957). *Verbal behavior*. Acton, MA: Copley Publishing Group.

Smerdon, B., & Cronen, S. (2000). *Teachers' tools for the 21st century: A report on teachers' use of technology*. Report No. NCES 2000102, U.S. Department of Education. Washington, DC: National Center for Educational Statistics.

Smith, B. (2003). The use of communication strategies in computer-mediated communication. *System, 31*, 29–53.

Smith, B. (2004). Computer-mediated negotiated interaction and lexical acquisition. *Studies in Second Language Acquisition, 26*, 365–398.

Smith, B., & Gorsuch, G. J. (2004). Synchronous computer mediated communication captured by usability lab technologies: New interpretations. *System, 32*, 553–575.

Son, J.-B. (2008). Using web-based language learning activities in the ESL classroom. *International Journal of Pedagogies and Learning, 4*(4), 34–43.

Sotillo, S. (2000). Discourse functions and syntactic complexity in synchronous and asynchronous communication. *Language Learning & Technology, 4*(1), 82–119. Retrieved from llt.msu.edu

Spiliotopolis, V., & Carey, S. (2005). Investigating the role of identity in writing using electronic bulletin boards. *The Canadian Modern Language Review, 62*, 87–109.

St. John, E. (2001). A case for using a parallel corpus and concordancer for beginners of a foreign language. *Language Learning & Technology, 5*(3), 185–203. Retrieved from llt.msu.edu

Stevens, V. (2004). Webhead communities: Writing tasks interleaved with synchronous online communication and web page development. In B. L. Leaver & J. R. Willis (Eds.), *Task-based instruction in foreign language education: Practices and programs* (pp. 204–227). Washington, DC: Georgetown University Press.

Stockwell, G., & Harrington, M. (2003). The incidental development of L2 proficiency in NS–NNS email interactions. *CALICO Journal, 20*, 337–359.

Sullivan, N. (1998). Developing critical reading and writing skills: Empowering minority students in a networked computer classroom. In J. Swaffar, S. Romano, P. Markley, & K. Arens (Eds.), *Language learning online: Theory and practice in the ESL and L2 computer classroom* (pp. 41–56). Austin, TX: Labyrinth Publications.

Susser, B., & Robb, T. N. (2004). Evaluation of ESL/EFL instructional websites. In S. Fotos & C. Browne (Eds.), *New perspectives on CALL for second language classrooms* (pp. 279–295). Mahwah, NJ: Lawrence Erlbaum.

Svensson, P. (2003). Virtual worlds as arenas for language learning. In U. Felix (Ed.), *Language learning online: Towards best practice* (pp. 123–146). Lisse, Netherlands: Swets & Zeitlinger.

Swain, M. (1985). Communicative competence: Some roles of comprehensible input and comprehensible output in its development. In S. Gass & C. Madden (Eds.), *Input in second language acquisition* (pp. 235–253). Rowley, MA: Newbury House.

Swain, M. (1998). Focus on form through conscious reflection. In C. Doughty & J. Williams (Eds.), *Focus-on-form in classroom second language acquisition* (pp. 64–81). Cambridge, Eng.: Cambridge University Press.

Swain, M. (2005). The output hypotheses: Theory and research. In E. Hinkel (Ed.), *Handbook on research in second language learning and teaching* (pp. 471–483). Mahwah, NJ: Lawrence Erlbaum.

Swain, M., & Lapkin, S. (1998). Interaction and second language learning: Two adolescent French immersion students working together. *The Modern Language Journal, 82*, 320–337.

Swain, M., & Lapkin, S. (2000). Task-based second language learning: The uses of the first language. *Language Teaching Research, 4*, 251–274.

Taylor, R., & Gitsaki, C. (2004). Teaching WELL and Loving IT. In S. Fotos & C. Browne (Eds.), *New perspectives on CALL for second language classrooms* (pp. 131–147). Mahwah, NJ: Lawrence Erlbaum.

Technology, Education, and Copyright Harmonization Act of 2002, Pub. L. No. 107–273, 116 Stat. 1758, 1910. (2002).

Tella, A., & Akande, S. (2007). Children['s] reading habits and availability of books in Botswana primary schools: Implications for achieving quality education. *The Reading Matrix, 7*(2), 117–142.

Terry, R. M. (1998). Authentic tasks and materials for testing in the foreign language classroom. In J. Harper, M. Lively, & M. Williams (Eds.), *The coming of age of the profession: Issues and emerging ideas for the teaching of foreign languages* (pp. 277–290). Boston: Heinle.

Thanasoulas, D. (2002). *The changing winds and the shifting sands of the history of English language teaching*. Retrieved from www.englishclub.com/tefl-articles/history-english-language-teaching.htm

The Copyright Act of 1976, Title 17 USC. Pub. L. No. 94–553, 90 Stat. 2541. (1976).

Thomas, M. (Ed.). (2009). *Handbook of research on Web 2.0 and second language learning*. Hershey, PA: IGI Global.

Thoms, J., Liao, J., & Szustak, A. (2005). The use of L1 in an L2 chat activity. *The Canadian Modern Language Review, 62*, 161–182.

Thorne, S. L. (2003). Artifacts and cultures-of-use in intercultural communication. *Language Learning & Technology, 7*(2), 38–67. Retrieved from llt.msu.edu

Thorne, S. L. (2008). Mediating technologies and second language learning. In D. Leu, J. Coiro, C. Lankshear, & M. Knobel (Eds.), *Handbook of research on new literacies* (pp. 417–449). Mahwah, NJ: Lawrence Erlbaum.

Tian, J., & Wang, Y. (2010). Taking language learning outside the classroom: Learners' perspectives of eTandem learning via Skype. *Innovations in Language Learning & Teaching, 4*(3), 181–197.

Toyoda, E., & Harrison, R. (2002). Categorization of text chat communication between learners and native speakers of Japanese. *Language Learning & Technology, 6*(1), 82–99. Retrieved from llt.msu.edu

Trotta, J. (2004). *Tiger information gap—an ESL speaking activity by James Trotta*. Retrieved from www.eslgo.com/resources/sa/ig_tiger.html

Tudini, V. (2003). Using native speakers in chat. *Language Learning & Technology, 7*(3), 141–159. Retrieved from http://llt.msu.edu

Tweney, D. (2010). Amazon sells more e-books than hardcovers. *Wired*. Retrieved from www.wired.com/epicenter/2010/07/amazon-more-e-books-than-hardcovers/

Tyler, A. (2008). Cognitive linguistics and second language instruction. In P. Robinson & N. C. Ellis (Eds.), *Handbook of cognitive linguistics and second language acquisition* (pp. 456–488). New York: Routledge.

Uden, L., & Beaumont, C. (2006). *Technology and problem-based learning*. Hershey, PA: IGI Global.

Valencia, S. W. (1990). Alternative assessment: Separating the wheat from the chaff. *The Reading Teacher, 43*, 60–61.

van Compernolle, R. A., & Williams, L. (2010). Orthographic variation in electronic French: The case of l'accent aigu. *French Review, 83,* 820–833. Retrieved from www.personal.psu.edu/rav137/preprints/FR.accentaigu.pdf

Van der Meij, H., & Boersma, K. (2002). Email use in elementary school: An analysis of exchange patterns and content. *British Journal of Educational Technology, 33,* 189–200.

Van Handle, D. C., & Corl, K. A. (1998). Extending the dialogue: Using electronic mail and the Internet to promote conversation and writing in intermediate level German language courses. *CALICO Journal, 15*(1–3), 129–143.

Van Patten, B. (2007). Input processing in adult SLA. In B. Van Patten & J. Williams (Eds.), *Theories in second language acquisition: An introduction* (pp. 115–135). Mahwah, NJ: Lawrence Erlbaum.

Van Selm, M., & Jankowski, N. W. (2006). Conducting online surveys. *Quality & Quantity, 40,* 435–456.

Van Waes, L., Leijten, M., & Neuwirth, C. M. (Eds.). (2006). *Writing and digital media.* Oxford, Eng.: Elsevier.

Volle, L. (2005). Analyzing oral skills in voice e-mail and online interviews. *Language Learning & Technology, 9*(3), 146–163. Retrieved from llt.msu.edu

Vonderwell, S. (2003). An examination of asynchronous communication experiences and perspectives of students in an online course: A case study. *Internet and Higher Education, 6,* 77–90.

Vygotsky, L. S. (1978). *Mind in society: The development of higher psychological processes.* Cambridge, MA: Harvard University Press.

Warschauer, M. (1996a). Comparing face-to-face and electronic discussion in the second language classroom. *CALICO Journal, 13*(2), 7–26.

Warschauer, M. (1996b) Computer-assisted language learning: An introduction. In S. Fotos (Ed.), Multimedia language teaching (pp. 3–20), Tokyo: Logos International.

Warschauer, M. (1996c). Motivational aspects of using computers for writing and communication. In M. Warschauer (Ed.), *Telecollaboration in foreign language learning* (pp. 29–46). Honolulu: University of Hawai'i Press.

Warschauer, M. (1999*). Electronic literacies: Language, culture, and power in online education.* Mahwah, NJ: Lawrence Erlbaum Associates.

Warschauer, M. (2004). Technological change and the future of CALL. In S. Fotos & C. Browne (Eds.), *New perspectives on CALL for second language classrooms* (pp. 15–26). Mahwah, NJ: Lawrence Erlbaum.

Warschauer, M. (2005). Sociocultural perspectives on CALL. In J. Egbert & G. Mikel (Eds.), *CALL research perspectives* (pp. 41–52). Mahwah, NJ: Lawrence Erlbaum.

Warschauer, M., & Healey, D. (1998). Computers and language learning: An overview. *Language Teaching, 31,* 57–71.

Warschauer, M., Shetzer, H., & Meloni, C. (2000). *Internet for English teaching.* Alexandria, VA: TESOL.

Weinstein, G. (2006). Learners' lives as curriculum: An integrative project-based model for language learning. In G. H. Beckett & P. C. Miller (Eds.), *Project-based second and foreign language education: Past, present, and future* (pp. 159–165). Greenwich, CT: Information Age Publishing.

Wiesel, T. N., & Hubel, D. H. (1963). Effects of visual deprivation on morphology and physiology of cells in the cat's lateral geniculate body. *Journal of Neurophysiology, 26*, 978–992.

Wiesel, T. N., & Hubel, D. H. (1965). Comparison of the effects of unilateral and bilateral eye closure on cortical unit responses in kittens. *Journal of Neurophysiology, 28*, 1029–1040.

Wigfield, A., & Asher, S. R. (2002). Social and motivational influences on reading. In P. D. Pearson (Ed.), *Handbook of reading research* (pp. 423–452). Mahwah, NJ: Lawrence Erlbaum.

Winn, P. (2009). *State of the blogosphere:Introduction*. Retrieved from technorati.com/blogging/article/state-of-the-blogosphere-introduction/

Wong, J., & Cohen, P. (1995). Two semesters of email keypaling: What works and what doesn't. In M. Warschauer (Ed.), *Virtual connections: Online activities & projects for networking language learners* (pp. 122–124). Honolulu: University of Hawai'i Press.

World Trade Organization. (1994). *Marrakesh agreement establishing the World Trade Organization. Annex 1C: Trade-Related Aspects of Intellectual Property Rights.* [Online]. Retrieved from www.wto.org/english/docs_e/legal_e/27-trips_01_e.htm

Wright, K. B. (2005). Researching internet-based populations: Advantages and disadvantages of online survey research, online questionnaire authoring packages, and web survey services. *Journal of Computer-Mediated Communication, 10*(3). Retrieved from jcmc.indiana.edu/vol10/issue3/wright.html.

Yanguas, I. (2009). Multimedia glosses and their effect on L2 text comprehension and vocabulary learning. *Language Learning & Technology, 13*(2), 48–62. Retrieved from llt.msu.edu

Yoon, H. (2008). More than just a reference: The influence of corpus technology on L2 academic writing. *Language Learning & Technology, 12*(2), 31–48. Retrieved from llt.msu.edu

Young, J. R. (2010). Reaching the last technology holdouts at the front of the class. *The Chronicle of Higher Education,* pp. A9–A10. Retrieved from chronicle.texterity.com/chronicle/20100730a?pg=9#pg9

Yu, M. C. (2004). Interlinguistic variation and similarity in second language speech act behavior. *The Modern Language Journal,* 88, 102–119.

INDEX